Lincoln's Supreme Court

Justices of the Supreme Court, 1865. Left to right, Justices Davis, Swayne, Grier, Wayne, Chase, Nelson, Clifford, Miller, Field. Justice Catron in inset.

Lincoln's
SUPREME COURT

BY DAVID M. SILVER

UNIVERSITY OF ILLINOIS PRESS

URBANA AND CHICAGO

Illinois Reissue, 1998
© 1956 by David M. Silver
Manufactured in the United States of America
P 5 4 3 2

This book is printed on acid-free paper.

Library of Congress Cataloging-in-Publication Data
Silver, David M. (David Mayer)
Lincoln's Supreme Court / David M. Silver. —
Illinois Reissue
p. cm.
Originally published: Urbana, Ill. :
University of Illinois Press, 1957.
Included bibliographical references and index.
ISBN 0-252-06719-3 (alk. paper)
1. United States. Supreme Court—History.
2. Constitutional history—United States. 3. United
States—History—Civil War, 1861-1865. I. Title.
KF8742.S54 1998
347.73'26—dc21 97-32780
CIP

The University of Illinois Press reissues these digital
editions to put significant works back into print.

To

Anita, Gregory, and Terrence

Preface

Although I am indebted to many friends for their encouragement in the preparation of this volume, it is to the late Professor James G. Randall of the University of Illinois that I owe the greatest appreciation. It was he who first guided me in a study of the Civil War in general and a study of the Supreme Court in particular.

This work describes and evaluates the Supreme Court's relationship to Lincoln and to the struggle that finally brought victory to the American Union.

The story includes many involvements. Not only does it concern itself with attempts by the Radicals to modify, pack, or destroy the Supreme Court, but it includes as well such diversified matters as the attitudes of the various members of the Court as the war opens, the politics behind the appointment of four Associate Justices and a Chief Justice, decisions of vital, war-related cases, examination of the normal business of the wartime Court, proposals to lure aged Democratic Justices into retirement, the role of the Justices on circuit, the revamping of the Court under its new Republican Chief Justice, Salmon P. Chase, and the absolution of its former Democratic head, Roger B. Taney.

It should be noted that this study is basically historical rather than legalistic. It proceeds upon the same principles that Professor Randall expressed in the preface to a work also closely related to legal problems. He stated: "In this . . . discussion my purpose has been to apply the canons of historical interpretation to legal material, making only such excursions into technical matters of law as the larger purposes of historical study require." [1]

Merely a list of persons who have assisted me would prove to be too long to include here. The following individuals, however, generously made special materials available: Mr. Edward S. Delaplaine of Frederick, Maryland; Mr. Gist Blair of Washington, D. C.; Mr. Alexander A. Lawrence of Savannah, Georgia; Miss Ola M. Wyeth of the Georgia Historical Society, Savannah; Mr. Daniel C. Knapp of Washington, D. C.; Dr. Louis A. Warren of the Lincoln Foundation, Ft. Wayne, Indiana; Mr. Jesse Cunningham of the Cossitt Library, Memphis, Tennessee; Mr. Albert G. Sogemeier, clerk of the United States district court at Indianopolis, Indiana; Mr. Howard E. Parker, clerk of the United States district

---

[1] James G. Randall, *Constitutional Problems Under Lincoln*, New York, 1926, viii.

court at Cincinnati, Ohio; and Mr. Charles Hallam, Associate Librarian, Library of the Supreme Court of the United States, Washington, D. C.

I am deeply indebted to the staffs of the following: the manuscript, law, and newspaper divisions of the Library of Congress; the justice department archives of the National Archives; the Maryland Historical Society; the Historical Society of Pennsylvania; the Illinois Historical Survey; the Library of the University of Illinois; the Indiana State Library; the Library of the Supreme Court of Indiana; the Indianapolis Public Library; the Louisville Public Library; and the Library of the Supreme Court of the United States.

Special mention must be made of the valuable suggestions offered by Professor Roy M. Robbins, Director of the Graduate Division, University of Omaha; Miss Corinne Welling, formerly a member of the English department of Butler University; Miss Gayle Thornbrough of the Indiana Historical Bureau, who read part of the manuscript; and Dr. Allan J. McCurry of the history department of Butler University, who read the entire manuscript. Of course, responsibility for the work is mine alone.

Completion of this study was greatly facilitated by a Butler University faculty fellowship for which I wish to express my deep appreciation.

The frontispiece photograph is from the Library of Congress, with the inset photograph of Justice Catron from the Lincoln National Life Foundation.

Butler University   DAVID M. SILVER

June 20, 1956

Contents

CHAPTER ONE

Pattern for Conflict

THE SUPREME COURT AWAITS LINCOLN

The fateful winter of 1860-61, characterized as it was by the national plunge over the precipice of dissolution, saw the Supreme Court of the United States, long a victim of inadequate quarters, move into spacious and majestic chambers. Brought from its dismal courtroom in the basement of the national Capitol, the Court was to enjoy new physical surroundings at the time that it was to suffer, along with the rest of the nation, the anguish of civil war.

The new home of the Supreme Court presented an imposing picture. Dominated from above by a vast ornamental dome, the chambers were given an inspiring luminosity by a skylight through which the sun could gleam and cast shadows upon the superb Potomac marble. The hall, which served formerly as the chamber of the United States Senate, was deemed "one of the handsomest in the capitol." Its semicircular shape lent itself admirably to service as a courtroom; its Potomac-marble pillars and pilasters gave it a rich atmosphere; its appearance of dignity and calm made it appropriate to the high Court. A large gilded eagle, with wings outspread, looked down over a raised dais upon which were the "comfortable armchairs of the Chief-Justice and his associates." A luxurious atmosphere was created by the "soft, heavy carpets [as well as] the cushioned benches for the spectators." Busts of the former Chief Justices—John Jay, John Rutledge, Oliver Ellsworth, and John Marshall —embellished the chambers and called upon history to bear witness to a glorious past.[1]

It was this Court, glorious in its past contribution to the republic, in new surroundings of dignity and honor and affluence, that awaited the attention of Abraham Lincoln, a President whose very election foreshadowed evil for it. What penalty would the Republicans inflict upon the Supreme Court that in 1857 had handed down the Dred Scott decision? Lincoln, himself, had warned that the Court must be forced to reverse the decision,[2] which provided that Negroes could not be

---

[1] John B. Ellis, *Sights and Secrets of the National Capital: A Work Descriptive of Washington City in All Its Various Phases* (New York, 1869), pp. 253-54.

[2] Roy P. Basler, ed., *The Collected Works of Abraham Lincoln* (New Brunswick, 1953-55), II, 494-96 (July 10, 1858). Cited hereafter as *Works*.

citizens and that slaves could be taken into any of the territories of the United States.

The urgency of the problems that faced the new President was unparalleled. The crisis of dissolution raced on with vehemence; the assault upon federal authority grew in its fierceness. Lincoln had no breathing spell in which to grasp control over the situation. For him vicissitude created injunction.

The Supreme Court, itself, presented perplexing difficulties to Lincoln. What would the role of the Court be? How would its members evaluate federal efforts to combat the South? How would the Chief Justice, Roger B. Taney, with views as expounded in the Dred Scott case, influence the thoughts and acts of the Court which was Democratic in majority? Within a short time three vacancies existed within its membership. At any point in American history the selection of three Supreme Court Justices by an incoming administration would be of vast significance, but at this juncture, with combat and trial and untried paths ahead, Lincoln's appointments and the decisions that he would make in relation to the nation's highest judicial tribunal were awaited with hope and fear.

Naturally, even before Lincoln's election, politicians had speculated about the role and personnel of the Court if the Republicans won. Typical of those who were concerned was T. Charlton Henry, brother of the mayor of Philadelphia, who had written Lincoln a week after the latter's nomination for the presidency that "your enemies here, [not only] are circulating the report that 'In religious opinions you are an open & avowed Infidel'" but in addition are charging "that you deny the authority of the Supreme Court. . . ." Lincoln was informed that "If these reports are untrue as I hope & believe they are you would confer a great favor upon me & . . . do good service to the cause of Republicanism, by addressing to me a few lines to that effect." [3]

Representative H. Winter Davis of Maryland, corresponding with his cousin David Davis of Illinois during the presidential campaign, suggested that upon the election of Lincoln, Republicans must await Supreme Court vacancies in order to reverse the Dred Scott decision, forecasting that "His [Lincoln's] time will come in filling the vacancies on the bench." Representative Davis proceeded to say that "If we now turn out the democrats from the Presidency in four or five years the Court will be reconstructed by new appointments & the Dred Scott [decision] will cease to be the opinion of the Court." [4]

When Lincoln became President there was a vacancy on the Supreme Court that represented unfinished business of the administration of

[3] T. Charlton Henry to Abraham Lincoln, May 26, 1860, Robert Todd Lincoln Collection of Lincoln MSS, Library of Congress. Cited hereafter as Lincoln MSS.

[4] H. Winter Davis to David Davis, September (?), 1860, ibid.

James Buchanan. Justice Peter V. Daniel, a Virginian and a member of the Court since his appointment by Martin Van Buren, died at Richmond on May 31, 1860, vacating a seat that was claimed by the Southerners, being one of five held by them at that time. It is not surprising that a spirited struggle ensued over the choice of a successor. Leading Southern Democrats demanded of Buchanan that he choose a Southerner to fill the post, but he made no choice during the fateful campaign and presidential election. And on December 4, 1860, when the Court met for its regular term, the seat was yet unfilled.

On that December day, with Washington engulfed in turmoil and vexation and with the nation facing disintegration, the Supreme Court met in its new chambers for the first time. At eleven o'clock the Marshal threw open the door leading from the Justices's quarters and announced, "The Honorable, the Judges of the Supreme Court of the United States." The audience arose, and the members of the Supreme Court, led by Chief Justice Taney, filed in "one by one, in their large flowing robes of black silk." At a sign from the Chief Justice the crier proclaimed: "All persons having business before the . . . Judges of the Supreme Court . . . are admonished to draw near and give their attendance, for the Court is now in Session. God save the United States, and this Honorable Court." [5]

It was customary upon the opening of a new term, if a member of the Court had died since the last meeting, for the Attorney General to address the Court in tribute to the deceased Justice. Consequently, Attorney General Jeremiah S. Black opened his remarks with a tribute to Justice Daniel. And Chief Justice Taney, taking recognition of Black's statement, replied for the Court, "His death has made our first meeting in this new hall a sad and painful one. . . ." [6] But the Court was saddened, too, for other reasons; bitter struggles, growing hatreds, and violent controversies ruled the day. But to these causes the Chief Justice did not allude.

In those days when each hour gave promise of events of unequaled import, rumors—unchecked, unbounded—swept ceaselessly through the national capital. Rumors concerned the President, the President-elect, Southern hotheads, Northern zealots, foreign governments, compromise, secession, the make-up of the Lincoln cabinet—no man, no topic, was safe from the wagging tongues. The Supreme Court, naturally, was not overlooked by the rumor-mongers.

Prior to the meeting of the December Term, 1860, there were whispers concerning Roger B. Taney, the eighty-four-year-old Chief Justice. Benjamin F. Butler, lawyer-politician of Massachusetts, was informed of Taney's "impending" resignation and was urged to participate in a

[5] Ellis, p. 258.
[6] 65 United States Reports, proceedings, vi. The reports of the United States Supreme Court are cited hereafter in abbreviated form, e.g., 65 U.S., proceedings, vi.

move to have the Boston bar petition President Buchanan in behalf of the appointment of Caleb Cushing, a leading Massachusetts Democrat, as Chief Justice.[7] Butler even went so far as to offer Cushing aid in getting the appointment although Taney, tireless as well as tenacious, had made no move to resign.[8] Taney's numerous enemies took joy in circulating rumors about him. From the standpoint of the Democratic party it might have been sound politics if Taney had resigned early enough in the Buchanan administration to have assured confirmation of a Democratic successor. His departure in 1860, however, by reason of the political passions of the last months of Buchanan's presidency, would not have been followed smoothly by confirmation of another Democratic Chief Justice.

As a matter of fact, Buchanan even delayed naming a successor to fill the Daniel vacancy until it was too late to secure senatorial confirmation. A month before the end of his presidency Buchanan submitted to the Senate the nomination of Jeremiah S. Black, but the Senate rejected the appointment. At an earlier date confirmation would have been possible, but senators from seceded states had now resigned and Democratic party strength was diminished. Furthermore, there was opposition to Black within the party itself. The vacancy had to await the new administration.

On the day that Lincoln assumed the presidency, Edwin M. Stanton, who had served in Buchanan's cabinet and who was later to serve the Lincoln administration as Secretary of War, took a dim view of events to come. Stanton, aware that the storm that imperiled the nation was to strike a blow at the Court, predicted at least one resignation from it. But all that Stanton could conclude as of March 4, 1861, was, "The inauguration is over & whether for good or evil Abraham Lincoln is now President of the United States." [9] Before Lincoln had served a month in the presidency, Stanton took even a dimmer view in a letter to former President Buchanan. He conjectured whether the Lincoln administration could sustain itself for four years and concluded, "Lincoln will probably (if his administration continues four years) [!] make a change that will affect the constitutional doctrine of the court." [10]

Nation, citizenry, Court—all awaiting the new President—stood at the brink of destruction. But all the doubters, all the faint in heart, all the

---

[7] Sidney Webster to Benjamin F. Butler, November 27, 1860, Cushing MSS., Library of Congress. The previous day Webster had telegraphed Cushing that the resignation of Chief Justice Taney had been announced. Webster to Cushing, November 26, 1860, *ibid*.

[8] Benjamin F. Butler to Caleb Cushing, November 30, 1860, *ibid*.

[9] Edwin M. Stanton to P. D. Lowe, March 4, 1861, Stanton MSS., Library of Congress.

[10] Edwin M. Stanton to James Buchanan, March 14, 1861, Buchanan MSS., Hist. Soc. of Pa.

pessimists were to observe Lincoln the statesman combat rebellion and sustain the integrity of the American Union. The heritage handed down from the time of Washington was to be preserved and rededicated. The years ahead were to be cruel but not futile.

Lincoln's Inaugural Address

A deeply troubled and sorely anxious nation awaited the arrival in Washington of President-elect Abraham Lincoln. The bold challenge of the South had to be answered. The nation waited impatiently: it anticipated both with hopefulness and with apprehension the inaugural address, an address that would lay down policies to determine the future of the nation. Would it dispel or intensify the uncertainty, the suspicion, and the confusion that saturated the land?

President-elect Lincoln and his party arrived in Washington several days before the inauguration. Comfortably installed at Willard's Hotel, the incoming Chief Executive busied himself by formulating policy for the new administration, by conferring with the endless throng of political leaders and office-seekers, and by paying the customary visits to the President, the cabinet, the Congress, and the Supreme Court. Secretary of State-designate William H. Seward sent word to Lincoln that "The Justices of the Supreme Court propose to receive your visit, either at their reception room in the Capitol at 3 o'clock P.M. or at their consultation room in Morrison's Buildings (on 4½ Street) at half past three, as you may prefer." Already Seward, who was to be so free in giving advice to the President, suggested which choice Lincoln should select, proposing that "Probably the former will be the better place if it will suit your convenience." [11]

President Buchanan and his cabinet received Lincoln with "cordial politeness." As could have been anticipated, political cohorts in the Senate and House welcomed Lincoln enthusiastically, while political enemies greeted him "somewhat sullenly." The Chief Justice and his brethren of the Court greeted President-elect Lincoln cordially though with restraint and "extended to him an affable recognition as the lawful successor in constitutional rulership." [12] In greeting the head of the Court, Lincoln came face to face with the man who would prove to be his chief judicial foe, a man who was to hold in ever-increasing disdain the policies that Lincoln would devise and carry into effect to protect and restore federal authority. But upon this occasion only gentlemanly affability and dignity were discernible.

To Taney, who had presided over the Supreme Court for some twenty-

---

[11] William H. Seward to Abraham Lincoln, February 25, 1861, Lincoln MSS.

[12] John G. Nicolay and John Hay, *Abraham Lincoln: A History* (New York, 1886), III, 317. See also New York *Times,* February 26, 1861, p. 1.

five years, fell the task of administering the oath of office to the new President. Taney had officiated at the inauguration of a long list of American presidents from Martin Van Buren to James Buchanan, and it was forecast by the Chicago *Tribune* that "The venerable Chief Justice ... who is in excellent health, will doubtless administer the oath of office on Monday next to Mr. Lincoln as impressively as he has heretofore administered it." [13] On March 4, 1861, the Supreme Court, with the throng assembled in front of the Capitol, heard the inaugural address, and the Chief Justice administered the oath of office to Abraham Lincoln.[14]

As Lincoln, aware of the little time allowed to gain a grasp over the ominous events that were swirling around him, looked out upon the crowd assembled to hear his inaugural address, what hopes, what apprehensions, what trepidations raced through his mind? His audience—the whole land, as well—hung on every word that he spoke. Here was the man on whom rested the salvation of the nation. Here was the man whose very existence from this fateful moment would be bound with the travail of a great nation.

Would Lincoln on this occasion see fit to challenge the Supreme Court? His election grew in part out of the decision of that Court in the Dred Scott case. In 1858 he had denounced the Court vigorously in his contest with Stephen A. Douglas in Illinois. His opportunity had now arrived. His adherents expected that he would state clearly the attitude of the new administration toward the Supreme Court, the Court that many held responsible for the national debacle. Lincoln did not entirely disappoint his followers, but it was with less than expected candor that he made known his attitude as to its future role. Some of the views that he expressed were his own; others were embodied in the address upon the counsel of William H. Seward.

The whole character of Lincoln's remarks about the Supreme Court indicated his intention to resist and menace it. But he did not pledge direct assault upon it, and he did not pledge to destroy or to nullify it. Rather, as though he were thinking aloud, he appeared to be trying to devise a thoroughly effective, though not deadly, means to combat the Supreme Court. "I do not forget the position assumed by some," declared the new President, "that constitutional questions are to be decided by the Supreme Court. . . ." But he carefully made the point that the Court might hand down a decision which later might be found erroneous and which should then be reviewed and reversed.

Lincoln did not hesitate to attack it for attempting to dictate govern-

[13] Chicago *Tribune,* March 4, 1861, p. 1.
[14] Carl B. Swisher, *Roger B. Taney* (New York, 1935), pp. 542-44.

mental policy. He lashed at the Court vigorously, maintaining that "the candid citizen must confess that if the policy of the government . . . is to be irrevocably fixed by decisions of the Supreme Court . . . the people will have ceased to be their own rulers, having to that extent practically resigned their government into the hands of that eminent tribunal." Lincoln did not only attack the Court itself for its role; he condemned those, as well, who used it to further their own political schemes and political aspirations: "Nor is there, in this view," stated the President, "any assault upon the court, or the judges. It is a duty, from which they may not shrink, to decide cases properly brought before them; and it is no fault of theirs, if others seek to turn their decisions to political purposes." [15] He condemned those who maneuvered for advantage resulting from a decision such as that handed down in the Dred Scott case. But his failure to propose concrete steps to be taken in relation to the Court served only to enhance uncertainties and to arouse the sanguinary desires of some of his Republican associates.

Upon the completion of the new President's address the Chief Justice, who had just heard the attack upon the Supreme Court, stepped forward to administer the oath of office to Abraham Lincoln, sixteenth president of the United States. The correspondent of the New York *Times*, with a fine appreciation of the dramatic scene that was being enacted, studied the Chief Justice during the inaugural and recorded that "Judge Taney did not remove his eyes from Mr. Lincoln during the entire delivery." Following the address, the *Times* correspondent reported, "Judge Taney stood up, and all removed their hats, while he administered the oath to Mr. Lincoln. Speaking in a low tone the form of the oath, he signified to Mr. Lincoln, that he should repeat the words." According to this observer, Chief Justice Taney was the first to shake hands with President Lincoln after the ceremony, although "The Chief Justice seemed very agitated, and his hands shook very perceptibly with emotion" as the oath was administered.[16]

Lincoln did not wish—actually he was unable—to commit himself as to any action to be taken concerning the Court. He intended to do whatever time and circumstances might dictate. To pledge to reconstruct it would be precipitous. To pledge to leave it alone might prove not only foolhardy and impossible but would be a breach of faith with his party. To pledge to disable or destroy it would not only be out of harmony with his own views, it would be an assault upon the American constitutional system, an assault that Lincoln would never make. To await further developments, particularly because of the events that were impending, was Lincoln's initial policy toward the Supreme Court.

---

[15] *Works*, IV, 268 (March 4, 1861).
[16] New York *Times*, March 5, 1861, pp. 1, 8.

In an attempt to evaluate Lincoln's statements about the Court, the New York *Times* explained that he adhered to the view that although Supreme Court decisions are binding upon the people, nothing forbids "Congress from changing the law, nor the people from changing the Constitution, nor the Supreme Court from afterwards reversing the decision if they see reason for doing so." [17] That is a sound but innocuous interpretation of his remarks. What if the Court were not impelled to reverse its view? What if circumstances make it impossible or too time consuming to amend the Constitution? Let public opinion, and the public will, provide the answer in the future—that was Lincoln's attitude as he grasped for the reins of government.

JUSTICES OF THE SUPREME COURT OF THE UNITED STATES[a]

AS THEY STOOD DURING THE TERMS OF 1861-62-63-64, TOGETHER WITH THE DATES OF THEIR COMMISSIONS AND TERMS OF SERVICE, RESPECTIVELY.

NAMES OF JUSTICES, AND WHENCE APPOINTED	BY WHOM APPOINTED	CIRCUITS, 1861-1864	COMMIS- SIONED	SWORN IN	TERMINA- TION
ASSOCIATE JJ. Nathan Clifford, Maine	President BUCHANAN	FIRST ME., N. H., MASS., RHODE ISLAND	1858 (Jan. 12)	1858 (Jan. 21)	Died 1881 (July 25)
Samuel Nelson, New York	President TYLER	SECOND VERMONT, CONN., New York	1845 (Feb. 14)	1845 (Mar. 3)	Resigned 1872 (Dec. 1)
Robert C. Grier, Pennsylvania	President POLK	THIRD NEW JERSEY AND PENNSYLVANIA	1846 (Aug. 4)	1846 (Dec. 7)	Resigned 1870 (Jan. 31)
CHIEF JUSTICES Roger Brooke Taney, Maryland	President JACKSON	FOURTH DEL., MD. & VA. (NORTH CAROLINA	1836 (Mar. 15)	1836 (Mar. 22)	Died 1864 (Oct. 12)
Salmon P. Chase, Ohio	President LINCOLN	Added July 15, '62) W. VA. added 1864	1864 (Dec. 6)	1864 (Dec. 15)	Died 1873 (May 7)
ASSOCIATE JJ. James M. Wayne, Georgia (From March 10, 1863 Vacant 1861, 1862)	President JACKSON	FIFTH ALABAMA & LA. Changed by Act of July 15, 1862, to S. C., GA., ALA., MISS. AND FLA.	1835 (Jan. 9)	1835 (Jan. 14)	Died 1867 (July 5)
James M. Wayne, Georgia (To March 10, 1863)	President JACKSON	SIXTH N. C., S. C. & GA., to July 15, 1862; after that	1835 (Jan. 9)	1835 (Jan. 14)	Died 1867 (July 5)
John Catron, Tennessee From March 10, 1863)	President VAN BUREN	LA., ARK., KY., TENN. & TEXAS	1837 (Mar. 8)	1838 (Jan. 9)	Died 1865 (May 30)

[a] From *Report of the Secretary of the Interior*, Dec. 6, 1864, published as Senate Ex. Doc. 1, 38th Cong., 2d session.

[17] *Ibid.*, March 9, 1861, p. 4.

JUSTICES OF THE SUPREME COURT OF THE UNITED STATES[a]

AS THEY STOOD DURING THE TERMS OF 1861-62-63-64, TOGETHER WITH THE DATES OF THEIR COMMISSIONS AND TERMS OF SERVICE, RESPECTIVELY.

NAMES OF JUSTICES, AND WHENCE APPOINTED	BY WHOM APPOINTED	CIRCUITS, 1861-1864	COMMIS- SIONED	SWORN IN	TERMINA- TION
Noah H. Swayne, Ohio	President LINCOLN	SEVENTH OHIO, IND., ILL. & MICH. to July 15, 1862; then OHIO & IND. one year; after that OHIO & MICH- IGAN	1862 (Jan. 24)	1862 (Jan. 27)	Resigned 1881 (Jan. 24)
John Catron, Tennessee (To March 10, 1863)	President VAN BUREN	EIGHTH KY., TENN. & MO. to July 15, 1862; then MICH., ILL. & WIS. one year; af-	1837 (Mar. 8)	1838 (Jan. 9)	Died 1865 (May 30)
David Davis, Illinois	President LINCOLN	ter that MICH., ILL., IND. & *WISCONSIN	1862 (Dec. 8)	1862 (Dec. 10)	Resigned 1877 (Mar. 4)
Samuel F. Miller, Iowa (From March 10, 1863 Vacant 1861, 1862)	President LINCOLN	NINTH ARK. AND MISS., to July 15th, 1862; after that MO., IA., KANSAS, MINN. & *WIS.	1862 (July 16)	1862 (Dec. 1)	Died 1890 (Oct. 13)
Stephen J. Field, California	President LINCOLN	TENTH CALIFORNIA, ORE- GON, & †NEVADA	1863 (Mar. 10)	1863 (Dec. 7)	Resigned 1897 (Dec. 1)

[a] From *Report of the Secretary of the Interior*, Dec. 6, 1864, published as Senate Ex. Doc. 1, 38th Cong., 2d session.
* By Act of February 9, 1863, Wisconsin was transferred to Ninth Circuit.
† By Act of February 27, 1865, Nevada was made part of Tenth Circuit.

THE COURT TORN ASUNDER

The month of April, 1861, with the nation in a critical situation, witnessed the Court torn asunder. To the one Supreme Court vacancy that Lincoln inherited from the Buchanan administration, there were now added two more vacancies. As if by an ironic injunction, only a month after the inaugural, death removed Justice John McLean of Ohio, long an occupant of the bench and one of the two dissenters from the majority in the Dred Scott decision. The other vacancy, however, effectually underlined the tragedy of the times: Justice John A. Camp- bell of Alabama resigned to join the Confederate cause.

McLean's death was not unexpected. He had served since his appoint- ment by Andrew Jackson, and the seventy-six-year-old friend of the Lincoln administration was known by his associates to be failing. He died at his residence in Cincinnati on April 4, 1861. The vacancy created by his death, coming as it did in the very early days of the Lincoln administration, was just one more distraction for the President. Even as the nation's fate rested in the balance, speculation as to McLean's successor added itself to the conjectures, guesses, and reflections saturating Washington.

It was the culmination of events at Fort Sumter—events long delayed but fearsomely anticipated—that forced the members of the Supreme Court, along with the rest of the nation, to choose sides and face the inevitable decision. After the fall of Sumter it was necessary to declare for the Union or against it. Three members of the Court, those whose states withdrew from the Union to combat federal authority, faced their decision with particular foreboding. Justice James M. Wayne of Georgia and Justice John Catron of Tennessee turned their backs upon secession despite intimidation, financial ruin, and cleavage from family and friends. But Justice John A. Campbell of Alabama resigned in order to help sustain the concept of states rights in its final thrust for supremacy.

Campbell, a prominent politician of Alabama, a competent lawyer, a man of affairs, and a slaveowner, was appointed to the Supreme Court by Franklin Pierce in 1853. Upon entering membership in the high Court, Campbell emancipated his slaves and proved to be temperate in viewing slavery. In the critical Dred Scott case, not unnaturally, he held with the majority, and he, along with his concurring brethren, was subjected to vilification.

Secession, when it came, troubled John Campbell sorely. He maintained that it was wrong; he stoutly argued for compromise; he rejected the desire for dissolution. That secession was a constitutional privilege and guarantee, he would not deny, but he rejected it as a feasible solution to the perplexities faced by the nation. He rejected it as unnecessary, undesirable, and unintelligent. In December, 1860, Justice Campbell, making the overture through his friend Montgomery Blair, offered to give Lincoln aid in refuting the imputations of the Southern conspirators.[18] But as the crisis unwound itself Justice Campbell served as an intermediary for the Southern cause.

In his role as agent for the South, Justice Campbell was completely disillusioned by negotiations with Secretary of State Seward. Seward had informed Campbell that Fort Sumter would be evacuated by March 20, 1861, but evacuation did not take place. Campbell's understanding, furthermore, on April 1 was that Fort Sumter would not be resupplied until Governor Francis W. Pickens of South Carolina was informed. On

---

[18] Montgomery Blair to Abraham Lincoln, December 14, 1860, Lincoln MSS.

April 7 Seward again assured Campbell, saying, "Faith as to Sumter fully kept—wait and see—."

Yet, on April 13 Lincoln announced that supplies would be brought to Sumter peaceably or by force. Campbell believed that he had been dealt with deceitfully. He heatedly called upon Secretary Seward for an explanation and stated with firm conviction that through him there had been systematic duplicity practiced upon General P. G. T. Beauregard and Confederate Secretary of War L. P. Walker. Justice Campbell declared to Seward that "no candid man who will read over what I have written and considers for a moment what is going on at Sumter, but will agree that to the equivocating conduct of the administration" must we attribute the great calamity that has overtaken the land.[19] How could Campbell have been aware that Seward was acting without the approval and consent of the President?

With these unfortunate circumstances Justice Campbell was on the verge of resigning from the Supreme Court, lured by duty to his state and smarting from what he deemed the chicanery of recent days. He delayed even yet, however. Members of the Court and others prominent in Washington convinced him that delay in withdrawing might contribute in some way to averting civil strife. To Justice Nathan Clifford, with whom he had discussed his intentions, he wrote, "Events at present look so threatening & the hopes of peace so remote that I suppose that it will soon become necessary for me to make my final decision[.] I there fore acquaint you with the fact, so that you should not be surprised by anything I should do[.]" He lamented that "I long apprehended that a collision of arms would take place at Sumter unless, there was something done to avoid it." [20]

Finally his irrevocable decision was made, and on April 25, 1861, he stated it in simple terms to the President of the United States: "I hereby resign the office of associate Justice of the Supreme Court of the United States—to take effect the 1st of May." [21] With no further official explanation—what was in his heart he left unsaid—Justice John A. Campbell was ready to leave the Court and the country he had served so well.

Deep in his heart Justice Campbell had the desire to pour forth his feelings with passion. Good taste dictated that he should reserve his intimate feelings for his friends rather than inflict them upon the President. To his brethren of the Court, however, he spoke with candor,

---

[19] John A. Campbell to William H. Seward, April 13, 1861, *ibid.*

[20] John A. Campbell to Nathan Clifford, April 18, 1861, Clifford MSS., Me. Hist. Soc.

[21] John A. Campbell to Abraham Lincoln, April 25, 1861, Papers of the Attorneys General, National Archives.

heatedly yet regretfully. He feared that his delay in resigning disgraced him in the eyes of those who awaited his decision, those who had expected that he would devote his strength and energy to the Southern cause.

To Justice Clifford he said what he could not bring himself to say to the President: "This administration seems determined to have a sectional war . . . I suppose the Congress at Montgomery will formally declare war—What will the end be?" Campbell admitted his regret in resigning, "principally as it diminishes the intimacy of those relations, which have grown up, among the members of the court & from which I have derived much happiness—" He condemned extremists both in the North and the South, lamenting that "The frightful excitement at the North has stimulated the administration to desperate measures & there is a party in the Confederate States equally desperate." The torment of the times Justice Campbell summed up in a pitiful lament characteristic of throngs of the citizenry, "Oh for peace[,] peace[.]" [22]

On taking leave of the Court, Justice Campbell wrote with tenderness and affection to the Chief Justice: "I should do injustice to my own feelings, if I were not to express to you the profound impression that your eminent qualities as a magistrate & jurist have made upon me." In the Chief Justice he found only "uprightness, fidelity, learning, thought and labor, . . . urbanity, gentleness, kindness, and tolerance." He said to Taney that from "[You] I have received all that I could have desired, & in leaving the court, I carry with me feelings of mingled reverence[,] affection[,] & gratitude." He closed "With the prayer that the remainder of your days be happy & their end peace." [23]

Thus he departed. His was no dramatic exit, no vehement abandonment of the Union. Campbell had mixed feelings in leaving the Court; he opposed the secession of Alabama; he resigned not to aid Alabama in war but to use every means in his power to prevent conflict. Although he ultimately served as Confederate assistant secretary of war, in a statement at Fort Pulaski after the end of the conflict he declared, "I . . . endeavored to avert the calamity. . . ." At the same time he revealed the reaction of some of his brethren of the Court at the time he resigned: "Chief Justice Taney, in my last interview with him 'acquiesced' in the propriety of the step. Mr. Justice Nelson regretted it, but thought it natural and proper." [24] He resigned to save his self-respect, his honor, and his reputation. On the bench of the Supreme Court the North distrusted him and the South despised him.

---

[22] John A. Campbell to Nathan Clifford, April 29, 1861, Clifford MSS.

[23] John A. Campbell to Roger B. Taney, April 29, 1861, Taney MSS., Md. Hist. Soc.

[24] Campbell's statement written at Fort Pulaski, July 10, 1865, quoted in Henry G. Connor, *John Archibald Campbell, Associate Justice of the United States Supreme Court, 1853-1861* (Cambridge, 1920), pp. 138-40.

The Court now lacked one-third of its normal personnel, but the President, harassed by demands and issues upon which the very existence of the nation depended, made no appointments. The burning need, demonstrated at Fort Sumter, was to prepare for war; all requirements of government were subordinated to military and political considerations in relation to that objective.

CHAPTER TWO

Inherited Court

OCTOGENARIAN CHIEF JUSTICE

Roger Brooke Taney, Chief Justice at the time of Lincoln's inauguration and one of the most controversial figures in American history, presided over a Court which was characterized both by strong personal animosities and by strong attachments and loyalties enhanced by a civil war. In a sense, despite the wrangling of the times, despite the passions and hatreds burning in men's hearts, and despite the vicious resentments he so often engendered by unpopular acts, the aged Chief Justice was the patriarch, the grand old man of the Court, though ranking second in seniority. How ironic it was that Taney, who was borne to the Court on a wave of unparalleled public resentment and who was swept roughly by the tempest that raged over Dred Scott, should live to be cast about viciously by the rage of civil war.

Taney, scion of a prominent Maryland family, was born in 1777. He attended Dickinson College, met the bar requirements in 1799, and promptly—due to the influence of family and friends—began a successful career in politics and the law. In 1816 he was elected to the Maryland senate where he played a prominent role in promoting banking and currency reform, as well as in advocating the just treatment of Negroes. Taney's interest in banking and financial problems led him into association with banking enterprises in Frederick, Maryland, and when he moved to Baltimore to practice law he continued his activities in that field.

At first Taney was friendly to the second Bank of the United States, which was chartered in 1816, because he felt it would serve to promote sound currency practices. But as counsel for the Union Bank of Maryland he began to feel the pressure of the national bank and to resent its policies. When Andrew Jackson invited him to serve as Secretary of the Treasury, Taney was of the opinion that if the Bank of the United States were to be rechartered, its powers should be clearly delimited. Later, he advised Jackson to veto renewal of the bank's charter and helped write Jackson's veto message. After the re-election of Jackson, Taney, out of resentment against its policies, urged Jackson to withdraw United States funds from the bank. And, as Secretary of the Treasury, Taney withdrew the funds, not out of subservience to Jackson but because of personal resentment against Mr. Biddle's bank.[1]

---

[1] Swisher, *Roger B. Taney*, pp. 252-53.

Soon after the United States Senate refused to confirm the nomination of Taney as Secretary of the Treasury—his appointment had been made when Congress was not in session—Jackson nominated him to a vacancy on the bench of the Supreme Court. But the Senate postponed indefinitely the vote on confirmation of that appointment. Upon the death of Chief Justice Marshall shortly thereafter, Jackson nominated Taney to be Chief Justice. Because of change in the political make-up of the Senate, this appointment was confirmed on March 15, 1836. Jackson had given Taney generous reward for political integrity and political usefulness.

Taney manifested, in spite of the controversies that haunted his career, an inherent affability and an admirable sincerity. He demonstrated broad tolerance by refusing to condone efforts to lead his wife, a Protestant, into his church, the Roman Catholic. His personal life was made difficult by the financial burdens of a family of six daughters and almost constant family illness. His wife and a daughter died in 1855, and his own health constantly harassed him. Perhaps the personal problems he faced contributed to the vast human understanding that he developed.

Taney's career on the Supreme Court was not stormy until the slavery controversy waxed hot. He was interested in colonizing Negroes in Africa and actively participated in that effort. He manumitted his own slaves and helped other slaves work their way to freedom,[2] but he believed slavery would continue as long as Negroes lived in the United States. He miscalculated badly the results that would accrue from the decisions handed down in the case of Dred Scott and the case of *Ableman v. Booth*, in which he delivered an opinion in 1859 strongly condemning efforts in Wisconsin to nullify the Fugitive Slave Act.

It is an irony of history that almost inevitably this man was on the unpopular or apparently undesirable side of controversies that raged during his public service. The resentment against him during the war years was almost boundless. As he was nearing the end of his career the Supreme Court entangled itself in the controversies that were raging around it, and the Justices were inevitably influenced by the frenzied conflict. Taney's views were not held by a majority of the Court during the war, but he never failed to state his convictions. Despite his advanced age and infirmity, Taney remained the head of the nation's highest judicial tribunal until death ended his career on October 12, 1864, in his eighty-seventh year.

As Chief Justice, Taney's views on the war were peculiar indeed. He deemed a peaceful separation of the North and the South preferable to a Union that was made possible only by military force and coercion. He denied to the federal government the power to sustain itself, the power to save itself from destruction. He maintained that the Constitution bestows no greater power upon the federal government in war than

---

[2] *Ibid.*, 94-95.

in peace. Taney's devotion to a government of laws was so great, so forceful, so complete, that he denied the right to suspend temporarily a part of the government of laws for the very purpose of restoring and securing for the future the unchallenged rule of law.

LOYALTY FROM GEORGIA

The senior member of the Supreme Court was Justice James M. Wayne of Georgia. A native of Savannah, he was graduated from the College of New Jersey (Princeton) in 1808, read law, and began practicing in 1810. He was a member of the house of representatives of Georgia, mayor of Savannah, a member of the Georgia supreme court, and ultimately a member of the national House of Representatives. Wayne served in Washington for three terms, following which Jackson appointed him to the Supreme Court. Significantly, he had supported Jackson's policies and had voted for the Force Bill at the time of the tariff controversy with South Carolina (he was the only representative from Georgia to support the bill.)

As a Justice, Wayne retained his strong Jacksonian views. In 1847, on the occasion of welcoming Daniel Webster to Savannah, he delivered an address in which he stated his devotion to the Union. As though a foreboding of the future disturbed his peace of mind, Wayne told the throng that "if, at any time hereafter, some dark cloud shall threaten our harmony, it will be made harmless by holding up to the people the remembrance of their fathers, united in the cause of American freedom." And he told Webster that upon his return to Massachusetts he should "tell those to whom you may speak that you have been among a people who, in the real respect which they feel and have shown to yourself, intended also to manifest their attachment to their Northern and Eastern brethren, and to show that their prevailing political feeling is devotion to our Union." [3]

When civil war came, James M. Wayne did not waver in his loyalty. His devotion to nation rather than to state cost him his personal holdings in Georgia. As an enemy alien his property was confiscated and turned over to his son, Henry C. Wayne, a Southern sympathizer and adjutant general of Georgia. Wayne was "Bred in the school of politics which made patriotism and Union a battle-cry, [and] long service on the Supreme Court in Washington and the natural conservatism of age served but to strengthen" the ties which made him loyal to the Union. His loyalty was costly almost beyond comprehension, and he suffered "Four

---

[3] Address of Justice James M. Wayne at Savannah on May 26, 1847, quoted in J. W. McIntyre, ed., *The Writings and Speeches of Daniel Webster* (Boston, 1903), IV, 98.

bitter-filled years. . . ." [4] His biographer, Alexander A. Lawrence, has said of him, "For a Justice from the lower South to uphold all of the war measures which came before the Court is one of the most interesting examples of judicial psychology. . . ." [5]

In the fall of 1861 Justice Wayne demonstrated his devotion to the policies that Lincoln devised to win the war. Acting under provision of a law empowering a Justice of the Supreme Court to issue a writ of habeas corpus, Wayne directed the clerk of the Court, William T. Carroll, to issue a writ in behalf of a petitioner, Edward A. Stevens, a soldier in the First Minnesota Regiment. The question at issue was whether Stevens was duly mustered into the army at Fort Snelling, since he entered it for three years during the period when its size was increased by presidential fiat, and before Congress convened in special session and confirmed Lincoln's acts. Wayne ordered the commander of the regiment, Colonel Willis A. Gorman, to produce Stevens at the Court chambers on August 14, 1861, so that a hearing could determine his status. [6]

Justice Wayne upheld the legality of the steps taken by the President. He stated his attitude toward the war and Lincoln's policies when he said, "It is my opinion that Congress has constitutional power to legalize and confirm executive acts, proclamations, and orders done for the public good, although they were not, when done, authorized by any existing laws." He affirmed that "such legislation by Congress may be made to operate retroactively to confirm what may have been done under such proclamations and orders. . . ." [7] Consequently, the Justice discharged the habeas corpus writ and remitted the petitioner to his military duty.

Commenting editorially on Wayne's decision, the New York *World* said that the ruling granted the executive powers for which "Judge Wayne will be severely criticized . . . but after all, it embodies the conclusions arrived at by those who believe that the integrity and perpetuity of the Union is worth maintaining by arms." [8] The Washington *National Intelligencer*, approving of Wayne's decision, pointed out that Justice Wayne, "who has thus honestly and frankly met a case which, had he chosen, might have given him an opportunity for cavilling at and em-

---

[4] Address of Alexander A. Lawrence, February 1, 1940, quoted in a letter to the author on February 13, 1940, from Miss Ola M. Wyeth, librarian of the Georgia Historical Society.

[5] Alexander A. Lawrence, *James Moore Wayne: Southern Unionist* (Chapel Hill, 1943), p. 183.

[6] James M. Wayne to William T. Carroll, August 10, 1861, Chase MSS., Hist. Soc. of Pa.

[7] Washington *National Intelligencer*, September 18, 1861, p. 3.

[8] Editorial, New York *World*, September 10, 1861, p. 4.

barassing [sic]" the government at a critical time, "is a native and citizen of Georgia" and like Justice Catron of Tennessee "an exile from his home, and proscribed for his faithfulness to the duties of his office." [9]

To Wayne the important consideration was to save the Union—to do so the Constitution had to adapt itself to the critical needs of the times. The ruling (its significance cannot be overstated) was a forecast of the Court's position on several occasions in the future while the war raged.

VIOLENCE AGAINST JUSTICE

At the beginning of the Civil War, Justice John Catron of Tennessee, like Justice Wayne a Union man of the South, sustained the efforts the Lincoln administration adopted to protect the Union. Catron made his contribution by maintaining federal judicial authority throughout his circuit, a circuit of the border states and one in which there was great zeal for secessionism. Here he upheld the position that the Union must be preserved; all considerations had to be tested in relation to that general objective.

Catron, third in seniority on the Court, was a native of Pennsylvania. He had had very few educational and economic advantages and at an early age went to Tennessee to live. He served under Jackson in the War of 1812, and after the war qualified for the Tennessee bar. As a lawyer he won a reputation practicing in the mountain districts of the state. Later he moved to Nashville, engaged in politics, and served in the judiciary of Tennessee. The day before Jackson left the presidency Congress increased the membership of the Supreme Court from seven to nine, and one of the last official acts of Jackson was to confer a Court appointment upon his fellow-Tennesseean. Catron, consequently, was one of the deans of the Court when civil war overcame the land. His service reflected his Jacksonian devotion to Union supremacy; to him there was no doubt as to the necessity of maintaining federal authority.

Following the December Term, 1860, (which ended on March 14, 1861) Justice Catron hurried from Washington to hold circuit court. Catron's circuit, consisting of Missouri, Kentucky, and Tennessee, was a hotbed of treason. The Justice was determined, however, to maintain the judicial authority of the United States.[10] He held circuit in Kentucky and then proceeded to Tennessee.

Catron's audacity was such that he attempted to hold circuit in Nashville even after the legislature of Tennessee had approved a military pact with the Confederacy. The marshal of the federal court in Nashville warned Catron to desist "or his life would pay the forfeit." Nonetheless, "The intrepid Judge commanded the marshal to do his duty in preparing

---

[9] Editorial, Washington *National Intelligencer*, September 18, 1861, p. 3.

[10] Editorial, Washington *Morning Chronicle*, February 1, 1865, p. 2.

for and opening the Court." The marshal finally confessed himself afraid to "discharge his duty, and flatly refused. Only then, did Catron give up his plan for circuit court." [11]

Announcing publicly that he intended to participate later in a special term of circuit court for Missouri, if it were possible to get through the Confederate line,[12] Catron finally made his way to St. Louis and held court. In a charge to the grand jury he denounced the traitorous acts of secessionists and denied writs of habeas corpus to men held on treason charges at Camp Jackson.[13]

His energy in behalf of the Union in Missouri was not unreported in Nashville. The Louisville *Journal* stated that upon his return to his home in Nashville personal animosity toward him surged violently—this was reward for faithful Union service in St. Louis. A vigilance committee visited him to warn that "he must either resign his office of judge or leave the State." The committee granted Catron twenty-four hours in which to decide; after that, it threatened, force would be applied. Within the hours of grace he "took his departure from Tennessee, leaving his aged wife behind him, as she was too sick and feeble to be removed." He had resolved to be loyal to the deep convictions he held; yet it was not easy for the aged jurist (he was over seventy years old) to incur the wrath of his neighbors. The *Journal* found this treatment of Catron "a gross and wanton outrage," since Tennessee could "have no apprehension that the residence of this aged judicial functionary among them was or could be dangerous to their State." [14]

Following his expulsion from Tennessee, Justice Catron held circuit court in Kentucky in the fall of 1861. Both civil and military officials in Kentucky sought and received his cooperation. Catron's desire was to uphold federal judicial authority, and when writs of habeas corpus were requested of him he decided each case upon its merits. Although he issued writs in behalf of persons arrested by the civil or military authorities in Kentucky, he did not demur when the military authorities quickly removed the prisoners to Fort Lafayette in New York. He heeded the opinion of United States Marshal A. H. Sneed, who had informed Lincoln, regarding some of the prisoners, that "it would be disastrous to have them released." [15] In some cases of military arrest Justice Catron met with the military authorities after he had granted writs of habeas corpus and agreed upon setting heavy bail and demanding oaths of allegiance before the prisoners were restored to freedom. Regarding this course, General

---

[11] Editorial, New York *Times*, July 13, 1861, p. 4.

[12] 70 U.S., memoranda, xii.

[13] Editorial, New York *Times*, July 13, 1861, p. 4.

[14] Washington *National Intelligencer*, August 19, 1861, p. 2 (reprinted from the Louisville *Journal*, August 13, 1861).

[15] A. H. Sneed to Abraham Lincoln, September 21, 1861, Lincoln MSS.

Robert Anderson informed Lincoln that it would "produce a good effect." [16] No greater cooperation could have been received from a federal judge. Catron was maintaining federal judicial supremacy when possible, but at the same time he assumed a policy of full cooperation with Union commanders who demanded that Southern sympathizers in Kentucky should be quieted.

The administration made strenuous efforts to hold Kentucky in the Union, and Catron wrote at length to Lincoln about Kentucky's turmoil. Catron offered him advice freely and expressed concern over judicial affairs. He related that "My K[entuck]y District Judge has left the state, and it is said is in Tennessee, which is true no doubt. His family has gone there. Will you inquire for me whether he has resigned his U[nited] S[tates] commission . . . a District Judge is much needed at this point." And he was curious about conditions in Washington, wishing "to hear from my friends . . . and to learn how City life is enjoyed; the city being a Camp. . . . this City [Louisville] is not much short of being a military camp also—"

Catron wrote of his devotion to the cause of the Union and told the President the story of his expulsion from Tennessee. He related that he had gone to Louisville, following the warning that had been served upon him to leave Tennessee, with the object of securing a residence "intending to return & send my furniture & bring my wife & servants—" Within a week the ailing Mrs. Catron and attendants followed the Justice to Louisville, "leaving 4 slaves behind—and every other species of property except her clothes & those of her attendants." Furthermore, Catron became acutely aware of the financial cost of his position when he "was notified of the act . . . passed at Richmond, forfeiting the goods, & lands of such who were even in K[entuck]y, as did acts prejudicial to the Confederacy. Mr. Benjamin's instructions may, & I think will, sweep mine in Nashville, worth over a $100,000. It covers my income on Houses & Stocks—" Justice Catron stood firm however; personal loss was secondary in this general maelstrom. He reaffirmed his stand to the President, neither requesting nor expecting any sympathy on the part of the North or the South. To Lincoln he declared his position boldly and vigorously: "I have to punish . . . Treason & will." [17]

"A PEACEFUL SEPARATION"

Fourth in seniority on the bench was Justice Samuel Nelson who was born in New York in 1792. Following graduation from Middlebury College, Nelson studied law and was admitted to the bar in 1817, beginning his practice in Cortland, New York. From 1823 to 1831 he was

---

[16] Robert Anderson to Abraham Lincoln, September 28, 1861, *ibid.*

[17] John Catron to Abraham Lincoln, October 9, 1861, *ibid.*

judge of New York's sixth circuit court; in 1831 he was elevated to the supreme court of the state, becoming its chief justice in 1837.

Nelson failed in an effort to become United States senator in 1845, but John Tyler nominated him to the Supreme Court that same year. As a member of the Court he gained a reputation as an authority on admiralty and maritime law, international law, conflict of laws, and patent law.

The position of Justice Nelson during the Civil War was exceedingly difficult. He maintained loyalty to the Union, but by persuasion he was allied with the conservative Northern Democrats. He was not only irked by President Lincoln's frequent use of arbitrary authority, but also he honestly doubted the advisability of coercing the Southern states.

When the conflict between the states began, he expressed his views frankly (just after the fall of Fort Sumter) to his brother Justice, Nathan Clifford, "Telegrapth [sic] just announcing Virginia is out—and forces south mustering—I disbelieve yet as to war—Necessity will compel a peaceful separation[.]" With such views Nelson might easily become very troublesome to the administration in the critical days ahead. "Too late in the age [continued Justice Nelson] for men to fight without any useful purpose—everybody agrees the Union can't be saved by this means." [18] It was fortunate, indeed, that President Lincoln did not agree with Justice Nelson.

In the deep gloom of 1862 when the Union was plunging from one disaster to another, when men of stout heart themselves were beginning to entertain doubts for the future, and when the administration seemed to be groping blindly for proper military leadership and adequate domestic policy, Justice Nelson expressed his despair more frankly. "*Proclamations* and *orders* thicken upon us from Washington—[he wrote to Justice Clifford]. The plunge of Emancipation is taken in one, and military despotism in the loyal states, in the other—no man can see the End—The darkness deepens—" [19] Justice Nelson was gaining a greater sense of the futility of the struggle. He could see no object in battling it out to the bitter end.

As the war progressed Justice Nelson continued to see no good in it. It was, he felt, futile and costly both in men and wealth. He believed that it was impossible to maintain a system such as the American Union unless it was voluntarily sustained. He believed that it was unjustifiable to exercise arbitrary authority to maintain a system based upon a govern-

---

[18] Samuel Nelson to Nathan Clifford, April 19, 1861, Clifford MSS.

[19] Samuel Nelson to Nathan Clifford, September 25, 1862, *ibid.* Despite his attitude toward the war, Justice Nelson was not reluctant to ask the administration for favors. See his request for an appointment for Henry Bennett of New York. Samuel Nelson to Abraham Lincoln, March 13, 1861, Lincoln MSS.

ment of laws—not a rule of men. Justice Nelson joined Chief Justice Taney in deeming arbitrary action unwise even if sustaining the Union depended upon it.

UNIONIST GRIER

Fifth in seniority on the bench of the Supreme Court was Justice Robert C. Grier. The eldest of eleven children of Reverend Isaac Grier and Elizabeth Grier, he was born in Cumberland county, Pennsylvania, in 1794. He was graduated from Dickinson College in 1812, taught there for a year, and then joined his father at Northumberland Academy. In 1815, upon the death of his father, he was appointed (as a youth of twenty-one) head of the academy. Here he taught Greek, Latin, mathematics, astronomy, and chemistry. Nevertheless, he found time to study law and was admitted to the bar in 1817.

Grier practiced in Danville, Pennsylvania, where he built up an extensive practice. It was so lucrative, in fact, that he was able not only to provide adequate support for his widowed mother but education for each of his brothers and sisters as well. In 1829 he married Isabella Rose, a member of a wealthy and prominent family. His legal career continued to prosper, and he became judge of the district court for Allegheny county. He served this court until 1846, when James K. Polk elevated him to the United States Supreme Court.

Grier was devoted wholeheartedly to the cause of the Union, though he was a Democrat. He revealed the full depth of his feelings about the war shortly after the tragic Union failure at the first battle of Bull Run in July, 1861. Grier wrote Justice Clifford that, despite illness, he "left home on the first of June" with his wife and daughter, "giving up my *annual trout* fish for the first time in *30 years—*" The Griers made their way South, finally arriving at Frankfort, Kentucky, where they visited "at my son in law's *Monroe*[.] sorry to learn he was a secessionist as insane as the others."

As to the debacle at Bull Run, Grier commented, "The result of this great battle will make a *long war of this*. We must conquer this rebellion or declare our republican government a failure, if it should cost 100,000 men & 1000 millions of money—" [20] That was the view of Robert C. Grier in the early stages of the war; that remained his view throughout the lengthy struggle.

DEVOTED DEMOCRAT

The Justice who ranked sixth in seniority after Campbell's resignation was Nathan Clifford. Clifford, the only son in a family of seven, was born at Rumney, New Hampshire, in 1803. He attended Haverhill Academy with the hope of preparing for entry into Dartmouth, but the death

---

[20] Robert C. Grier to Nathan Clifford, July 24, 1861, Clifford MSS.

of his father ended those plans. He studied law, passed the bar requirements in 1827, and began practice in Newfield, Maine. Here he married
Hannah Ayer, the daughter of a leading citizen.

Clifford's political career began in 1830 when he was elected to the
house of representatives of Maine. In 1838 he was elected to the national
House of Representatives, in which he served two terms. President Polk
appointed him Attorney General in 1846. He served Polk, too, as a
negotiator of the peace treaty that ended the Mexican War.

With Whig victory in 1848 Clifford retired from public life and
practiced law in Portland. Both in 1850 and 1853 he failed in attempts
to become a United States senator from Maine, but his public career was
not at an end. He had served in Polk's cabinet with James Buchanan,
who was Secretary of State, and when Buchanan was President he appointed his friend Clifford to the United States Supreme Court. Clifford
was affiliated with the pro-slavery Democrats. After strong opposition in
the Senate, the nomination was confirmed, and Clifford was seated on
January 21, 1858. As a member of the Court he specialized in commercial
and maritime law and Mexican land titles.

The role Justice Clifford found himself in during the Civil War was a
hard one. Generally he was aligned with the conservative Democrats.
He was loyal, but he was troubled by policies adopted by the administration to sustain the Union. As was later said of his role, "It is hard to
conceive of a more difficult position than the one occupied by Judge
Clifford during the war." He sought to uphold his ideals and concepts
of law, and his effort in addition to support "the government in the
prosecution of the war, was a task to try the nerves and tax the strength
of a very giant." [21] In general Clifford was critical of the administration's
use of arbitrary power, and he refused to recognize that in wartime it
could exercise emergency authority.[22]

Perhaps Justice Clifford's views on the problems of the war are explainable partly by the profound respect he had for Chief Justice Taney.
Six months after he was elevated to the Court, he wrote to his wife that
"having just received a beautiful letter from Ch[ief] Jus[tice] Taney I
thought I must send it to you & trust you will keep it as one among the
most valuable letters we ever received. . . . Every word of it breathes
sincerity and friendship—He is truly my friend & that is honor enough
at present." [23]

---

[21] Philip G. Clifford, *Nathan Clifford: Democrat (1803-1881)*, (New York, 1922),
p. 285.

[22] Despite Clifford's lack of cooperation with the administration, he wrote William
Whiting, who served as solicitor for the war department, seeking a commission for
Samuel Gilman, Jr. of New York City. See Nathan Clifford to William Whiting,
December 19, 1863, Lincoln MSS.

[23] Nathan Clifford to his wife, June 21, 1858, quoted in Clifford, *Nathan Clifford*,
p. 274.

Thus, of the six Justices who remained upon the bench in the early days of the war, three—Wayne, Catron, and Grier—were friendly to the Lincoln administration and its efforts to combat secession, and three—Taney, Nelson, and Clifford—were largely unfriendly to the administration. Fortunately there were three vacancies, and the administration would use them to its best advantage.

Lincoln chose to move slowly in making readjustments in regard to the Supreme Court. The most radical Republicans would have tried to destroy it or increase its size in order to swamp its Democratic members. But Lincoln was to deal patiently with it. His patience did not indicate lack of determination, but rather, an unusual restraint. A heavy burden rested upon those who directed the war effort and upon those whose responsibility it was to interpret the American constitutional system during a time when a section of the nation challenged with arms the supremacy of the Federal Union.

CHAPTER THREE

Declarations of Defiance

RUMORS OF COURT APPOINTMENTS

The inauguration of Abraham Lincoln unleashed a flood of speculation concerning appointments to the Supreme Court. Newsmen, congressmen close to the administration, Democrats—all speculated whether Southern ire might be quieted by elevation of persons who represented sentiments of border-state restraint. Would not such appointments demonstrate statesmanship characterized by political sagacity? Might not such appointments lead away from the raging passions that directed men's actions at the moment?

Until the events at Fort Sumter had swept away all hopes of such soothing action, rumor hurled itself upon rumor. Secretary of State Seward urged Lincoln to appoint Congressman George W. Summers of Virginia in order to strengthen Unionist sentiment and help sway the decision that Virginia was facing.[1] Pointing out that the deceased Justice Peter V. Daniel was from Virginia, Seward declared, "Summers nomination, being from the same state as well . . . would totally demoralize disunion in the Border states—Pray think of it." [2]

But the greatest pressures developed for John J. Crittenden of Kentucky, recently a United States senator, but now a member of the House. Rumors circulated that the appointment of Crittenden would be a brilliant political stroke, one that would fully reassure the Southerners. No other single act, declared the New York *Times*, would at the moment "so much reassure Conservative Southern men." [3] Governor Thomas H. Hicks of Maryland wrote Lincoln only a week after the inauguration, "if it could only be true, that he or some such man shall be appointed by you, it would be hailed by the unionists throughout the south . . . as a practical interpretation of the declaration, that your Inaugural meant peace—" [4]

Republican senatorial ranks and the cabinet as well split sharply over the desirability of appointing a man such as Crittenden. Secretary of the Treasury Salmon P. Chase opposed the move bitterly. Senator Lyman Trumbull of Illinois and other senatorial leaders were vexed. Lincoln

---

[1] Nicolay and Hay, *Abraham Lincoln*, III, 423.

[2] William H. Seward to Abraham Lincoln, March 9, 1861, Lincoln MSS.

[3] New York *Times*, March 7, 1861, p. 1.

[4] Thomas H. Hicks to Abraham Lincoln, March 11, 1861, Lincoln MSS.

could not have adopted a policy such as this (even if he so desired) because of the numerous, forceful, disquieted Republican leaders.[5]

Two members of the newly formed cabinet, Secretary of the Treasury Salmon P. Chase and Attorney General Edward Bates, were discussed in April as possible appointees to fill Court vacancies, and the Chicago *Tribune* reported a growing movement to elevate Secretary Chase.[6] "Your name is used freely here this morning [a friend in Columbus informed the Secretary] in connection with the Supreme Judgeship. . . . I wish I knew your feelings on this subject[.]"[7] A cabinet quarrel involving Chase and Seward was recounted by the New York *Times*, which explained that Chase might welcome an opportunity to depart from the cabinet. But it doubted this turn of events since an alteration in the Lincoln cabinet at such an early date would be forthright testimony of confusion and discord.[8]

Yet others were rumored for Supreme Court appointment. Joseph Holt, Kentucky politician and lawyer who had served Buchanan first as Postmaster General and finally as Secretary of War, was mentioned in the press as a possible appointee. Rumors of Court appointment hovered also over former Senator Thomas Ewing of Ohio; Judge William Y. Gholson of the supreme court of Ohio; Stephen T. Logan, Illinois jurist and former law partner of Abraham Lincoln; and Noah H. Swayne, an Ohio lawyer and politician.[9]

Broader considerations of strategy than alluded to in the press and in private correspondence were involved in Supreme Court appointments however. Appointments to the Court would have no effect whatsoever upon the constantly increasing challenge to federal authority. Furthermore, appointments, in the final analysis, depended upon a reorganization of the circuit system of the United States, a circuit system that was badly antiquated and one that, on account of the secession of the Southern states, would be vastly modified. Until the circuit system was reorganized

---

[5] New York *Times*, March 11, 1861, p. 1 (reprinted from the Baltimore *American*).

[6] Chicago *Tribune*, April 10, 1861, p. 2.

[7] D. Rees to Salmon P. Chase, April 5, 1861, Chase MSS., Library of Congress.

[8] New York *Times*, April 9, 1861, p. 1.

[9] A letter from former President Millard Fillmore to Lincoln's commissioner of agriculture, Isaac Newton, dated November 18, 1861, in which Fillmore urged the appointment of Isaac Hazlehurst of Pennsylvania to the Supreme Court, is to be found in the Lincoln MSS. Fillmore wrote the letter during the period when the three Supreme Court vacancies awaited Lincoln's attention. "His neighbors must know him much better than I, [wrote Fillmore] but from all my acquaintance I have the highest opinion of his integrity, talents and legal ability, and if there is no objection to his locality I do not see how the President can do better than to appoint him." Another letter in behalf of Hazlehurst, from James Pollock to Simon Cameron, November 28, 1861, found its way into the Lincoln MSS.

to meet the needs of the United States in 1861, appointments would be delayed unless resignation or death so depleted the Court that it could not function. The Chicago *Tribune* informed its readers that although the Republicans had intended to reorganize the circuits quickly, dissolution of the Union posed additional questions. The *Tribune*—it was heartily joined by other Republican papers as well as Republican leaders —was toying with the thought that in a reorganization the North should be assigned a majority of the Supreme Court Justices.[10] At the time there were five circuits in the South and four in the North.

With the events at Fort Sumter military problems took precedence over all nonmilitary matters. Along with all political problems that could be pushed aside, Supreme Court appointments as well as the broader task of reorganizing the circuit system were delayed. The question of the structure of the judiciary could not compete at the moment with more pressing matters.

LINCOLN AND TANEY CLASH

The administration was unable, nevertheless, to wash its hands of judicial problems. Soon after the war began, the question of personal rights and civil liberties thrust itself forward. There were many Southern sympathizers in the North, and Lincoln believed that they had to be dealt with summarily. He concluded that it was the President, in his executive capacity, who must cope with Northern traitors. But Chief Justice Taney determined that the role of the judiciary must remain unaltered even in civil war and that those whose loyalty was questioned should be tried in the usual manner before the civil courts. Consequently the President and the Chief Justice defied each other. Within six weeks they were matching wits in a bitter controversy over civil liberties. The prosecution of the war was to provoke a constantly recurring battle over the proper role of the judiciary in wartime.

The city of Washington, situated between Virginia and Maryland, was in a precarious situation from the beginning of the secessionist movement. With the vote of secession by the Richmond convention on April 17, 1861, to sustain the security of the national capital became a basic Union objective. With Virginia lost to the cause, it was absolutely essential that Maryland remain loyal, but Maryland had much pro-Southern sentiment within it.

Following the fall of Fort Sumter the situation in Maryland became acute. Mayor George W. Brown of Baltimore kept Lincoln informed as to the agitation within the city, and finally, in utter frustration, wrote,

---

[10] Chicago *Tribune*, March 9, 1861, p. 1; see also Richard H. Dana, Jr. to Charles Sumner, March 9, 1861, Sumner MSS., Widener Library.

"I . . . earnestly request that no more troops be permitted . . . to pass through the city." [11] On April 26, with the Maryland legislature scheduled to meet the next day, President Lincoln wrote General Winfield Scott, ·the commanding general of the army, that the legislature would probably take steps to oppose Union authority and that "I therefore conclude that it is only left to the commanding General to watch, and await their action. . . ." [12]

Lincoln was in dire need of troops and to transport them through a semi-hostile Maryland was a difficult problem. To combat disloyal elements and bring their activities under control, Lincoln on April 27, 1861, no longer deeming it advisable to delay, directed General Scott to suspend the writ of habeas corpus whenever necessary in the area from Washington to Philadelphia. [13]

Maryland was a part of the circuit over which Chief Justice Taney presided, and at this critical time Taney was engaged in holding circuit court at Baltimore. The cause of the clash between the President and the Chief Justice was the arrest of John Merryman, president of the Maryland State Agricultural Society, a man of family, position, and property, who was seized by military authorities on the morning of May 25, 1861, on the charge of being an active secessionist sympathizer and taken to Fort McHenry. Merryman associated with forces that were opposed to the Union and enunciated secessionist sentiments. The arrest was made under the authority of General George Cadwalader who was the military head of the area.

The day of the arrest a petition was filed in the circuit court at Baltimore requesting the court to issue a writ of habeas corpus in behalf of Merryman and direct it to General Cadwalader, commanding him to produce the prisoner before the court "with the cause, if any, for his arrest and detention. . . ." [14] Chief Justice Taney promptly issued the writ and made it returnable "at eleven o'clock, on Monday, the 27th of May, at the circuit court room, in the Masonic Hall, in the city of Baltimore, before me, chief justice of the supreme court of the United States." [15]

General Cadwalader sensed immediately that this case involved him in weighty responsibility, and he was unwilling to proceed until he made certain the attitude of the President toward the interference of the Chief Justice. Therefore he communicated with army headquarters

---

[11] George W. Brown to Abraham Lincoln, April 18, 1861, Lincoln MSS.

[12] Abraham Lincoln to Winfield Scott, April 25, 1861, copy in Lincoln's hand, *ibid.*

[13] "Proclamation Authorizing Suspension of the Writ of Habeas Corpus," *H.R. Exec. Doc. No. 6*, 37th Cong., 1st sess., p. 3.

[14] 17 Federal Cases, 145. This compilation of cases heard by United States district and circuit courts from 1789 to 1880 is cited hereafter as Fed. Cas.

[15] *Ibid.*, 146.

and asked for instructions from Lieutenant Colonel Edward D. Townsend, assistant adjutant general.[16]

At the hour appointed by the Court, Colonel Lee, a military aide,
appeared at the courtroom to present the Chief Justice with Cadwalader's
return to the writ. The answer sent by the General was in every sense
appropriate and respectful. Cadwalader informed Taney that under the
direction of the President he was bound to take steps to interfere with
Merryman's actions because the public safety was at stake. In a spirit of
friendly cooperation and mutual respect the General wrote, "those who
should co-operate in the present trying and painful position . . . should
not, by any unnecessary want of confidence in each other, increase our
embarassments [sic]." He urged the court to postpone further action,
pending instructions he awaited from the President.[17]

Chief Justice Taney was not impressed either by Colonel Lee or by
the letter of explanation sent by General Cadwalader. Ignoring the letter,
he asked Colonel Lee if John Merryman had been brought into court
as ordered; upon a reply in the negative Taney ruled that the General
"has acted in disobedience to the writ, and I therefore direct that an
attachment be at once issued against him, returnable before me here, at
twelve o'clock tomorrow [the twenty-eighth of May]." [18] Before leaving
for Court on the twenty-eighth, Taney remarked that he would not be
surprised if he were in prison by nightfall, but he intended to do his
duty.[19]

General Cadwalader, in the meantime, was fortified in his position,
having received instructions from Lieutenant Colonel Townsend. He
was informed that "The general-in-chief [Winfield Scott] directs me to
say . . . that you will hold in secure confinement all persons implicated
in treasonable practices. . . ." [20] Consequently the General resisted Taney's
writ of attachment by directing that the marshal of the court be denied
entrance to Fort McHenry.

At noon on the twenty-eighth a throng gathered in front of the
Masonic Hall, and the courtroom, too, was densely crowded.[21] This
judicial controversy had served to incite the populace, a populace already
frenzied by secessionist flirtations or Unionist urges. The marshal, Washington Bonifant, made his report to the court. He informed the Chief
Justice that he presented himself at the outer gate of the fort, sent in
his name, but received the reply, "no answer." Bonifant reported, "I

---

[16] *War of the Rebellion: Official Records of the Union and Confederate Armies*
(Washington, 1880-1901), ser. II, vol. I, 574. Cited hereafter as *Offic. Rec.*

[17] 17 Fed. Cas. 146.

[18] *Ibid.*

[19] Swisher, *Roger B. Taney*, p. 552.

[20] *Offic. Rec.*, ser. II, vol. I, 576.

[21] New York *World*, May 29, 1861, p. 4.

could not serve the writ. . . . I was not permitted to enter the gate." [22]
Taney received the news with vexation and told the marshal that a *posse
comitatus* could have been summoned, though such a body would have
been of little avail against superior military force.

The Chief Justice was thoroughly aroused. His first step was to rule
in behalf of Merryman, stating that "It is . . . very clear that John Merryman . . . is entitled to be set at liberty. . . ." [23] His next step was to deliver
a sweeping denunciation of arbitrary military arrest. He made the occasion an opportunity to bring all the prestige and dignity of his high
office to bear upon the question of denial of judicial processes in matters
of military arrest. He called for a government of laws and issued a ring-
ing defense of civil liberties. He denounced the use of arbitrary and
unconstitutional power by the Chief Executive. In regard to the claim
that the President could suspend the writ of habeas corpus, the Chief
Justice said, "I certainly listened to it with some surprise. . . ."

Taney, trumpeting a defiance of the President that was calculated to
precipitate either a head-on collision or presidential submission, pointed
out that if General Cadwalader merely had acted upon his own authority
the case would not have assumed constitutional significance. But on the
contrary, he declared, the General acted under the explicit instructions
of the highest military authority in the nation, authority that itself was
under the direct orders of the President. It was that fact that made the
cause of John Merryman a *cause célèbre*.

Taney declared that since the President was exercising a power that
he did not possess, "a proper respect for the high office he fills, requires
me to state plainly and fully the grounds of my opinion." Citing the
Constitution, he maintained that Congress alone was granted authority
to suspend the writ of habeas corpus. "He certainly does not faithfully
execute the laws," scornfully continued the Chief Justice, "if he takes
upon himself legislative power, by suspending the writ of habeas corpus,
and the judicial power also, by arresting and imprisoning a person without due process of law." Taney could find no justification for emergency
presidential powers whether "for self-defence in times of tumult and
danger" or not.

The Chief Justice made no defense of John Merryman; he made no
argument in behalf of John Merryman's acts. He emphasized that both
the United States district court and the United States circuit court in
Baltimore were functioning in the fullness of their authority. He declared
that the United States district attorney should have begun proceedings
before a United States commissioner and if the evidence had been deemed
sufficient, Merryman should have been brought to trial. The Chief Justice

---

[22] 17 Fed. Cas. 147.
[23] Chief Justice Taney's decision covers pages 147-53 of 17 Fed. Cas.

said that the federal courts alone had jurisdiction over men such as John Merryman.

Taney summed up his position in the following statement:

... great and fundamental laws ... have been disregarded and suspended ... by a military order, supported by force of arms. ... I can only say that if the authority which the constitution has confided to the judicial department and judicial officers, may thus, upon any pretext or under any circumstances, be usurped by the military power, at its discretion, the people of the United States are no longer living under a government of laws but every citizen holds life, liberty and property at the will and pleasure of the army officer in whose military district he may happen to be found.

He declared that he could not make the decision of his court effective because he faced a military force "too strong for me to overcome." Furthermore he provided a way for the President to withdraw gracefully from the position that had been chosen. Taney stated that he realized that the officer "who has incurred this grave responsibility may have misunderstood his instructions, and exceeded that authority intended to be given him." Consequently the Chief Justice ordered the clerk "to transmit a copy" of all of the proceedings in the case, including the decision, to the President of the United States. And Taney concluded, "It will then remain for that high officer in fulfillment of his constitutional obligation to ... determine what measures he will take to cause the civil process of the United States to be respected and enforced."

This, then, was Taney's declaration of defiance. This was his position and from it he would not retreat. A man of less zeal for the law would never have enunciated such views at so critical a time. But the Chief Justice, despite the weight of his years, interpreted this as his duty and would not shirk his responsibility as he saw it.

The decision of the court, with all its venom and sting, made a deep impression upon the press, recording as it was the daily events of dissolution. It was widely quoted and widely commented upon editorially. Leading Northern dailies found Taney's views incomprehensible. The Chicago *Tribune*, in an editorial titled "Old Taney," stated that when Taney delivered the Dred Scott decision he was already in his dotage and that the Merryman decision was evidence that in the intervening years his faculties had brightened none whatsoever.[24] Horace Greeley's New York *Tribune* criticized Taney vigorously. It declared that the Chief Justice wretchedly "takes sides with traitors ... throwing about them the sheltering protection of the ermine." It warned that "when Treason stalks abroad in arms let decrepit Judges give place to men capable of detecting and crushing it." And it expressed the hope that no occasion would present itself to General Cadwalader necessitating the arrest of the aged Chief Justice! [25]

[24] Editorial, Chicago *Tribune*, May 30, 1861, p. 1.
[25] Editorial, New York *Tribune*, May 29, 1861, p. 4.

Taney was deemed a meddler by the New York *Times*. His interposition was condemned as officious and improper, presenting "the ungracious spectacle of a judicial and a military authority of the United States at variance, the soldier eager to punish, and the jurist to exculpate a traitor." It expressed no surprise that the author of the Dred Scott decision "should soil the ermine of justice . . . and go through history as the Judge who draggled his official robes in the pollutions of treason."[26]

It was the tone of Taney's decision that offended the New York *World*, which felt it was "uncalled for and in bad taste." Taney had violated, in its opinion, the "decorum which ought to regulate the bearing of the first judicial officer of the government toward its first executive officer."[27] As to bringing Merryman to trial in Maryland, the New York *World* declared that an uproar would have resulted, stemming from the turmoil already rampant within the state. "It is hard even for a chief justice [continued the New York *World*] to confess that his 'occupation's gone,' and to concede that the sergeant of the guard is more in place than a tipstaff. But such a time may have come."[28] At this point the *World* maintained that emergency expanded the powers of the federal government; however, it would change its views as the war progressed.

Two Washington newspapers, the *Evening Star* and the *National Intelligencer*, joined in a greater understanding of the position of the Chief Justice. The *Evening Star* found Taney correct according to the "strict letter of the law," but his decision, it maintained, "exhibits a determination on his part palpably to ignore the existing state of the country."[29] The *National Intelligencer* referred to Taney's decision as an "able and lucid opinion" defending the rule of law. But Lincoln's action, it affirmed, resulted "from what he believes such an impervious public necessity as is held to justify him in transcending the letter of the Constitution."[30]

"Impervious public necessity"—that was the theme of those who justified Lincoln's position in the Merryman case. The heart of the question was whether the Constitution expanded in wartime to provide special presidential authority. The diametrically opposed position on the part of Chief Justice and President gave promise of more quarrels in the future— quarrels of equal rancor and equal import.

Taney continued to hold circuit court in Baltimore after he had disposed of the Merryman case, but he made no further official comment

[26] Editorial, New York *Times*, May 29, 1861, pp. 4-5, and *ibid.*, May 30, 1861, pp. 4-5.

[27] Editorial, New York *World*, May 29, 1861, p. 5.

[28] *Ibid.*, June 5, 1861, p. 5.

[29] Editorial, Washington *Evening Star*, May 29, 1861, p. 2.

[30] Editorial, Washington *National Intelligencer*, June 8, 1861, p. 3.

upon it. In his personal correspondence, however, he did not hesitate to express the full extent of his resentment. To his close friend, former Congressman George W. Hughes of Maryland, who had expressed Southern sentiments in a speech in the House on February 5, 1861, he wrote that he wished no conflict with President Lincoln "and would be glad, as you will readily suppose, to pass the brief remnant of life that may yet be vouch-safed to me in peace with all men." Nevertheless he expressed the firm intention of meeting all official responsibilities despite personal consequences.[31]

A few days later, in a letter to former President Franklin Pierce, the Chief Justice revealed fully his personal reaction to the civil conflict and unparalleled turmoil. He acknowledged with satisfaction Pierce's "cordial approbation of my decision." He explained that he felt a great sense of responsibility in the Merryman case due to ". . . the present state of the public mind inflamed with passion & seeking to accomplish its object by force of arms." He said his duty was clear and that he would not evade it, adding,

The paroxism [sic] of passion into which the country has suddenly been thrown—appears to me to amount almost to delirium. I hope that it is too violent to last long—and that calmer and more sober thoughts will soon take its place—and that the north as well as the south will see that a peaceful separation with free institutions in each section—is far better—than the union of all the present states under a military government & a reign of terror—preceded too by a civil war with all its horror & which end as it may will prove ruinous to the victors as well as the vanquished—But at present I grieve to say—passion—& hate—sweeps every thing before them—[32]

How would this Chief Justice view cases involving the war and efforts of the Lincoln administration when they arrived for adjudication before the Supreme Court? There could be no doubt. The Lincoln government could expect no support from the Chief Justice. To Taney the solution was "peaceful separation."

Ensuing events only served to strengthen the enmity that was felt by the Chief Justice toward the Chief Executive. He came to look upon Lincoln's position as deliberately provocative. He exhibited his resentment when he refused to accompany the members of the Court on January 1, 1862, in the customary call upon the President. "Mr. Carroll [he wrote to Justice James M. Wayne] has given me your message—I expect some friends tomorrow—and as there is no established Etiquette which requires the court to wait on the President on the 1st of January, as a matter of official courtesy, I am sure my Brethren will excuse me for

---

[31] Roger B. Taney to George W. Hughes, June 8, 1861, quoted in Samuel Tyler, *Memoir of Roger Brooke Taney, L.L.D.* (Baltimore, 1872), pp. 430-31.

[32] Roger B. Taney to Franklin Pierce, June 12, 1861, Pierce MSS., Library of Congress.

not joining them tomorrow[.]" [33] The Chief Justice could not submerge his feelings; to Abraham Lincoln he desired to pay no visit.

In almost the same days that Taney clashed with the administration over the case of John Merryman, United States District Judge Samuel Treat at St. Louis had a somewhat similar experience.[34] Treat issued a writ of habeas corpus in behalf of Captain Emmet McDonald, who was arrested under the authority of General William S. Harney, and directed it to the general. But Harney refused to surrender the prisoner and informed Treat that he had asked Washington for instructions.[35] When it became clear that the military authorities would not give heed to his order, Treat handed down an opinion not unlike the Merryman decision.[36]

Knowing that Taney was involved in a similar battle, he sent the Chief Justice a copy of his decision. Taney reciprocated by sending to Treat a copy of the Merryman decision. And Taney declared, "It exhibits a sad & alarming condition of the public mind when such a question can be regarded as open to discussion: and no one can foresee to what disastrous results the inflamed passions of the present day may lead—" [37]

It will be remembered that the Chief Justice had directed that a copy of the Merryman decision be sent directly to the President. What method would be selected by Lincoln to answer the Chief Justice? Would he simply be ignored? Would the answer be of a public or private nature? These questions remained unanswered for many days, and the President kept his silence.

In the meanwhile several federal district attorneys felt the need for a statement of policy by Attorney General Bates, and in response to a question from one of them, Bates declared on June 4, 1861, "As yet, the Government has not come to any definite resolves." Nonetheless, he was willing to offer advice. "The President [he wrote] is required by the Constitution . . . to Suppress insurrection. . . . Draw your own inferences." [38]

The reply of President Lincoln to Chief Justice Taney, when it arrived, consisted of two parts: Lincoln answered the Chief Justice in the July fourth message to the special session of Congress, and Attorney General Bates issued an opinion, twenty-six pages in length, dealing with the powers of the President in time of emergency.

[33] Roger B. Taney to James M. Wayne, December 31, 1861, copy made from recollection on January 2, 1862, Taney MSS., Md. Hist. Soc.

[34] Judge Samuel Treat of St. Louis should not be confused with Judge Samuel H. Treat, who was federal district judge at Springfield, Illinois.

[35] New York *Times*, May 16, 1861, p. 1.

[36] 16 Fed. Cas. 33.

[37] Roger B. Taney to Samuel Treat, June 5, 1861, Treat MSS., Mo. Hist. Soc.

[38] Edward Bates to George A. Coffey, June 4, 1861, Attorney General's Letter Books, National Archives.

In the message to Congress the President explained that in order to combat "such individuals as . . . might . . . [be deemed] dangerous to the public safety," he considered it a "duty" to empower generals in certain cases to suspend the writ of habeas corpus.[39] Such action, however, had "purposely been exercised but very sparingly." The President, obviously referring to the Chief Justice and even quoting from a portion of the opinion Taney delivered, said that the whole country had had its attention *"called to the proposition that one who has sworn to 'take care that the laws be faithfully executed' should not himself violate them."* [40] Lincoln explained that in nearly one-third of the states federal law was being violated, and that he did not intend to permit the habeas corpus writ, which was made in "such extreme tenderness of the citizen's liberty. . . ." to assist those who were attempting to destroy Federal authority.

This man who had long before demonstrated a remarkable ability to phrase questions, asked, *"are all the laws, but one to go unexecuted, and the government itself go to pieces, lest that one be violated?"* [41] And he posed yet another question: *"Even in such a case, would not the official oath be broken if the government should be overthrown, when it was believed that disregarding the single law, would tend to preserve it?"* [42]

As to whether the Congress or the President could suspend the writ, Lincoln said that he could not believe that "the framers of the instrument intended, that in every case, the danger should run its course, until Congress could be called together" because an emergency could arise in which it might be impossible for Congress to assemble. He promised that a more lengthy exposition on the subject would be made public shortly by the Attorney General. As to whether Congress should legislate upon this subject, Lincoln submitted that to the judgment of the legislators. With logic and dignity the Chief Executive had answered the Chief Justice.[43]

The day after the President answered Taney, Attorney General Bates delivered his opinion on arbitrary arrest.[44] Bates interpreted the President's responsibility as hinging upon the very nature of the presidential office. He declared that since a president has the responsibility to "preserve, protect, and defend the Constitution," there is implied in that responsibility the power to fulfill his oath. As Bates pointed out, the means whereby a president will combat insurrection are not prescribed by the Constitution, the discretion of the president prevailing. "I am clearly of

---

[39] Lincoln's message of July 4, 1861, is to be found in *Works*, IV, 421-41.

[40] My italics.

[41] My italics with the exception of "but one."

[42] My italics.

[43] Edward S. Corwin, *The Twilight of the Supreme Court: A History of Our Constitutional Theory* (New Haven, 1934), pp. 133-34.

[44] Edward Bates to Abraham Lincoln, July 5, 1861, Lincoln MSS.

the opinion [the Attorney General ruled] that, in a time like the present
. . . the President has the lawful discretionary power to arrest and hold
in custody persons known to have criminal intercourse with the insurgents." Exceptional times call forth exceptional powers—this was the full
answer of Abraham Lincoln and his Attorney General to the challenge
by Chief Justice Taney.

In view of the bitterness engendered in relations between the Chief
Executive and the Chief Justice, it is of interest to examine the denoue-
ment of the Merryman case. In midsummer, 1861, Attorney General
Bates sent an order of Secretary of War Simon Cameron to the United
States district attorney at Baltimore, William M. Addison. It directed the
military authorities at Fort McHenry to deliver Merryman to the marshal
of the district court if the marshal were properly equipped with a warrant for his arrest on the charge of treason.[45] Merryman was subsequently
indicted for treason and his case was remitted in November, 1861, to the
United States circuit court for Maryland. He was required to put up the
sum of $20,000 as a guarantee that he would not renew anti-Union ac-
tivities. The case went no further; it was continued by the court and
ultimately dropped. This was typical of the treatment accorded such
cases by the Lincoln administration.[46] When Merryman was no longer
capable of harming the Union, Lincoln, who sought no tyranny, gladly
washed his hands of the Merryman controversy. But neither the President
nor the Chief Justice had a change of heart, and their differences endured.

Special Session and the Judiciary

There was a single objective set up for the special session of the Thirty-
Seventh Congress which assembled on July 4, 1861: it must enact legislation to combat the incorrigible South. The war had begun in April; the
administration had resisted the Southern conspiracy in the weeks that
followed; the President had clashed with the Chief Justice. Lincoln was
now ready to present his program to Congress for approval. In the days
ahead the Congress dealt largely with matters pertaining to the coming
of war—mobilization of both human and economic resources.

But the Congress did not restrict itself solely to the military problems
that beset the nation. It turned to many of the normal problems of government, and relative to the federal judiciary, it gave indication that it
would be willing to take extensive action. The administration, however,
was not ready for Congress to enter into the complexities of judicial
reorganization or reform. The President did not even make a move to

---

[45] Edward Bates to William M. Addison, July 12, 1861, Attorney General's Letter
Books.

[46] James G. Randall, *Constitutional Problems Under Lincoln*, rev. ed. (Urbana,
Illinois, 1951), p. 162, n. 43.

fill any of the three vacancies existing on the bench. The administration preferred to hold in abeyance a multitude of matters—including judicial ones—until problems could be more carefully thought through and policies formulated.

Proposals to change judicial procedures and to alter judicial districts were introduced into the special session nonetheless. Among the most important were: a bill to prohibit disloyal citizens from suing in the courts; a bill to form new federal judicial districts; and a bill to facilitate removal of certain proceedings from state courts to the federal courts. In addition, resolutions were introduced, looking toward the regular session of Congress in December, asking Secretary of the Interior Caleb B. Smith to provide Congress with information as to the number of federal cases that were heard from 1850 to 1860, the number of days each Supreme Court Justice was on circuit in each year of the decade, the number of cases on the federal dockets in January, 1860, and the number of vacant federal judgeships. These resolutions obviously involved the assembling of data that would be used by the Congress as ammunition against the federal judiciary.

Steps were taken at the special session to eliminate at once two weaknesses in the federal judicial system. One weakness pertained to delay in hearing cases in districts where the judgeship was vacant or the judge was ill; [47] the other involved the need to relieve the government of heavy expense in appealing California land title cases to the Supreme Court.[48]

With these tasks accomplished, judicial matters were cast into the background. It was not that all matters pertaining to the judiciary were satisfactory, but rather, that problems of the war came first. Before many months other judicial problems—proposals to abolish the Supreme Court, pack it, or reorganize it, and the question of appointments as well—would have their day before the Congress and the President. But when the special session adjourned in August, they remained untouched.

THE SUPREME COURT MEETS

As December, 1861, approached, the Supreme Court as well as the Congress made ready to resume their activity. The Court was rapidly approaching its day of Armageddon. The Attorney General was busy preparing for the first term of Court during his tenure, and in his diary recorded facts in relation to the forthcoming meeting. He spent almost the whole of November 27 concerning himself with the Court. He visited William T. Carroll, the clerk, "and rec[eive]d many kind suggestions . . . about the details of business." He examined the docket and visited the

---

[47] *Cong. Globe*, 37th Cong., 1st sess., appendix, p. 42; 12 Stat. 318.

[48] Edward Bates to S. S. Blair, July 31, 1861, *Cong. Globe*, 37th Cong., 1st sess., p. 455.

courtroom. He paid a call upon Chief Justice Taney and "had a conversation much more pleasant than I expected." He visited, too, with Justice Wayne "and had an agreeable talk." He inferred, erroneously, from his conversations that "little business will be done, and that not in as strict order as is usual." [49] Could his inference have been the result of wishful thinking? The Court, under the headship it enjoyed, could not be expected to put itself on any part-time basis.

The Court shared with the general citizenry a feeling of expectancy in relation to the President's first annual message which was to be submitted on December 3. Naturally the message would include recommendations that would affect the judiciary. Filling the three vacancies would inevitably involve some reorganization of the circuits. Would administration hotheads seek to assault the Court? What thoughts must have been racing through the minds of the aged Chief Justice and his associates?

The Supreme Court opened its regular term on December 3. Attorney General Bates delivered a memorial to the deceased Justice McLean. And the new Attorney General did not lose the opportunity to address to the Court stirring observations on the turmoil that swept the nation.

Bates lamented, "Oh! that today it were my delightful offices to bring you good tidings, and to publish to you peace." [50] He remarked that since the first meeting of the Court "no term has yet been held under circumstances so gloomy and sorrowful." He declared that "Even this august tribunal . . . the revered dispenser of our country's justice, shares with us in feeling the common sorrow, and suffers in our common calamity." Attorney General Bates referred to the vacancies, saying that two Justices who recently occupied seats were "beyond the reach of malice," but another, "has been swept away from his high position by the turbulent waves of faction and civil war." Bates pointed out that normally vacancies would have been filled more promptly; the Court itself bore testimony of the troubled times.

But Bates saw more tragedy in the situation than the vacant seats implied. He told the Court that its "lawful jurisdiction" was restrained, that its "just power" was diminished, and that its "beneficient authority to administer justice" was denied. He said that he beheld a "ghastly spectacle" as he looked over the nation. He lamented that since insurrection engulfed the land, "your just and lawful power is practically annulled, for the laws are silent amidst arms" and the drum drowns out the voice of "legal justice."

---

[49] Howard K. Beale, ed., *The Diary of Edward Bates, 1859-1866*, American Historical Association, *Annual Report for 1930*, vol. IV, (Washington, 1933), 204-05 (November 27, 1861). Cited hereafter as Bates, *Diary*.

[50] Attorney General Bates's remarks to the Supreme Court are to be found in 66 U.S. 8-10.

Chief Justice Taney replied for the Court. He acknowledged the high tribute that had been paid to the former Justice but remained quiet concerning the eloquent display that the Court had just experienced. He expressed neither sympathy with nor approval of Bates's comments on the war, nor did he even dignify the Attorney General's remarks by disclosing whether the Court accepted them in the spirit in which they were presented.

LINCOLN REVEALS HIS HAND

On the same day, December 3, within the same building that sheltered the Court and not far removed from its meeting place, Congress assembled to receive Lincoln's first annual message. The President was now ready to deal with judicial problems, and in the course of his message which dealt with a multitude of matters, he presented a plan of action. He was fully aware, remarked the New York *Tribune*, that he "was elected on the grounds of distinct antagonism to . . . the Supreme Court," and he was not going to break faith with those who depended upon him to deal with it. To have broken faith, it added, would have proved him "a dissembler, a trickster, a liar and a fool." [51] But Lincoln, true to his personal feelings in the matter, kept faith.

The President explained that although three vacancies existed, he delayed making appointments because two of the Justices had resided in areas overrun by insurrection, the result being that successors could not have functioned in their circuits.[52] He said, too, that he had been unwilling to throw all of the appointments into the hands of the North, "thus disabling myself from doing justice to the South on the return of peace." Furthermore, it occurred to the President that it would be equitable, from the point of view of territory and population, to grant to the North one additional circuit by consolidating the Southern states into fewer circuits. Lincoln declared that the circuit of Justice McLean, a circuit over which he presided for thirty years, grew into a vast empire during his tenure. The population rose from 1,470,000 in 1830 to 6,151,000 in 1860, resulting, said Lincoln, in a circuit "altogether too large for any one Judge. . . ." And he emphasized that what was true of the McLean circuit was true of the others.

Of equal importance was to determine what to do to improve the federal circuit system. Lincoln fully comprehended this problem. It is interesting to see him, confronted by the military threat that was to haunt almost all of the days of his presidency, planning improvement in the federal judicial system. It was in reality an expression of faith that

[51] Editorial, New York *Tribune*, November 27, 1861, p. 4.

[52] Lincoln's first annual message is to be found in *Works*, V, 35-53 (December 3, 1861).

federal authority would be maintained. The same faith was evidenced by other nonmilitary wartime legislation passed by Congress during the Civil War.

Lincoln told Congress that the federal judicial system had been outgrown and was in need of alteration. The system even lacked unity in that not all states had circuit courts presided over by Supreme Court Justices. Lincoln believed that this condition could not be remedied without a change of the system "because the adding of judges to the Supreme Court, enough for the accommodation of all parts of the country, with circuit courts, would create a [Supreme] court altogether too numerous for a judicial body of any sort." And as Lincoln pointed out, the larger the country grew the greater the evil in this regard would be. In typical Lincolnian style the President concluded: "Circuit courts are useful, or they are not useful. If useful, no State should be denied them; if not useful, no State should have them. Let them be provided for all, or abolished as to all."

Having presented the problem, the President suggested three possible solutions. To start with, Lincoln said, *"Let the Supreme Court be of convenient number in every event."* [53] How the Radicals and hotheads did hang on every one of those words! To them this inferred that the number of Supreme Court Justices might be increased.

Lincoln's best proposal was to "let the supreme judges be relieved from circuit duties, and circuit judges [be] provided for all the circuits." From every point of view of judicial procedure this was the soundest recommendation. An alternative, said Lincoln, would be to divide the nation into circuits of convenient size, "the supreme judges to serve in a number of them corresponding to their own number, and independent circuit judges to be provided for the rest." And lastly—a poor suggestion in view of the fact that the federal courts were already laden with judicial proceedings—Lincoln proposed that we "dispense with circuit courts altogether, leaving the judicial functions wholly to the district courts and an independent Supreme Court." As to which he favored, the Chief Executive remained silent.

The President's public statements in 1861 concerning the Supreme Court and the federal judiciary were now at an end. Lincoln saw that the nation had developed beyond the capacities of its judicial system; in his recommendations he had included the possibility of a thorough revision. Radicals in the Congress were delighted with the prospect of reorganizing the circuits. They wished to remold the Court, to punish it for its past role, and to protect the war effort from its interference. This was Lincoln's answer to the Court's challenge: revise the federal circuit system and in the process remold the Supreme Court. His approach was

---

[53] My italics.

subtle. No one could deny the inadequacy of the system as it existed. This attack upon the Court was oblique rather than frontal; Lincoln had demonstrated political acumen. The Supreme Court now faced the Congress, and little delay could be expected before the legislators would make known their wishes in regard to the highest judicial tribunal of the land.

CHAPTER FOUR

Disaster Stalks

SHATTER THE COURT

Lincoln's first annual message touched off an attack upon the Supreme Court seldom equaled in American history. Elements existed within the Republican party that wished to mutilate the Court if not destroy it. Taking heart at the President's utterances, these elements—they had waited with evil intent—believed that the Court was in its final death throes. But their attempt to wreck the Court failed, and they had to satisfy themselves with efforts in the course of circuit reorganization to reduce the number of circuits allotted to the Southern states. This meant fewer Southern Justices at least, and the Court would begin to reassume "respectability" in the eyes of its antagonists.

From the beginning of the administration a part of the Republican press was contemptuous of the Supreme Court. The Chicago *Tribune* started the ball rolling on March 4, 1861, and it did not let up in its persistent criticism. The *Tribune* was a leader of the view that no Republican victory was complete until that Court which had enunciated the "evil" principles of the Dred Scott decision had been forced to bow before the new party in power. "That bench-full of Southern lawyers, which gentlemen of a poetical temperament call 'an august tribunal,'" said the Chicago *Tribune* in an editorial, "is the last entrenchment behind which Despotism is sheltered." It proposed two plans of attack: let a national convention be called to modify the power of the Court through constitutional amendment, or reconstruct the Court "by the dropping off of a few of its members, and the *appointment of better men in their places*." [1]

Many Republicans soon proposed additional methods by which to attack the Court. John Jay, a leading New York Republican and grandson of the first Chief Justice, suggested reorganization of the Supreme Court on the basis of new circuits which would reflect the 1860 census. [2] The New York *Tribune* devised a Court-packing plan which would have given Lincoln mastery at once. It hoped for prompt action by the special session of Congress that met on July 4. Recognizing the "anomalous condition," the *Tribune* proposed to increase the Supreme Court to thirteen.

[1] Editorial, Chicago *Tribune*, March 4, 1861, p. 2 (my italics).
[2] John Jay to Charles Sumner, March 18, 1861, Sumner MSS.

That would assure Republican control because three vacancies already existed and increasing the Court to thirteen would enable Lincoln to appoint seven new Justices. At one stroke a majority of the United States Supreme Court would be appointees of Lincoln.

Detailed recommendations of circuit changes were proposed by this newspaper. It suggested that New England and the Northwest have two circuits each, that New York City and its environs constitute a circuit, that the rest of New York state form a circuit, that Pennsylvania make up a circuit, and that California and Oregon compose a circuit. Reference to a circuit on the Pacific coast was the first proposal of that nature. The *Tribune's* suggestions meant eight circuits for the free states rather than four; five circuits would remain assigned to the border states and to the South.[3] One of Lincoln's correspondents made similar proposals. It was suggested to the President that the Court be increased to twelve Justices, apportioning "them according to population and business, giving one to the States of the Pacific." "This . . . will give the administration six important appointments," said the correspondent, "which may aid in bringing treason to terms, as well as provide judicial machinery for punishing traitors—" [4]

The day after Congress heard the President's first annual message Radicals led by Senator John P. Hale of New Hampshire, a leading abolitionist who had been among the first antislavery men elected to the United States Senate, began a bitter attack upon the Supreme Court. The Radicals had awaited impatiently the President's remarks and now Senator Hale did not equivocate. He introduced a resolution which proposed: "*Resolved:* That the Committee on the Judiciary be instructed to inquire into the expediency and propriety of abolishing the present Supreme Court of the United States, and establishing instead thereof another Supreme Court. . . ." [5] The Radicals had unveiled their plan to scuttle the Taney Supreme Court. This was to be the Chief Justice's recompense for Dred Scott and John Merryman.

Senator Hale took the floor on December 9, 1861, to give the Senate a demonstration of rationalization rarely equaled even in a legislative body where attributing creditable motives to one's actions is often developed to a fine art.[6] John P. Hale had the boldness to give new interpretation to that portion of the Constitution which creates the Supreme Court. He said that many people interpret the Constitution as providing specifically

[3] Editorial, New York *Tribune*, June 10, 1861, p. 4.

[4] Samuel A. Foot to Abraham Lincoln, June 4, 1861, Papers of the Attorneys General.

[5] *Cong. Globe*, 37th Cong., 2nd sess., p. 8.

[6] This senatorial attack upon the Supreme Court is to be found in the *Cong. Globe*, 37th Cong., 2nd sess., pp. 26-28, 37, and 155.

for a Supreme Court, but he declared that the Constitution provides that "The judicial power of the United States shall be vested in one Supreme Court, and in such inferior courts as the Congress, may, from time to time, ordain and establish." [7]

The New Hampshire senator demanded of Congress that it act in accordance with constitutional provision, that it "look this thing right in the face, right in the eye, and march up to their duty and establish a Supreme Court as the Constitution requires them to do 'from time to time,' yes sir, 'from time to time.' " With sophistry Hale boomed out to his colleagues in the United States Senate: "My idea is that the time has come; that this is one of the very times the framers of the Constitution contemplated."

Senator Hale condemned the Supreme Court for a multitude of reasons. The Senator charged that it failed in its duty to the nation; he found it devoid of everything that could be expected of it; he found that it lacked the confidence and respect of the people. He charged that if the rebels were successful in annihilating federal authority Union soldiers "would be judicially pronounced by this very Supreme Court trespassers and rioters."

Senator Hale assigned the blame for the Supreme Court's position not to the Court alone but to the manner in which members of the Court were appointed. He found that appointment was made not because men were properly qualified but "because they were not learned, and were never likely to be." The determining factor in appointment, Senator Hale maintained, was politics, and the Supreme Court had become a "part of the machinery of the old Democratic party."

As a case in point, Senator Hale cited the circuit of which his state was a part. He charged, referring to Justice Clifford, "A man was imposed upon us against all but the unanimous voice of the people." Clifford was appointed, explained Hale, because "he was known to sympathize with the men who were for forcing . . . [slavery] doctrines upon the country."

It was the contention of Hale that the Supreme Court had based its decisions upon the desires of the Democratic party rather than attempting "to study and find out and declare the law." And it was his contention that the Senate should pass his resolution so that inquiry could be pursued since "there are certainly as sound judges on the Judiciary Committee as there are in the Supreme Court, and a good deal sounder." The Senator made one additional point. He said that he was not criticizing all of the members of the Court. "Indeed, I would not undertake to say," concluded this abolitionist from New Hampshire, "that there is not a good man on the bench of the Supreme Court. I am far from going to that extent."

---

[7] U.S. Constitution, Art. III, sec. 1.

A reply to Senator Hale came promptly from Senator Lafayette S. Foster of Connecticut, a member of the committee on the judiciary. Although he was not fully out of sympathy with Hale's sentiments, Foster took sharp issue. Foster questioned the value as well as the propriety of such an open attack upon the Supreme Court.

He stated that if "any . . . officer of the Government is derelict in duty" the proper procedure is to impeach him, adding that existing evils could not be corrected by "these denunciatory charges." Foster asked Hale what benefit would come from saying that the Supreme Court "is bankrupt" and that it "has lost the confidence of the country and deserves to have lost it." The result of this denunciation would be, said the Senator, that Court decisions would be disobeyed.

Next the Senator from Connecticut turned to the proposition that the Supreme Court could be abolished, according to the "from time to time" provision. Foster denied that Congress had authority to abolish the nation's highest judicial tribunal. Even if the Taney Court could be dissolved, said the Senator, new Justices would be appointed by a "fallible President," confirmation would be voted by a "fallible Senate," and "we shall be subject . . . to very much the same evils that we have been subject to for eighty years past."

In conclusion Senator Foster emphasized the need for a new attitude of respect and cooperation among the branches of the federal government. In the crisis confronting the nation, he asserted, mutual assistance and counsel were more to be desired than perpetual conflict. How improper it would be, he averred, if the Justices suddenly were to say publicly that Congress is a "corrupt body," that its members "were elected by bribery and trickery," and that its enactments were "not worthy of public respect."

Foster's reply to Hale indicated the more rational view of the Republican party in regard to the Supreme Court, and Foster's view was the more popular. The Republican party saw as yet no need to deal in an extremist manner with the Court. That day might arrive, but the Senate was to conclude that with three vacancies to be filled there was no need to treat the Court harshly. But criticism of the Supreme Court having been touched off by the Hale proposal, a pyrotechnical display resulted.

Republican Senator Jacob Collamer of Vermont entered the fray to state in opposition to the resolution, "I can hardly conceive of anything more radical. . . ." Collamer denied that the resolution was a harmless one merely seeking information. He believed that its underlying objective was not to inquire about the Supreme Court but to abolish it.

A major weakness in Hale's proposal was demonstrated by Senator Orville H. Browning of Illinois, an intimate associate of Lincoln during the Illinois days. "If you repeal the Supreme Court out of existence to-day for the purpose of getting rid of obnoxious judges," said Browning, "and reorganize it, and have new judges appointed, the very moment there is a change in the political complexion of Congress the same 'town-meeting proceeding' " will recur. In fact, Browning predicted, once tampering with the Supreme Court began, every time the political make-up of Congress changed the Court would be abolished and a new one which would reflect the political tincture of the Congress would be created. It would be more appropriate, urged the Illinois senator, to have the committee on the judiciary "to inquire into the expediency of repealing the Constitution!"

Senator Collamer sought to avoid prolonged debate; he moved that Hale's resolution be amended to provide merely that the portion of the President's message which pertained to the courts be referred to the Senate committee on the judiciary.

But Senator Hale, unhappy with this turn of events, gained the floor and proceeded to answer the criticism that his resolution had provoked. Almost with mockery he dismissed Senator Browning's protest against "the time when Congress shall lay its hand upon this tribunal." Chiding Browning for his naive faith, Hale rejected the view that "when degeneracy has stalked over the land, we can look, as to a star of hope to this Supreme Court to save us from overthrow and destruction."

Senator Hale renewed his attack but in a more cunning manner. He sought to allay fears by telling the Senate, "this is a resolution of inquiry, simple, harmless, eminently necessary; one that the heart of the people calls for, as I think it does for no other measure, unless it be a little activity in our Army—" He tried to reassure those who were alarmed. He explained that on one occasion in his state it was found desirable to abolish the state supreme court in order to create a better one! Continuing, he said that if the senators intended to sit it out "stolid," "immovable," "convinced that everything is the best that can be had," then "I am content," but "I want inquiry."

Senator Hale challenged the Senate to meet the need that confronted it and to direct the committee on the judiciary to inquire whether the United States of 1861 could not improve upon the wisdom of 1789. "I think that the Supreme Court of the United States," explained Senator Hale, "in its very organization has a radical and fatal error, one that we inherited from the British constitution." That error, he declared, consisted of permitting Justices to hear cases first on circuit and then later to pass upon their own findings, sitting in Washington as the Supreme Court. Justices "look on those cases as their own children, that they are bound to take care of when they come up to be reviewed on the bench," charged the Senator. His line of attack was changed: he had started attacking the Court on., the basis of political partisanship; he concluded by criticizing circuit procedure of the federal judiciary. When the Senate had heard Senator Hale out, Vice President Hannibal Hamlin put to the Senate the question of agreeing to the Collamer amendment. And the Senate adopted the Hale resolution as modified by it. Hale's first attempt was a failure.

Not to be outdone, Hale at once offered a second resolution which directed the committee on judiciary to inquire into the "*expediency and propriety of abolishing the present judicial system of the United States.*" [8] Hale was hopeful of keeping his attack alive. He surmised that a less direct assault upon the Supreme Court would have greater appeal. Although this resolution was forced to lie over, the Senate accepted it the next day. It remained to be seen whether Hale would enjoy further success.

While the two resolutions were before the committee, a part of the Republican press, led by the New York *Tribune*, renewed its cry for revamping the Supreme Court. The *Tribune* expressed the view that "The present rebellion . . . is due quite as much to an unsound and unwise decision of the Supreme Court as to any other single cause." It maintained that the Court was grossly sectional; it held that "The present is a favorable opportunity to restore a just equilibrium between the sections, and, at the same time, bring back public confidence to the Court. . . ." The *Tribune* altered its earlier proposal and called for increasing the Court to eleven rather than thirteen, concluding that this, along with reshuffling the circuits, would suffice. "Our sole object now," it declared, "is to impress upon Congress the transcendent importance of embracing this opportunity to thoroughly reform our Federal judiciary." [9]

But Hale and the Radicals and the radical press lost. On December 20 Senator Lyman Trumbull, chairman of the committee on the judiciary, asked that the Senate discharge the committee from further investigating the expediency of abolishing the judicial system of the United States. Trumbull explained that the committee had reported a bill in relation to circuit reorganization and had decided to take no action in reference to revamping the entire federal judiciary. Hale announced that he would not object, and the committee was discharged.

The more conservative element of the Republican party had prevailed; there was to be no frontal attack upon the United States Supreme Court at this time. Hale, of course, was dissatisfied and said, "I want to take occasion to say, with highest respect for the Judiciary Committee, that in my humble judgment they have come far short of what they ought to." In this way, nonetheless, the Radical attempt to abolish the Supreme

[8] My italics.
[9] New York *Tribune*, December 12, 1861, p. 4.

Court was thwarted. Few of his colleagues would join Hale in the views he had professed.[10] The Senate rejected violence against the Supreme Court because Republican leaders saw that they could well afford to be patient since it was composed largely of aged Justices and already had three vacancies. Resignation or death could be relied upon shortly to provide additional opportunity to deal with it. The less impatient Republicans counseled delay; they felt time itself would contribute to the solution of the problem of Supreme Court membership. The modification of the circuits was to be the limit of the action taken at this time, and to that complex task the Congress turned itself.

FEDERAL JUDICIAL CIRCUITS

In 1860	*After July 15, 1862*
1. Rhode Island, Massachusetts, New Hampshire, Maine	1. Rhode Island, Massachusetts, New Hampshire, Maine
2. New York, Vermont, Connecticut	2. New York, Vermont, Connecticut
3. Pennsylvania, New Jersey	3. Pennsylvania, New Jersey
4. Maryland, Delaware, Virginia	4. Delaware, Maryland, Virginia, North Carolina
5. Alabama, Louisiana	5. South Carolina, Georgia, Florida, Alabama, Mississippi
6. North Carolina, South Carolina, Georgia	6. Louisiana, Texas, Arkansas, Kentucky, Tennessee
7. Ohio, Indiana, Illinois, Michigan	7. Ohio, Indiana
8. Kentucky, Tennessee, Missouri	8. Michigan, Wisconsin, Illinois
9. Mississippi, Arkansas	9. Missouri, Iowa, Kansas, Minnesota

POLITICS RIDES THE CIRCUITS

The revamping of the circuit system became a main consideration of the Thirty-Seventh Congress despite its preoccupation with problems relative to the war. The President had laid the problem before the legislature to be dealt with as it saw fit. There was to be lengthy delay before Congress completed its action, however, as the whole process of reorganization became filled with political considerations. Every congressman realized that filling the Court's vacancies depended upon the regrouping of the states into new circuits. Consequently, a congressional battle of great magnitude was fought before reorganization was completed.

For an aspirant to secure one of the vacant seats on the Supreme Court, victory first had to be won in the congressional fight over the circuits, and politics was given full rein. Ultimately an impatient press strongly condemned the intrigue. But so far as political leaders who were campaigning in behalf of particular candidates were concerned, it was of vital consequence to them to see to it that states with equally prominent

[10] Charles Fairman, *Mr. Justice Miller and the Supreme Court: 1862-1890* (Cambridge, 1939), p. 41.

aspirants were thrown into different circuits rather than into the same one—otherwise the possibility of dominating over an appointment was seriously threatened.

The bill to reorganize the circuit system was introduced into the Senate on December 9, 1861, by John Sherman of Ohio. The bill, arising out of the recommendations of President Lincoln, was referred to the committee on the judiciary. The process had begun. Senator Trumbull reported it with an amendment barely ten days later. The committee on the judiciary was ready to push action promptly.[11]

Immediately after the Christmas holidays the Senate turned its attention to circuit reorganization. On January 6, 1862, Senator Trumbull took the floor to explain existing conditions and to discuss the proposals that were being made.

The circuit system, as it was then constituted, was composed of nine circuits in which the nine members of the Supreme Court held circuit court in conjunction with federal district judges.[12] Ordinarily a Supreme Court Justice presided over the circuit in which he was a resident. Twenty-five years had elapsed since there was an extensive modification of the circuits, and certain states, including Texas, Florida, Wisconsin, Iowa, Minnesota, Kansas, and the states of the Far West had never been assigned to any circuit. In these states circuit court was presided over by district judges who were granted special power for this purpose or by a special circuit judge.

Senator Trumbull explained that although the bill under consideration did not propose to bring the states of the Far West into the regular circuit system, it was the object of the bill "to equalize the judicial circuits of the United States." The committee, further stated Trumbull, largely basing its action upon the desire to distribute population in the circuits approximately equally, modified the bill introduced by Senator Sherman.

The committee recommended that the three Northern circuits remain unchanged. The three had a combined population of 10,601,244. The First Circuit, presided over by Justice Clifford, was composed of Rhode Island, Massachusetts, New Hampshire, and Maine. The Second, presided over by Justice Nelson, was composed of New York, Vermont, and Connecticut. And the Third, presided over by Justice Grier, was composed of Pennsylvania and New Jersey.

It was in recommendations to condense the Southern and border circuits that the plan of the committee revealed itself. The suggested

---

[11] The ensuing debate in the Senate is to be found in the *Cong. Globe*, 37th Cong., 2nd sess., pp. 187-88 and 469.

[12] In the Chase MSS. in the Historical Society of Pennsylvania there is a memorandum written by Chase, titled, "Organization and Changes of Circuits," which lists the changes in the circuits from 1789 to 1866.

Southern and border circuits were: the Fourth, presided over by Chief Justice Taney, to consist of Maryland, Delaware, Virginia, and North Carolina. The Fifth, presided over by Justice Wayne, to consist of South Carolina, Georgia, Alabama, Mississippi, and Florida. The Sixth, presided over by Justice Catron, to consist of Louisiana, Texas, Arkansas, and Tennessee. The combined total population of the three would be 9,902,266, which compared well with the population of the first three circuits.

The committee, in harmony with Republican desires to increase the number of Northern circuits, proposed to assign the three remaining circuits to the Middle West. The proposed middlewestern circuits were: the Seventh, Ohio and Kentucky; the Eighth, Wisconsin, Michigan, Indiana, and Minnesota; and the Ninth, Illinois, Missouri, Kansas, and Iowa. The combined total population, 10,219,388, would compare favorably with the population of the other three Northern circuits and of the three Southern circuits. Senator Trumbull stated that the three vacancies on the Supreme Court would be filled from the Middle West and the new Justices would be assigned to these circuits.

He also clarified the situation as to California and Oregon. He stated that they were left out of the reorganization plan because "They have a peculiar system there. They have a circuit system of their own with a circuit judge who is not a judge of the Supreme Court." These states could not be brought within the system, added Senator Trumbull, unless a tenth circuit was added. A tenth circuit would require a tenth Justice, and the committee did not feel that a circuit for the Far West was justified as "it would be a very small circuit compared with the others."

Senator Sherman rose to object to the arrangement by which Ohio and Kentucky were placed together. He stated that although Ohio and Kentucky were once part of the same circuit, they were divided and the division proved successful. He declared that Ohio's relations were chiefly with Michigan and Indiana, and he served notice that he would battle to restore such a circuit to the bill. This battle and other battles of a similar nature were to delay completion of circuit reorganization for many months.

Trumbull replied that it was of little concern to him where Ohio was placed, but that for purposes of requisite population, business, and the shape of the circuit, the committee's recommendations should be accepted.

Following this exchange of views, the Senate, sitting as the Committee of the Whole, accepted the committee report. Senator Benjamin F. Wade of Ohio attempted to delay further consideration of the bill, although Senator Trumbull pointed out that there was need for action, declaring, "The Supreme Court has but six judges on the bench. The other three ought to be appointed." He added that he presumed that "they will not be appointed until some bill passes on the subject, and I think it would be best to act upon it as early as we conveniently can."

While the Senate was considering the circuit bill, renewed speculation as to final decisions in relation to Supreme Court appointments and judicial circuits was intense. John P. Usher of Indiana, who was later to serve Lincoln as Secretary of the Interior, speculated that if the bill passed, Secretary of the Treasury Chase might be appointed to the bench. But Usher had doubts as to whether the bill would pass. "[I] will not be surprised if Tr.[umbull] himself finally opposed the bill to defeat the combinations made," Usher stated.

Speculating further, Usher predicted that if the bill passed, Lincoln would name Chase to fill the Ohio circuit, Secretary of the Interior Caleb B. Smith to fill the Indiana circuit, and Orville H. Browning to fill the Illinois circuit.[13] The New York *Tribune* also predicted the appointment of Smith but hedged in predicting the Illinois appointment, believing the choice lay between Orville H. Browning and David Davis.[14]

When Wade succeeded in delaying senatorial action, President Lincoln, aware of the inability of the six Justices of the Supreme Court to maintain a quorum because Taney and Catron were ill, concluded that he must take action, and so he made his first appointment to the Court, nominating Noah H. Swayne of Ohio. (Swayne's appointment is discussed in Chapter 5). Now the Supreme Court could continue to function, and the Congress could continue its leisurely pace in revamping the circuits.

The Senate renewed its consideration of the circuit bill on January 24, the day it confirmed Swayne's nomination. The entire question of circuit reorganization was reopened because the Senate agreed to Senator Wade's motion to reconsider acceptance of the report of the committee on the judiciary.

At this time Senator James W. Grimes of Iowa proposed several alterations in the bill. Grimes sought a Supreme Court appointment for his friend Samuel F. Miller, a Republican leader in Iowa, and if Iowa were in a circuit with Illinois, Miller would have to compete with such Supreme Court aspirants as David Davis and Orville H. Browning. Grimes believed that the placing of Iowa in a circuit with Illinois would be fatal to Miller's chances and consequently worked diligently to bring about some change.

He proposed that the Ninth Circuit be composed of Missouri, Iowa, Kansas, and Minnesota; in addition, he suggested other changes, the most important of which were that Ohio and Michigan should be placed together and that Illinois be grouped with Indiana and Wisconsin. Grimes

---

[13] John P. Usher to R. W. Thompson, January 20, 1862, Thompson MSS., Lincoln National Life Foundation, Fort Wayne, Indiana.

[14] New York *Tribune*, January 23, 1862, p. 5.

admitted that his proposed Ninth Circuit would be small in population but it was "rapidly increasing," and he explained that the states he grouped in it had a simplified legal code in common. Grimes shrewdly reassigned Ohio, hoping that this would bring him the support of Ohio's senators.

The Senate was not impressed with Grimes's proposals and rejected them, finally accepting the proposals of the Trumbull committee. The senatorial snarl on the circuits was broken. But the battle was to rage on, the scene shifting to the House of Representatives.

Members of the House also had begun, after hearing the President's message, to consider reorganization of the circuits. Representative John A. Bingham of Ohio, a member of the committee on the judiciary, introduced a reorganization bill on December 11, 1861.[15] As reported from the committee, this bill, like the one in the Senate, contemplated the consolidation of Southern and border states into fewer circuits and the creation of new circuits for the Middle West.

Representative William Kellogg of Illinois condemned this piecemeal reorganization, demanding that a revision be provided for the whole country. Others, including Representative Roscoe Conkling of New York, expressed dissatisfaction, and the House delayed taking action. As a matter of fact, the House marked time until the senatorial bill, passed on January 24, 1862, was referred to it for action.

Those forces that were lobbying for favorites now turned their big guns on the House of Representatives. The intensity of the struggle increased, and the rivalries threatened to prevent the passage of any reorganization bill whatsoever.

A leading actor in the struggle in the House was James F. Wilson of Iowa, whose recent appointment to the committee on the judiciary was to prove highly advantageous to the cause of Samuel F. Miller. Wilson waged a skillful battle to place Iowa in a circuit in which Miller would not encounter competition with other leading aspirants. Under the leadership of Representative Wilson the bill that the Senate referred to the House was bottled up in the committee on the judiciary during the months of February, March, April, and May, 1862.

During the months of delay, those interested in forcing action to place Iowa in a circuit with Missouri, Minnesota, and Kansas sought through every legislative strategem to win their objective. The legislature of Iowa, itself, passed a resolution on March 10, 1862, urging Iowa's congressional delegation to battle for a suitable circuit,[16] and finally it even petitioned Congress to grant its wishes.[17]

---

[15] *Cong. Globe*, 37th Cong., 2nd sess., p. 33.

[16] *Sen. Misc. Doc. No. 73*, 37th Cong., 2nd sess., p. 1.

[17] Petition to Congress, referred to the Senate committee on the judiciary on March 26, 1862, Thirty-Seventh Congress, United States Senate Files, National Archives.

At last on June 4 the reorganization bill was reported to the House. The committee on the judiciary recommended significant changes: the Seventh Circuit would consist of Ohio, Kentucky, and Michigan; the Eighth, Indiana, Illinois, and Wisconsin; and the Ninth, Missouri, Iowa, Kansas, and Minnesota.[18]

Representative Wilson explained that it was proper that a circuit should be formed consisting of certain trans-Mississippi states, and it was as a consequence that he urged setting up a circuit composed of Missouri, Iowa, Kansas, and Minnesota. Arguing the need for such a circuit, Wilson declared that no other part of the nation was growing so rapidly. He said that the states he wished to join with Iowa had similar legal codes and that the commerce and trade of these four states were connected with the Mississippi and Missouri rivers.

John F. Potter of Wisconsin rose promptly to challenge Wilson's assignment of Wisconsin. Wilson countered that the change regarding Wisconsin simply made for a more compact and symmetrical circuit! This circuit-juggling provoked Representative Kellogg to make a keen analysis, declaring: "I fear that too many mantles for Supreme Court judges have already been cut out, and made up. If it were not for that, there would be little trouble in arranging the States in compact circuits."

The Chicago *Tribune*, impatiently awaiting legislation pertaining to the judiciary, finally asked editorially, "What has become of the bill reorganizing the Supreme Court?" The *Tribune* demanded to know why the bill has "been let sleep for three months past." "Some half a dozen Western States," lamented the *Tribune*, "are in no district at all. The twenty millions of the people of the free States are represented by four judges in the Court, while the nine millions of whites in the South have *five* judges." It demanded of Congress that it take action and not "leave the court in this wretched condition." [19]

As adjournment of Congress loomed, the reorganization bill finally gained momentum, and the House moved rapidly toward passage of the bill. Representative John W. Menzies of Kentucky and Representative Horace Maynard of Tennessee succeeded in having Kentucky placed in the same circuit as Tennessee. Following this decision, the House accepted the bill, amended to meet the desires of Representative Wilson. The Iowans had accomplished in the House what they had failed to accomplish in the Senate. Each branch of Congress had its own plan; it remained to be seen which would bow to the wishes of the other.

THE IMPASSE BROKEN

With Senate and House at odds, even the keenest political forecasters

[18] The ensuing debate in the House of Representatives is to be found in the *Cong. Globe*, 37th Cong., 2nd sess., pp. 2561-65.

[19] Editorial, Chicago *Tribune*, June 5, 1862, p. 2.

were unable to predict what the final action would be. Although the
House of Representatives on June 12, 1862, requested agreement of the
Senate, almost two weeks elapsed before Senator Trumbull reported
the bill and asked the Senate to disagree. He maintained that the House
bill disregarded the aim to equalize population in the circuits.[20]

Senator Joseph A. Wright of Indiana was displeased particularly by
Indiana's assignment. He declared that he spoke for the senators from
Indiana, Ohio, and Michigan and explained that they opposed both the
House version and the Senate version. "The people of Indiana, from the
time they have been a State," declared Senator Wright, "have been
connected with Ohio. Their judge has been ours. The judge of the circuit
of Ohio can go to my city in four hours; he can go to Michigan in five
hours." Wright argued that Indiana, Ohio, and Michigan grew up together and that they had similar judicial processes. "Why not allow us,
then, to be together in one circuit?" asked Senator Wright.

The Senate was ready to make its decision and accepted the House
bill, except that it adopted the request of Senator Wright and joined
Indiana with Ohio and Michigan, and assigned to Kentucky Indiana's
former position with Illinois and Wisconsin. The Senate had acceded
very largely to the wishes of the House. The efforts of Senator Grimes
and Representative Wilson were successful. Their dilatory tactics had
brought victory. All that remained was to obtain final approval by the
House.

A few days later, however, Representative Wilson moved that the
House insist fully upon the terms of its bill, and he asked that a conference
be held with the Senate. Senators Jacob Collamer of Vermont, Joseph
A. Wright of Indiana, and John C. Ten Eyck of New Jersey represented
the Senate in the resulting conference. Representatives John A. Bingham
of Ohio, James F. Wilson of Iowa, and Robert Mallory of Kentucky
represented the House.

Following meetings of the conference committee in which a number
of readjustments were made in the circuit assignments, the House of
Representatives accepted the committee's recommendations. Circuit reorganization was nearing enactment into law.

But in the Senate a final acrimonious debate resulted when Senator
Wright reported the terms agreed upon by the committee on conference.
His report particularly provoked the senators from Michigan because
they resented alteration of Michigan's position. Senator Jacob M. Howard
of Michigan charged that the conference committee had written a new
bill. He was joined by his colleague, Senator Zachariah Chandler, in
demanding that delay be granted in order to allow for fuller considera-

---

[20] The ensuing debate in the Senate is to be found in the *Cong. Globe*, 37th Cong.,
2nd sess., pp. 3089-90, 3255, 3277, and 3298.

tion. Senator Wright urged the Senate to proceed because Congress was anticipating adjournment, but Senator Ten Eyck supported the move for delay so that no one could charge that the committee forced "snap judgment" upon the Senate.

The next day Senator Howard renewed his attack upon dividing Michigan from Ohio and cited the similarities between the two states in regard to commercial activities, legal codes, and modes of practice. But Senator Wright argued that if, after months of congressional debate, the unanimous report of the committee on conference were disregarded, the reorganization bill might die.

Before the final vote on the conference report the Senate rejected an effort by Senator Henry M. Rice of Minnesota to postpone action until the following December. Then the Senate accepted the conference report. The circuit reorganization bill was passed. Lincoln's signature completed enactment on July 15, 1862.

The new law provided no changes in the first three circuits, but it did provide vast alteration for the rest. The new Fourth consisted of Maryland, Delaware, Virginia, and North Carolina. The new Fifth embraced South Carolina, Georgia, Alabama, Mississippi, and Florida. The new Sixth included Louisiana, Texas, Arkansas, Kentucky, and Tennessee. The new Seventh contained Ohio and Indiana. The new Eighth consisted of Michigan, Wisconsin, and Illinois. And the new Ninth included Missouri, Iowa, Kansas, and Minnesota.

The main battle, that involving the creation of a trans-Mississippi judicial circuit, was won by Representative James F. Wilson and Senator James W. Grimes. They delayed and jeopardized circuit reorganization, but they succeeded in their demands. Their next step was to influence President Lincoln to select their favorite for appointment to the Supreme Court. That would crown their efforts with the fullest measure of success.

In reviewing the accomplishments of this session of the Thirty-Seventh Congress, the New York *Tribune* receded from its bloodthirsty demands for packing the Supreme Court and declared of the Congress, "It has reorganized the Supreme Court, adapting it to the growth and wants of the country." [21] But the entire country was not yet included in the circuit system, and politics, not genuine need, had dictated the regrouping of the states into circuits.

The answer of the majority of the Republican party to the demands for packing the Supreme Court had finally arrived. The Republican party concluded that regrouping the states and taking advantage of the Supreme Court vacancies—different procedure might be deemed necessary at a later date—would result in the modifications that seemed

[21] Editorial, New York *Tribune*, July 22, 1862, p. 4.

necessary. President Lincoln soon turned to the problems of Supreme Court appointments to complete the process. This was sound policy by a party which sought to sustain the American system of government rather than to destroy it. But the Radicals were unwilling to admit defeat; they sensed that some day a somewhat different policy would be adopted. And in this they were not in error.

CHAPTER FIVE

Quorum and Marked Seat

SWAYNE SATISFIES THE QUORUM

Abraham Lincoln was to be privileged to appoint five men to the United States Supreme Court, and a Lincoln appointee was to linger on the bench until 1897. Consequently, Lincoln's direct influence upon the Court may be said to have endured until that time. Before Lincoln's individual appointments to the Supreme Court and his relationship with the Court are examined, it will be of value to look at the general character of his Supreme Court appointments.

Two main factors controlled the administration's appointments to the Court: Lincoln's demand that the selectees have sound views toward the great political issues of the Civil War, and the political forces that guided his selections. Lincoln did not regard legal training and judicial experience as primary requirements. This was in harmony with his policy of refusing to grant to the Court the right to provide the final answer on questions that were of political nature. He believed that many men rather than few could meet the requirements for membership on the bench.

An analysis of the previous experience of Lincoln's appointees reveals how little their past activity guided him. Noah H. Swayne, David Davis, and Stephen J. Field each had served in state legislatures; Noah H. Swayne and Salmon P. Chase had served in state administrations; both Swayne and Chase had served in national administrations. Only one of the five, Chase, had served in Congress. Samuel F. Miller had held no public office prior to his appointment. Only two had previous experience on the bench: Davis had served in the state courts of Illinois, and Field had served in the state courts of California.[1] President Lincoln demanded sound views on the war rather than extensive service in the state courts or the lower federal courts.

Lincoln sought men who were trustworthy thinkers on problems of the war and men who were prominent in the profession of law. But he sought men whose selection would be good politics, as well. And he had to select men who were geographically available, the circuit system making this demand upon him. It was customary to appoint a man

[1] Cortez A. M. Ewing, *The Judges of the Supreme Court, 1789-1937, A Study of Their Qualifications* (Minneapolis, 1938), pp. 86-87.

resident in the vacant circuit. This custom, of course, was not observed in selecting a Chief Justice.

Appointments to the Supreme Court were among those tasks of President Lincoln that did not demand immediate attention. Since the Supreme Court was not in session from March 14, 1861, to December 2, 1861, there was no necessity for presidential action until the later date. But upon the reassembling of the Court in December it was soon demonstrated to the President that he could not long delay naming at least one Justice. As the Congress proceeded to discuss circuit reorganization, it became quite clear to the President that it would be impossible to rely upon early congressional action. The circuit bill was enmeshed in too much political intrigue for that. And soon it became almost obligatory for him to take action.

The urgent situation developed out of the condition of the Court itself. In addition to the three vacancies there were temporary absences resulting from the illness of Chief Justice Taney and Justice Catron. At times it was impossible to maintain in attendance five Justices, the number necessary to constitute a quorum.[2] Lincoln had to make at least one appointment so that the Court could maintain the legal number necessary to function. Furthermore, he began to realize that cases involving the war, particularly the question of the legality of the blockade, would soon reach the Court so it might be well to start to fill the vacancies.[3]

Consequently, President Lincoln nominated Noah Haynes Swayne of Ohio on January 21, 1862. The choice of an Ohioan to replace Justice McLean of the Ohio circuit served to solve the problem of an adequate number of Justices to maintain a quorum without disturbing the congressional action being taken in relation to the circuit system.

As a young man Noah H. Swayne had developed a violent hatred for the institution of slavery. Born in Virginia in 1804, he attended a Quaker academy at Waterford, following which he began the study of medicine at Alexandria. Upon the death of his teacher he abandoned medicine, studied law, and was admitted to the bar in 1823.

When he was ready to practice, Swayne moved to Ohio because he opposed slavery. He settled in Coshocton where his success was immediate, and he received appointment by President Jackson as United States district attorney for Ohio in 1830. In 1832 Swayne married Sarah Ann Wager of Harper's Ferry, Virginia, who emancipated her slaves upon her marriage. Ultimately they moved to Columbus where he earned an outstanding reputation as a corporation counsel. When Lincoln

---

[2] New York *Tribune*, January 23, 1862, p. 5.

[3] Ernest Bates, *The Story of the Supreme Court* (Indianapolis, 1936), p. 168.

appointed him, Swayne was at the height of his legal career and in intimate contact with the leading Republicans of Ohio.

Lincoln's selection of Noah H. Swayne is explainable by many factors. It is true that Swayne had no judicial experience. But the Ohio circuit was vacant, and it was reasonable to expect Lincoln to select an Ohioan to fill it. Justice McLean had even expressed the hope that his good friend Swayne might succeed him. And Lincoln owed a vast debt of gratitude to Ohio Republicans: on the third ballot in the Republican convention of 1860 it was four Ohio votes that tipped the scale in his behalf. The governor of Ohio, William Dennison, urged the appointment as did Ohio's senators, John Sherman and Benjamin F. Wade. The entire Ohio delegation to the national House of Representatives added its voice as well.

Swayne's views on the war and his opposition to slavery naturally recommended him to the President, but his appointment also was made desirable by the fact that he was prominent as a corporation counsel. It was true that "The war could not be prosecuted to a successful conclusion without the support of Big Business," and Lincoln at least satisfied business interests at the same time that he satisfied the Ohio politicians.[4]

Swayne was mentioned as an aspirant for nomination to the Court shortly after the death of Justice McLean. He revealed in a letter in the summer of 1861 to Samuel J. Tilden, a leading New York corporation lawyer and prominent Democrat, the effort that was being made to influence Lincoln. Swayne wrote, "An Indiana friend urged my appointment on Mr. Lincoln a few days ago very strongly. He [Lincoln] spoke of me . . . in much more flattering terms than I deserve—but said nothing as to his purpose." Swayne, who was soon to go to Washington on business, promised Tilden, "While there I shall learn fully 'the lay of the land' and will write you again." [5] Tilden was active in helping to obtain for Swayne the support of the New York bar which declared that business relations between New York and the Ohio circuit justified its effort in his behalf.[6]

An attempt was made to enlist the aid of Secretary of the Treasury Chase. One of Swayne's friends wrote Chase that if he did not desire the seat Swayne should receive it. This friend concluded, "Among the men *who are moving for it in* this region of the country I think he is the most fit." [7] And Governor Dennison telegraphed Lincoln: "I trust you will

---

[4] *Ibid.*

[5] Noah H. Swayne to Samuel J. Tilden, July 3, 1861, Tilden MSS., N.Y. Pub. Lib.

[6] Draft of a petition of the New York bar to Abraham Lincoln, July 6, 1861, *ibid.*

[7] Aaron F. Perry to Salmon P. Chase, December 2, 1861, Chase MSS., Library of Congress.

favor the organizing of Ohio[,] Indiana[,] & Michigan into a federal Judicial circuit & will find it consistent with your sense of duty to promptly appoint Col[onel] N. H. Swayne as successor of Judge McLean." [8]

Less than a fortnight before the appointment was forthcoming Swayne wrote an illuminating letter to Senator Wade. Apparently one of the main fears of Swayne's supporters was that John J. Crittenden of Kentucky would be given the appointment to placate the South. But Swayne wrote, "The President has always from the first frankly said that he must appoint Browning. He has never in any conversation with any of my friends named the Gentleman referred to [Crittenden]." Swayne, who was aware that appointments were largely dependent upon the circuits formulated, continued, "He [Lincoln] has said repeatedly that if the circuits were divided & Ohio disjoined from Illinois that he would appoint me. He has never made any other condition." Swayne even revealed to Wade that Lincoln's suggestion to the Congress that the Ohio circuit was too big and ought to be divided was put into the presidential message at "the instance of a friend of mine."

This informative letter indicates, too, that Swayne not only feared Browning and Crittenden but Secretary Chase as well. He told Wade, "Mr. L.[incoln] has said . . . that Gov[.] C[hase] was not & would not be in the least in my way." Swayne was hopeful, too, because he could not see the propriety of appointing Crittenden, "It would not be treating the loyal & republican state in which we live—well—to appoint the Judge of our circuit from Kentucky." [9]

When the Senate received the nomination of Swayne, it moved swiftly, confirming the appointment on January 24, 1862.[10] The new Justice arrived in Washington on January 25, took the oath of office in open Court on January 27, and assumed his place on the nation's highest tribunal.[11]

Swayne was not well known outside of the Middle West at the time. That he was little known in the East is indicated by the fact that for several days following his appointment important Eastern newspapers misspelled his name. The Washington *National Republican* gave his name as "Noah A. Swain" as did the Baltimore *Sun*. The New York *Tribune* used the same erroneous spelling in announcing confirmation of the appointment.[12]

---

[8] William Dennison to Abraham Lincoln, December 14, 1861, Lincoln MSS.

[9] Noah H. Swayne to Benjamin F. Wade, January 10, 1861, Wade MSS., Library of Congress.

[10] Nomination of Noah H. Swayne, January 21, 1862, Papers of the Attorneys General.

[11] Minutes of the United States Supreme Court, January 27, 1862, Clerk's File, Library of the U.S. Supreme Court.

[12] Washington *National Republican*, January 23, 1862, p. 2; Baltimore *Sun*, January 23, 1862, p. 2; New York *Tribune*, January 25, 1862, p. 5.

The press reacted favorably to Swayne. The Chicago *Tribune*, expressing surprise that the President took action before circuit reorganization was complete, said that he undoubtedly had satisfied himself concerning Swayne and that "from what we know we believe he will . . . [fulfill] the expectations of the people." [13] The Washington *National Intelligencer* overflowed with praise for Swayne and complimented Lincoln for making such an excellent appointment. The *Intelligencer* declared, "To great legal training and eminence in the walks of his profession . . . he adds . . . the qualities of mind which singularly fit him for the able and impartial dispensation of justice." [14] The Washington *National Republican* was particularly impressed by the fact that "Twenty years ago he inherited twenty-five slaves, whom he forthwith liberated." [15] The Washington *Evening Star* emphasized Swayne's Southern birth as well as the role he played in giving Ohio "its material eminence." In all, it concluded, he would "surely prove as efficient on the Supreme Court bench, as in every other position he has previously" held.[16]

Upon the bench of the Supreme Court, Justice Swayne found his duties arduous. It was necessary for him to plunge into the activities of the Court; there was no opportunity to enter slowly upon his new responsibilities. When he was appointed he was fifty-eight years old, the Chief Justice was over eighty, and four of the five Associate Justices were around seventy,[17] so it is not surprising that he soon came to shoulder his full share of responsibilities. To his friend Thomas Ewing, formerly United States senator from Ohio, Swayne wrote three weeks after he had entered upon his duties, "I have delivered . . . opinions which were satisfactory to my brethren. The work is hard but very amicable." [18] He was to lament at a later date, "My Judicial duties here leave me scarce a moment to Spare." [19] Swayne's "settled habits of labor and research" soon acquired for him a great amount of work, and he quickly became a valuable member of the Supreme Court of the United States.[20]

Even though Noah Swayne had been elevated to the Court, he retained a keen interest in the political intrigue that permeated Washington. Evidence indicates that he was interested in the remaining Court vacancies, in obtaining favors from leaders in the Lincoln government, in the political well-being of the administration, and in the problem of arbitrary arrest.

---

[13] Chicago *Tribune*, January 23, 1862, p. 1.

[14] Editorial, Washington *National Intelligencer*, January 27, 1862, p. 3.

[15] Washington *National Republican*, January 24, 1862, p. 2.

[16] Editorial, Washington *Evening Star*, January 23, 1862, p. 2.

[17] 103 U.S., memoranda, xi-xii.

[18] Noah H. Swayne to Thomas Ewing, February 22, 1862, Ewing MSS., Library of Congress.

[19] Noah H. Swayne to Henry C. Carey, February 4, 1865, Edward Carey Gardiner MSS., Henry C. Carey Section, Hist. Soc. of Pa.

[20] 103 U.S., memoranda, xi-xii.

Attorney General Bates recorded in his diary that he met at length with Swayne "To day, at my office—and tonight at my house" to discuss the Supreme Court vacancies. Bates and Swayne canvassed the effort in progress to "gerrymander" the circuits so as to give both Caleb B. Smith and Orville H. Browning a seat.[21]

A letter written by Justice Swayne in 1862 indicates the interest he retained in politics, and the high political circles in which he circulated. Written only a few months after his elevation to the Supreme Court, it was addressed to Secretary of War Edwin M. Stanton. "I can not allow myself to use language sufficiently strong [wrote Justice Swayne] to express fully the pride—the confidence—the gratitude—and the affection with which you are regarded by the entire body of our people." Swayne urged Stanton to continue his great work and told him that "while you live" you will be aware of the high esteem of your fellow countrymen and "when you die, every good man in the land, will be prepared to say of you, as was said of another—'More than any man *living*—I envy *him* his grave—with its honors.' "[22]

Justice Swayne was not reluctant to intervene with leaders in Washington when he felt justified. One such occasion presented itself when he sought the aid of his friend Stanton in behalf of Willie W. Foote, son of onetime governor of Mississippi, Henry S. Foote. The youth, who had entered the Confederate army when he was sixteen, was taken prisoner at Fort Donelson. Swayne wrote Stanton that he and Governor Foote were as close as brothers "until this most wicked & causeless rebellion separated us." He asked that the boy, who was being held at Camp Chase, be permitted to return home. In the letter Mrs. Swayne added a note. Asking that she be forgiven for trespassing, she wrote, "His youth must be his apology—for being mislead."[23]

Justice Swayne retained an abiding interest in the political well-being of the Lincoln administration. During the period when Republican resentment and revolt manifested themselves so violently prior to the election of 1864, Swayne had unshakable faith in Lincoln. Fearing interception of his messages, during this period he had the Attorney General take them to Lincoln for him. To Bates the Justice commented on the Wade-Davis fight against the President, "The Wade & Davis pronouncement will hurt no one but themselves. I feel warranted in saying that it will not . . . [lose] Mr. Lincoln a vote in Ohio." He said he hoped for early victories from Grant, Sherman, and Farragut to alter the situation within the party and to swamp the Copperheads.[24]

---

[21] Bates, *Diary*, p. 244 (March 26, 1862).

[22] Noah H. Swayne to Edwin M. Stanton, April 19, 1862, Stanton MSS.

[23] Noah H. Swayne to Edwin M. Stanton, April 11, 1862, *ibid.*

[24] Noah H. Swayne to Edward Bates, August 19, 1864, Lincoln MSS.

Shortly before the election of 1864 Swayne wrote Henry C. Carey of Philadelphia, a noted economist of the time, "Every thing looks well for the good cause here. No doubt is Entertained, by any loyal man—so far as I know—of the result in Ohio. What is the prospect in Pennsylvania?" [25] Before Lincoln's second inauguration Carey sent Swayne a lengthy letter advocating high tariff and expressing fear of Great Britain's manufacturing ability.[26] Swayne saw that the letter, which stated, "Let the revenue laws remain . . . as they are and Lincoln's second administration will be one of . . . bankruptcy, and he will prove to . . . [be] the *last president* of the American Union," reached Lincoln's hands.[27]

Justice Swayne had an abiding interest in the subject of arbitrary military arrest. His correspondence on this subject is a tribute to the traditional American respect for a rule of law. Justice Swayne intervened in a case of arbitrary arrest, and in the course of correspondence concerning it, he enunciated a healthy attitude toward legal processes. It is significant that he, a Lincoln appointee to the Court, should have made these comments to Lincoln.

Admitting that it was with reluctance that he came to the decision to write Lincoln, Swayne declared that he wished to bring to his attention a charge that "has originated in malice or misconception." Swayne said that military authorities arbitrarily threatened to exile to the South a Mr. Harris. This provoked him to state: "While the guilty should not be spared—care should be taken that the innocent and the guilty are not confounded. In my judgement [sic] he is Entitled to a hearing. If found guilty, he must take the consequences. If innocent, he should be discharged."

Justice Swayne respectfully requested the President to direct General Stephen G. Burbridge to grant Harris a hearing. "I intend no reflection [continued Justice Swayne] upon the military authorities. The best motives have doubtless, guided their conduct . . . [and] nothing but my firm conviction of the innocence of the accused could have induced me thus to interpose." [28] President Lincoln, consequently, ordered General Burbridge to have the case fully examined as "Judge Swayne of the . . . Supreme Court appeals to me in favor of . . . Harris." [29] A short time later the Justice was pleased to learn that the prisoner was freed, apparently before Lincoln intervened, on the basis of unquestioned innocence." [30]

---

[25] Noah H. Swayne to Henry C. Carey, September 30, 1864, Gardiner MSS., Carey Section.

[26] Henry C. Carey to Noah H. Swayne, January 29, 1865, Lincoln MSS.

[27] Noah H. Swayne to Abraham Lincoln, January 29, 1865, *ibid.*

[28] Noah H. Swayne to Abraham Lincoln, August 19, 1864, *ibid.*

[29] Abraham Lincoln to S. G. Burbridge, September 4, 1864, *Works*, VII, 534.

[30] Noah H. Swayne to Abraham Lincoln, August 30, 1864, Lincoln MSS.

Justice Swayne also interested himself in Confederate Captain John Y. Beall who was condemned to death as a spy. This was not a case in which arbitrary arrest was concerned; it was one in which the Justice appealed to Lincoln for mercy. Swayne explained that he did not know the facts of the case, but that he did know the family of the young man. "I will add, [proceeded the Justice] that if you have *erred* on the side of mercy— the error has met with the approbation of good men of all parties. . . . In this case I have no doubt you will do what you think right & I can neither ask nor desire any thing more. I am confined to my room today or I would not trouble you with this note." [31] For Justice Swayne, of course, this was truly an errand of mercy even though it was Lincoln's decision that Beall must die.

Without any reflection upon Lincoln, his first appointee to the Supreme Court feared that with the rule of law in abeyance, injustice might creep into the American system. And without hesitation he made his views known to the President. Furthermore, he even saw fit to ask of Lincoln charity toward an apprehended foe. The American system which Lincoln sought to preserve was safe in such hands. Justice Swayne's respect for legal processes and his willingness to mix charity with the dictates of the law were among his most laudable characteristics. Nonetheless, as the legal problems growing out of the war made their way to the Supreme Court, Justice Swayne firmly upheld the policies Lincoln deemed necessary to save the Union.

A SEAT MARKED

Lincoln's second appointee to the Supreme Court, Samuel Freeman Miller, received a medical degree in 1838 and practiced medicine in Kentucky for more than a decade. From the time of his college days, however, he had a keen interest in politics. This interest led him to study law surreptitiously, while practicing medicine, and he was admitted to the bar in 1847. Miller, as were most of his neighbors, was a Whig party member. Although he was born in Kentucky in 1816, he opposed slavery and looked forward to the day when his state, through a process of gradual emancipation, would be free.

When Kentucky retained the institution of slavery in its constitution of 1849, Miller determined to establish himself and his family elsewhere. He settled in Keokuk, Iowa, formed the law firm of Reeves and Miller, and became active in the Republican party. In 1861 he was a candidate for the Republican nomination for governor of Iowa, and at the time of his appointment by Lincoln he was chairman of the Republican district committee at Keokuk.

Two factors governed the choice of Miller for appointment to the

---

[31] Noah H. Swayne to Abraham Lincoln, February 15, 1865, *ibid.*

Supreme Court: creation of a trans-Mississippi circuit which included Iowa and development of overwhelming pressures in his behalf. Miller's cohorts in the Congress fought the battle of circuit reorganization with both skill and resourcefulness. And Miller's friends at home flooded the President with a deluge of recommendations, even though at the time Miller was practically unknown outside his adopted state.

Recommendations came to Lincoln's desk in behalf of Miller from the governor of Iowa, the United States senators from Iowa, the United States representatives from Iowa, the Iowa state bar, the Iowa state legislature, the attorney general of Iowa, the Iowa state supreme court judges, and a multitude of others. Miller's friends, who even saw to it that petitions from "Iowa State Citizens" were added to the pile, left no stone unturned.

The recommendations that poured in upon Lincoln appealed to every motive that could influence him. Bypassing the trite, it is interesting to examine some of the most original. Lincoln was asked to select Miller as a compliment to Iowa "whose devotion to our Union is so . . . deserving." [32] Francis Springer, former judge of the first judicial district of Iowa, was certain that he expressed "the opinion of the Bar and Bench" when he declared that "as a jurist [albeit Miller had no experience as a judge] he has no superior in the State." [33] The Iowa attorney general recommended Miller as an "earnest Patriot and conscientious Republican," and added that he *has never held a public office.*" [34]

The President was told that the "loyal, thinking people of Iowa would be gratified" by Miller's appointment.[35] Judge George C. Wright of the Iowa supreme court wrote, "In the full prime and vigor of healthy manhood . . . devoted to his country at all times & all the more in this hour of her greatest peril, I deem him in every way qualified." [36] And this was not all that came to the President's desk in behalf of Samuel Miller.

Meant for the President's eyes, too, was a letter from J. C. Hall, former judge of the Iowa supreme court, which said that if the circuits were reorganized "Iowa of course will expect Some appointment upon the Bench." [37] Edward Johnstone, who told the President that he had opposed Miller politically, wrote to endorse him for the Supreme Court, remarking, "The Citizens of the Upper Mississippi Valley believe that this region . . . is entitled to be represented on the Federal Bench." [38]

---

[32] Daniel F. Miller to Abraham Lincoln, December 10, 1861, Lincoln MSS.

[33] Francis Springer to Abraham Lincoln, December 11, 1861, *ibid.*

[34] C. C. Nourse to Abraham Lincoln, December 14, 1861, *ibid.*

[35] Caleb Baldwin to Abraham Lincoln, December 16, 1861, *ibid.*

[36] George C. Wright to Abraham Lincoln, December 16, 1861, *ibid.*

[37] J. C. Hall to James W. Grimes, December 16, 1861, *ibid.*

[38] Edward Johnstone to Abraham Lincoln, December 20, 1861, *ibid.*

And yet the letters came. At the end of a letter that was lavish with praise for Miller, Judge James M. Love of the federal district court for Iowa said, "I beg leave to add that in what I have just said I have spoken not the language of mere empty compliment and inconsiderate commendation." [39] Amusingly, Joseph C. Knappe wrote to Lincoln urging the appointment, saying that Miller "has had an extensive practice in the United States District Court for . . . Iowa, in which Court, for Eight years—and until removed by your Excellency—I discharged the duties of United States Attorney . . . Mr. Miller and myself—as you will of course infer—differ politically. . . ." [40]

Interviews that two champions of Miller had with Lincoln throw considerable light upon the appointment. John A. Kasson of Des Moines, whom Lincoln had appointed first assistant postmaster general and who later was elected to Congress, was requested by Miller to call upon Lincoln and intervene in his behalf. Kasson learned that Miller's reputation had not extended as far as Springfield and that the President had Miller confused with Daniel F. Miller who had represented Iowa in the Thirty-First Congress (1849-1851). He proceeded to correct the President's misunderstanding and to sketch for him the career and qualifications of Samuel F. Miller.[41]

The other interview with Lincoln was held by Governor Samuel J. Kirkwood of Iowa, Senator James Harlan, and several members of the Iowa delegation to the House of Representatives. Senator Harlan explained that they had come in regard "to that appointment." And the Governor remarked that the appointment would be "a very fit and proper one to be made." But no one, as yet, had mentioned the office or the name of the man who was to be appointed. This gave the President an opportunity to poke a little fun at his visitors. Kirkwood had found Lincoln obliging in the past, especially in relation to military appointments. Lincoln "picked up his pen, and drawing a paper to him as if to make the appointment in compliance with their wishes, said to them, 'what is the office and whom do you wish to be placed in it?' "

The Iowans were almost overcome. Senator Harlan quickly stated their request: "We wish to have Mr. Miller of Iowa chosen by you to the vacancy on the Supreme Bench." Lincoln, who was well aware of their hopes, replied, " 'Well, well,' . . . replacing the pen and pushing back his paper, 'that is a very important position and I will have to give it serious consideration. I had supposed you wanted me to make some one a Brigadier General for you.' " Lincoln had had his little joke at the expense

---

[39] J. M. Love to Abraham Lincoln, January 1, 1862, *ibid.*

[40] Joseph C. Knappe to Abraham Lincoln, January 4, 1862, *ibid.*

[41] John A. Kasson to Charles Aldrich, November 10, 1893, quoted in *Annals of Iowa*, January, 1894, I, 252.

of the Iowans, but with the interview at an end they had no assurance that their request would be granted.[42]

Lincoln acceded to their wishes the day after he signed the circuit reorganization bill. On July 16, 1862, President Lincoln nominated Samuel F. Miller to the Supreme Court. The nomination was "read, considered, and confirmed" the day it was received by the Senate. Iowa's politicians had tasted the fruits of their talents twice within two days. They got their trans-Mississippi circuit, and they got the appointment for Samuel Miller, too.

The newspapers reacted in a confused manner to this appointment. Some of them were unable to decide whether the new Justice was Samuel F. Miller or Daniel F. Miller. The confusion is significant evidence of the obscurity of the new appointee. Some newspapers apparently knew or could learn so little about Miller that they could carry only a statement that the appointment was made.[43] The New York *Tribune* went so far as to correct the dispatches, saying, "Mr. Miller's name is printed *Samuel* in the dispatches, but we presume it is Daniel F. Miller, the first Whig member of Congress ever chosen from Iowa." [44] In discussing the appointment in an editorial titled "New Supreme Judge," the Chicago *Tribune*, however, properly identified Miller as a Republican leader of Iowa and referred to him correctly as Samuel F. Miller.[45]

The confusion in the East did not clear up quickly. Months after the appointment was made the Washington *Morning Chronicle* quoted comments from the New York *Post* which discussed Daniel F. Miller as a member of the United States Supreme Court. The *Chronicle*, referring to the new Justice as a "sterling patriot," said, "A blunder similar to the above was recently made by the same Journal which lashed itself into a fierce rage over its own exclusive announcement that the late Secretary of the Interior [Caleb B. Smith] had been placed upon the Supreme Bench. Is ignorance of the *personnel* of the Supreme Court a specialty of the *Post*?" [46]

Justice Miller received his commission from Attorney General Bates on July 19 and was administered the oath of office by Chief Justice Taney on July 21. When Taney administered the oath, he saw standing in front of him a man of striking appearance, "large, well built, with massive head,

---

[42] H. W. Lathrop, "Judge Miller's Appointment to the Supreme Court," *Iowa Historical Record*, January, 1891, VII, 17.

[43] Washington *Daily Globe*, July 17, 1862, p. 4; Washington *Evening Star*, July 17, 1862, p. 2; Baltimore *Sun*, July 17, 1862, p. 2; New York *Times*, July 17, 1862, p. 5; New York *World*, July 17, 1862, p. 1; New York *Herald*, July 17, 1862, p. 1; Chicago *Tribune*, July 18, 1862, p. 1.

[44] New York *Tribune*, July 18, 1862, p. 4.

[45] Editorial, Chicago *Tribune*, July 21, 1862, p. 2.

[46] Editorial, Washington *Morning Chronicle*, January 24, 1862, p. 2.

clear-cut features, and a pair of bright, penetrating eyes." [47] He was a man who made friends easily, delighted in good companionship, excelled as a conversationalist, and had a good sense of humor.

Previously, Miller had held no public office. Of course it was not by deliberate design that Lincoln chose a man without previous public experience, but it is highly significant that lack of public service did not prevent Lincoln from naming him. Despite the critical statement that Miller's "preponderant qualification was that he was chairman of the Republican district committee at Keokuk," [48] selection of Miller was not out of harmony with Lincoln's concept of what qualified a man for elevation to the Supreme Court.

In the Robert Todd Lincoln collection there are few communications sent by Justice Miller to the President, but two of them reveal Miller's relation to the administration. In one Miller recommended to Lincoln appointment of Caleb Baldwin of Council Bluffs, Iowa, to be a director of the Union Pacific railroad. [49] The other was a telegram in which Miller called Lincoln's attention to a case of arbitrary arrest. Here, again, one of Lincoln's Supreme Court appointees interested himself in arbitrary arrest. In a telegram from St. Louis, Miller told Lincoln that J. G. Turner of Richmond, Kentucky, had been arrested and sent to Memphis. "I know nothing of the facts [telegraphed Miller] and have satisfactory assurances that Judge Breck & Curtis T. Burnam of whose devoted loyalty there can be no doubt & who are his neighbors say that he is wrongfully arrested[.]" Miller added that the prisoner was over seventy years of age and asked Lincoln to modify the order so as to send Turner to Washington, Indiana, where he had a son. In conclusion Miller said he believed that in this way "all useful purposes may be subserved without cruelty[.] This I Earnestly beg may be done[.]" [50]

In an address before the Iowa State Bar Association at Des Moines in 1879 Justice Miller admitted how little known he was when he was elevated to the bench. He attributed his appointment to the heartiness and "unanimity with which the bar of my own State recommended" it. He declared that he had always been gratified that Democrats of the Iowa bar joined Republicans to back his candidacy. [51]

---

[47] Horace Stern, "Samuel Freeman Miller," *Great American Lawyers* (Philadelphia, 1909), VI, 548-49.

[48] Ewing, *The Judges of the Supreme Court*, p. 105. A leading student of Miller's career, Charles N. Gregory, states that Miller, fully aware of his limited legal preparation, proceeded in the early days of his service on the Supreme Court to study every reported case heard by the Court from its first term to the time that he took his seat. Charles N. Gregory, "Samuel Freeman Miller, Associate Justice of the Supreme Court of the United States," *Yale Law Journal*, April, 1908, XVII, 428.

[49] Samuel F. Miller to Abraham Lincoln, September 26, 1863, Lincoln MSS.

[50] Samuel F. Miller to Abraham Lincoln, October 8, 1864, *ibid*.

[51] Address of Mr. Justice Miller Delivered Before the Iowa State Bar Association at Des Moines, May 13, 1879, quoted in *Albany Law Journal*, July 12, 1879, XX, 25.

At a later date Justice Miller wrote Mrs. James W. Grimes, widow of the Senator, a lengthy letter explaining the story of his appointment and the role that Senator Grimes played in obtaining it. He said that it was known that his appointment depended upon establishment of a trans-Mississippi circuit and that Senator Grimes, Senator Harlan, and Representative Wilson all fought for its creation. He added that Grimes secured the signatures of twenty-eight senators on a petition urging the appointment. And Representative Wilson, whose assistance "was especially efficient," circulated a similar petition in the House which was signed by one hundred and twenty members.[52]

Miller, whose legal training left so much to be desired, was a self-made jurist with little systematic approach to the law. His strength on the bench rested in the capacity he had to think independently and logically. Although he came to the bench with strong antislavery bias and could well have been immoderate, he practiced self-restraint as a Justice.[53]

Justice Miller proved to be "second to none" in the difficult task that the Supreme Court faced during the Civil War—the task of seeing that "no just power of the General Government should be lost, and on the other [hand], no just right of a State or of a citizen should be sacrificed." [54] Although Miller had the task of overcoming inadequate training and lack of experience in governmental responsibilities, this liability was so well surmounted that he finally was to rank with a half-dozen other Supreme Court Justices "who, after Marshall, have impressed their personalities upon our constitutional law." [55]

---

[52] Samuel F. Miller to Mrs. James W. Grimes, August 28, 1888, *Iowa Historical Record*, April, 1891, VII, 88-89. Miller stated that these petitions were presented to Lincoln but admitted that at a later date the President declared ". . . in my presence that no such recommendations for office had ever been made to him." *Ibid.*

[53] Fairman, *Mr. Justice Miller and the Supreme Court*, p. 67.

[54] 137 U.S. 704-05.

[55] Charles Fairman, ed., "Justice Samuel F. Miller and the Barbourville Debating Society," *Mississippi Valley Historical Review*, March, 1931, XVII, 595.

CHAPTER SIX

Our Mutual Friend

THESE COVETED IN VAIN

There remained, after the appointment of Miller, only one vacancy. Strenuous efforts were made by four candidates to obtain it, and Lincoln found himself besieged by powerful politicians. One candidate, Secretary of the Interior Caleb B. Smith, had small chance at best after the circuit reorganization placed Indiana and Ohio together. But the other three aspirants, Orville H. Browning, David Davis, and Thomas Drummond, all longtime associates of Lincoln during the Illinois days, fought an energetic battle to secure the remaining vacancy.

Orville H. Browning, whom Governor Richard Yates appointed senator from Illinois to replace Stephen A. Douglas, who died on June 3, 1861, sought a Supreme Court seat almost from the time of Lincoln's inauguration. In the early days of Lincoln's presidency and in fact until Lincoln passed over him in filling the Court, Browning was a devoted correspondent of the President, sending him lengthy letters of political gossip and political advice.

The Lincoln administration was hardly more than a month old when Browning wrote Lincoln seeking appointment. He said that friends wished to circulate petitions in his behalf but that he did not believe it proper to pursue a seat on the Supreme Court. Browning said to Lincoln that Lincoln knew him "about as well as I know myself." With candor he told Lincoln, "If, then, you shall think me competent to the duties of the office, and shall be at all inclined to gratify me in any thing, I say frankly, and without any sort of disguise, or affection, that there is nothing in your power to do for me which would gratify me so much as this."

Browning felt a strong personal distaste for what he was doing and told Lincoln that he was unwilling for everyone to know that he had solicited the post. "I am willing *you* shall know that I do desire the office —I am *not* willing that the world shall," he wrote the President. He feared that his ambition might become publicly known, and he asked Lincoln to spare him that humiliation. He pointed out that although powerful pressures would be exerted, "I know that you can do as you please, and that the great body of people will not care a fig who the appointee is." Ending with the thought that "The whole matter is in your hands,"

Orville H. Browning was ready to rest his case.[1] After this outburst Browning continued writing letters to the President (usually four pages), but he did not again refer to his desire for a justiceship.

Early in June, 1861, however, a letter signed by Eliza H. Browning and carefully marked "Sub Rosa" made its way to Lincoln.[2] She informed him that her husband was not well; he had suffered a rupture during strenuous speaking engagements in Lincoln's behalf! With the admission that her husband would be aghast if he were aware that she was involving herself in his behalf, she determined to ask Lincoln for consideration nonetheless.

Eliza Browning wrote Lincoln that no man—not even David Davis— had a better claim upon him than her husband. She said that she asked for the appointment because "*I* know my husband to be one of the *Wisest*[, and] *best* men in the Nation[.] I know him to be, an unselfish Patriot, & not a *miserable* office Seeker." She declared that he had in the past never been fully appreciated "owing in part, to his Great Modesty, and unselfishness in not pushing himself forward." She scourged that "class of cold[,] heartless politicians" in Illinois who consistently opposed him and "left no Stone unturned to defeat him." Upon this appeal she hoped that Lincoln would decide to "Gratify a sincere friend and devoted wife."

Clandestine though efforts of the Brownings were, certain politicians gained knowledge of their appeals. William H. Bradley, clerk of the United States district and circuit courts at Chicago, an opponent of Browning, wrote Representative Elihu B. Washburne of Illinois that Browning "took the Senatorship to aid himself in his efforts to secure the Judgeship." And Bradley informed Washburne, "(I know confidentially that he wrote to Mr. Lincoln about the Judgeship a long letter— which please do not mention)."

Bradley was well informed in other regards, too. He said that he heard that the plan was to satisfy Ohio with the appointment of Swayne and to leave "this circuit for Mr. B.[rowning]." Bradley hoped for the appointment of Thomas Drummond, United States district judge at Chicago, in whose court he functioned. He told Washburne, "I think Mr. Lincoln would like to give it to Judge Drummond but I fear Mr. B.[rowning] will worry it out of him." [3]

The followers of David Davis, too, looked upon Browning as their greatest threat. Ward H. Lamon, a law associate of Lincoln in the Illinois days, wrote to William W. Orme, who practiced law in Bloomington, Illinois, and was a champion of David Davis, that "I have said all I dared

---

[1] Orville H. Browning to Abraham Lincoln, April 9, 1861, Lincoln MSS.

[2] Eliza H. Browning to Abraham Lincoln, June 8, 1861, *ibid.*

[3] William H. Bradley to Elihu B. Washburne, July 10, 1861, Washburne MSS., Library of Congress.

without injury—in the direction of my first allegiance." Lamon feared that Browning and Smith would be appointed to the Supreme Court and that Davis would be made Secretary of the Interior, but Lincoln would not discuss the matter with him.[4]

While awaiting the decision, David Davis expressed his sentiments freely. He wrote Orme that Hawkins Taylor, prominent Iowa Republican, informed him that the word in Washington was that Browning and Smith would be elevated to the Court. Regarding it all, Davis concluded, "Caleb B. Smith, I expect is fighting with Browning, & it is fine gratitude for me for what I done [sic] for him—" Davis revealed that so many friends were supporting him that he was beginning "to feel some desire about it, though feeling great distrust of my ability to fill the office acceptably. . . . The Interior Department has no charm for me—not a bit—" [5]

Joseph Medill, a leading Illinois Republican who was associated with the Chicago *Tribune*, wrote Senator Trumbull bluntly that "You may safely tell your senatorial associate Browning that he represents only the secesh [secessionists] of Illinois—Republicans detest and despise him." Medill said that Lincoln must be kept from the error of appointing Browning, that "His elevation to the Supreme Bench will be the most unpopular act of Mr. Lincoln's life and he ought to be informed of it, before he does the deed." [6]

The hesitancy of the administration caused comment all along the line. Apparently the President was sorely in travail over filling the Illinois circuit. Chief Justice Taney, himself, was finally to comment on the prospective appointment: "I learned from him [Justice Miller] & Mr. Bates who introduced him, that the appointment of Mr. Browning to the vacant circuit, although probable was not certain." Taney said that he understood that Judge Thomas Drummond and another person were strong rivals of Browning and that there was "some hesitation" on the part of the President.[7] That Taney could not recollect the name of David Davis is quite remarkable. But at any rate, Lincoln had them all guessing, including the Chief Justice.

President Lincoln did have a dilemma to solve: he had been closely associated with Browning and Davis, and both men could make strong claims upon him. Probably the view expressed by Joseph Medill, which was the view of the Radicals, strongly influenced Lincoln as he watched

[4] Ward H. Lamon to William W. Orme, February 10, 1862, Orme MSS., Ill. Hist. Survey.

[5] David Davis to William W. Orme, February 23, 1862, *ibid*.

[6] Joseph Medill to Lyman Trumbull, July 4, 1862, Trumbull MSS., Library of Congress.

[7] Roger B. Taney to Nathan Clifford, August 2, 1862, Clifford MSS.

Browning act out his senatorial role. Browning became less an administration stalwart than could have been expected. If Browning hesitated as a Senator to support the administration, would he prove more devoted to Lincoln as a member of the Supreme Court? There was some chance, also, that if Browning resigned his senatorship, Illinois would replace him with a Democrat.[8]

Judge Drummond, too, was boomed energetically by friends who sought his elevation to the Supreme Court. When Noah H. Swayne was appointed while the circuit battle raged, William H. Bradley wrote to Washburne that Drummond's friends preferred to see disagreement over the circuits continue unless "our Friend Judge Drummond stands an equal chance for one of the Circuits."[9] He stated that Drummond and the new Secretary of War, Edwin M. Stanton, were close friends and that something might happen "to make the way more clear for Judge D[rummond]."

Friends of Drummond insisted that he write a letter to Representative Washburne that could be placed in Lincoln's hands at the proper time.[10] Judge Drummond obliged them, but he wrote with reluctance as it was his opinion that a Supreme Court appointment should be conferred without active solicitation by candidates. Lincoln at one time had practiced in the court over which he presided, and it was that fact which convinced him that it would not be inappropriate to seek the post. And so Drummond wrote that he needed the additional income the appointment would bring, that he and Lincoln were personal friends, and that his experience on the federal bench justified his request. He said that appointment by Lincoln would gratify him, and that if he failed it would "grieve me to find I did not stand so high in his good opinion as I hoped." One great apprehension stood out in Drummond's mind; he feared that his lengthy service on the federal judiciary—he had served over a decade—tended to disconnect him from party ties.

Drummond's position in the matter was that of a gentleman. "If the President is disinclined, [he warned Washburne] under all circumstances . . . to appoint me, it would be unfair and ungenerous to press him on the subject."[11] Judge Drummond was unwilling to wangle the appointment out of his friend Lincoln.

As to Caleb B. Smith, even if a different circuit arrangement had been concluded, there is no evidence that his candidacy was seriously considered by the President. Edward Bates explained Smith's interest in the

---

[8] Baltimore *Sun*, January 24, 1862, p. 4.

[9] William H. Bradley to Elihu B. Washburne, January 28, 1862, Washburne MSS.

[10] J. R. Jones to Elihu B. Washburne, June 21, 1862, *ibid.*

[11] Thomas Drummond to Elihu Washburne, June 21, 1862, *ibid.*

Court by the fact that he was the object of considerable criticism. Bates recorded in his diary, "I hear that there is a strong combination against him—I hear of no charge in particular, only some alleged abuse of patronage and lack of vim. *Note.* He is very anxious to be translated to the Supreme Bench." [12] No matter what the political considerations were, Secretary Smith was failing in health and believed that judicial duties would be less strength consuming than a post in the cabinet.[13]

DAVID DAVIS TRIUMPHS

President Lincoln filled the last of the three original vacancies by the appointment of David Davis on October 17, 1862. It is not surprising that the President was subjected to unparalleled pressures both in behalf of Davis and against him. The Robert Todd Lincoln collection and other sources as well give insight into the maneuvering that produced the appointment.

During his lengthy career in the state judiciary of Illinois David Davis had presided over a court in which several men practiced who later were to gain prominence: Lyman Trumbull, Orville H. Browning, Stephen A. Douglas, Abraham Lincoln, and others. Born in Maryland in 1815, Davis attended Kenyon College in Ohio, studied at Yale, and began his legal practice in Pekin, Illinois. Soon he moved to Bloomington where he turned promptly to politics and was elected to the Illinois legislature in 1844. In 1848 he became judge of the eighth circuit of Illinois, a post he held until 1862. Judge Davis and lawyer Lincoln became close friends, and events finally brought them into close political cooperation. Judge Davis worked strenuously for Lincoln in the senatorial campaign of 1858, and in the Republican convention of 1860 Davis marshaled the forces in favor of Abraham Lincoln.

The intimate relationship between Davis and Lincoln at the time of "President-making" is well revealed by the Robert Todd Lincoln collection. From the Republican convention in Chicago in 1860 David Davis telegraphed Lincoln: "Am very hopeful[.] dont be Excited[.] nearly dead with fatigue[.] telegraph or write here very little[.]" [14] And after his efforts were successful, Davis telegraphed the new presidential nominee, "Write no letters & make no promises till You see me[.] write me at Bloomington when to see you[.] I must see you soon[.]" [15] Judge Davis

---

[12] Bates, *Diary*, p. 228 (February 2, 1862).

[13] Shortly after he failed to get the appointment, Secretary Smith asked to retire from Lincoln's cabinet. He requested appointment as United States district judge for Indiana, a post to which he was named after the death of Judge E. M. Huntington.

[14] David Davis to Abraham Lincoln, May 17, 1860, Lincoln MSS.

[15] David Davis to Abraham Lincoln, May 18, 1860, *ibid.*

had established Lincoln headquarters in the convention city at the Tremont House and had paid the expenses himself. As the campaign progressed Davis continued his interest in the cause of Lincoln. On August 12, 1860, he wrote Lincoln, "You will be elected Pres[i]d[en]t[.] There is no longer a doubt of it in my mind—" He was convinced, he told Lincoln, that the Democrats no longer had any hope or any confidence.[16]

An amusing letter written to Lincoln by Ward H. Lamon described the reaction of Judge Davis to the good news resulting from state elections in Pennsylvania and Indiana in October, 1860. When the election returns came, Lamon related, Judge Davis was trying an important criminal case, but the Judge terminated it by "Kicking over the Clerk's desk, turned a double somersault [some feat for Davis with his excessive weight!] and adjourned court until after the presidential Election—" [17]

When the election was over, Davis remained close to the President-elect and accompanied him to Washington. It was natural that after the inauguration friends of Davis urged Lincoln to name him to one of the three vacancies upon the Supreme Court. H. Winter Davis of Maryland wrote Lincoln only two days after the inauguration to urge the appointment. The former representative said, "I venture to press on you the peculiar fitness both in experience, learning, judicial habits & judicial cast of mind of the Hon. David Davis." He added that on the basis of maturity, capacity, and age, Judge Davis merited selection. And he suggested to Lincoln that "No appointment would better grace your administration." [18] This letter was the beginning. Letters of similar nature were to be directed to Lincoln constantly until the appointment of Davis was forthcoming.

Friends of Judge Davis demanded the appointment as a matter of justice and reward; they admitted frankly their estimate of Lincoln's indebtedness to Davis. Upon the death of Justice McLean, Lawrence Weldon, who had been appointed by Lincoln to be federal district attorney for the southern district of Illinois, asked why Judge Davis should not be appointed, "especially when he was so instrumental in giving position to him who now holds the matter in the hollow of his hand?" Weldon argued that Lincoln could "do nothing less than to tender" the justiceship to Davis.[19] And along similar lines, H. C. Whitney told Lamon: "Justice, gratitude[,] reason[,] and patriotism may say, if Judge Davis is to be

[16] David Davis to Abraham Lincoln, August 12, 1860, ibid.

[17] Ward H. Lamon to Abraham Lincoln, October 10, 1860, ibid.

[18] H. Winter Davis to Abraham Lincoln, March 6, 1861, ibid.

[19] Lawrence Weldon to Ward H. Lamon, April 6, 1861, quoted by Harry E. Pratt, "David Davis, 1815-1886," MS., doctoral dissertation, University of Illinois, 1930, p. 92. Cited hereafter as Pratt, "David Davis."

snubbed by such men as Chase & —————— it is a d--n pretty pass, a man has come to in the house of his friend." [20]

Judge Davis, fully aware of all this effort, was not too friendly at first to the idea of his friends. As an experienced jurist, he was disturbed by the circuit activities which were a part of the responsibilities of a member of the Supreme Court. He knew well the laborious tasks performed by judges.[21] "The position that Judge Drummond holds, [Judge Davis wrote at this time] I would prefer it to the Supreme Judgeship because I know I could discharge the duties of the one satisfactorily, but am diffident about the other." [22]

But his associates became more and more disturbed as Lincoln failed to appoint him. Leonard Swett, law partner of William W. Orme, found it incomprehensible that Lincoln should fail to appoint Davis and told Lamon so.[23] Finally Swett, who could stand the delay no longer, went to Washington to see Lincoln personally and to suggest that if he would appoint Davis, he could "plead what is done for him as an estoppel to me and my friends at any time. . . ." [24]

Six months later Swett, continuing his campaign for Davis, wrote the President a letter that was bold to the point of bordering the limits of propriety and enclosed a letter from John T. Stuart, Lincoln's first law partner. Stuart told Lincoln that the appointment of Davis would be pleasing "*especially* to the circle of *your old personal friends.*" [25] But Leonard Swett, assuming a daring position, wrote Lincoln in a manner that only an associate of long duration and closest intimacy could adopt.

Swett declared that a group of friends in Illinois had been interested in Lincoln's success and that Judge Davis was its leader. The group, stated Swett, wished Lincoln to acknowledge his indebtedness to Davis. Swett asked the President to consider what Davis would do if "your elevation had rested in the power of Judge Davis as his does now in yours? . . . Now should not a man in power remember those men, and discriminate in favor of those men, who throughout life have been as true as steel to him. Is this not common justice[?]" [26] Leonard Swett's efforts did not languish. He saw to it that as the year 1862 began an almost constant stream of letters in behalf of Judge Davis found its way to Lincoln.

As his friends pressed his candidacy more energetically in 1862, Davis began to express desire for the appointment, although he could not forget that the duties were arduous. He admitted to his friend Orme that perhaps

---

[20] H. C. Whitney to Ward H. Lamon, April 13, 1861, *ibid.*, p. 93, n. 10.

[21] David Davis to Ward H. Lamon, May 17, 1861, *ibid.*, p. 95.

[22] David Davis to Ward H. Lamon, April 14, 1861, *ibid.*, p. 94.

[23] Leonard Swett to Ward H. Lamon, July 26, 1861, *ibid.*, p. 93.

[24] Leonard Swett to Abraham Lincoln, August 15, 1861, Lincoln MSS.

[25] John T. Stuart to Abraham Lincoln, January 24, 1862, *ibid.*

[26] Leonard Swett to Abraham Lincoln, January 25, 1862, *ibid.*

he was not self-confident enough, but that he feared he could not fulfill the responsibilities "without hard study," nonetheless adding that he believed Browning to be no better qualified. Reflecting upon Browning's prospects, Judge Davis added, "If Mr. Lincoln does appoint Mr. Browning, as I believe he will, will it not be a fine commentary on human friendships & human gratitude—" [27]

For six months following the appointment of Noah H. Swayne the Davis supporters flooded Lincoln with entreaties. Innumerable arguments were presented to the President, but always prominent was the thought that Davis merited it on the basis of devotion. Clifton H. Moore, a one-time partner of Davis, wrote the President that he was at the Chicago convention with Davis, that Davis fought valiantly for Lincoln's nomination, and that the appointment should be made "upon the ground of his eminent service to you." [28] Lincoln was informed, also, that "I *believe* he done [*sic*] much towards elevating you to the position you now occupy." [29] Lincoln was told as well that appointment of Davis would remove the impression that "his service and merits have not been appreciated by your administration." [30]

It fell to John M. Scott of Bloomington, who was to succeed Davis as judge of Illinois's eighth judicial district, to write Lincoln the most lengthy lecture on his duty toward David Davis. He wrote Lincoln that the public expected the appointment, that the relations of Lincoln and Davis had been such that justice dictated the appointment, and that if Davis "*is not appointed*" the public mind would question Lincoln's magnanimity. Scott disposed of Browning by telling Lincoln that "to appoint *one* not heretofore your most steadfast friend with the hope of *making him such* is neither wise in politics or morals." [31]

Curiously, after the appointment of Samuel F. Miller, Lincoln delayed filling the remaining vacancy. It would have been natural to expect that he would have filled the two vacancies at the same time. But the painful decision was not yet made. Newspapers speculated as to the meaning of this delay, but the New York *Tribune* concluded that Judge Davis was still the most likely appointee, although it suggested that William A. Howard, a prominent Michigan lawyer, or Senator James R. Doolittle of Wisconsin might get the post. The fact that Lincoln left the one circuit open, however, said the *Tribune*, "is regarded as virtually the defeat of Senator Browning's aspirations to a seat on the bench." [32]

President Lincoln at last was ready to act even though Congress had

[27] David Davis to William W. Orme, January 27, 1862, Orme MSS.

[28] Clifton H. Moore to Abraham Lincoln, January 29, 1862, Lincoln MSS.

[29] L. P. Lacey to Abraham Lincoln, January 30, 1862, *ibid.*

[30] Oliver L. Davis to Abraham Lincoln, February 3, 1862, *ibid.*

[31] John M. Scott to Abraham Lincoln, February 11, 1862, *ibid.*

[32] New York *Tribune*, July 18, 1862, p. 4.

adjourned on July 17, 1862, and no appointment was anticipated until it reassembled. On August 27, the President sent Judge Davis news that he promptly answered with deep satisfaction. "Your note of the 27th ult., [wrote Judge Davis] Stating that you had made up your mind to appoint me Supreme Judge is just received—" Judge Davis said that he could not adequately express his "thankfulness and gratitude." [33]

Apparently this offer of appointment was a secret of the President and Judge Davis. It was not mentioned in the press. Since the Senate was not in session, official nomination, it appeared, would await the meeting of Congress in December. It is interesting to note, however, that the men who led the fight for Davis ceased firing their ammunition in the direction of the Executive Mansion.

The President finally became unwilling to delay the nomination until the Senate reassembled, so he requested Attorney General Bates to give an opinion as to whether a vacancy on the Court could be filled during a recess. On October 15 the Attorney General ruled that the power in question had been exercised in the past. Consequently on October 17 President Lincoln appointed Davis to the Supreme Court. Writing to William W. Orme on October 21, Davis related that "Mr. Lincoln has sent me my commission under his own frank, accompanied by a cordial letter inviting me to Washington." [34]

David Davis wrote exuberantly to President Lincoln on October 30. Perhaps he delayed acceptance for two weeks to rebuke Lincoln for the hesitation in making the appointment. Davis acknowledged the commission, "I need not repeat to you the expression of my thanks for this mark of your favor & for the manner of conferring it—" He said that he had not expected the appointment to be made until December and informed Lincoln that he had intended "going to Washington Sometime in Nov[embe]r—" but that "The tenor of your note will hasten my departure."

Still the politician, Davis wrote Lincoln of the political situation in Illinois (the congressional election of 1862 was but a few days away). He said that he feared bad results and related that "swett is working hard as mortal man ever did work to accomplish his object—" Davis admitted that "My greatest fear is of Sangamon County." [35]

Did the dark political situation in Illinois (as elsewhere) influence both Lincoln's choice for the Illinois circuit as well as the timing of the appointment? Was the appointment of Davis interwoven with the political storm that swirled around Lincoln in the congressional election of 1862? The nature and timing of the appointment would make it appear so.

---

[33] David Davis to Abraham Lincoln, September 1, 1862, Lincoln MSS.

[34] David Davis to William W. Orme, October 21, 1862, Pratt, "David Davis," p. 92.

[35] David Davis to Abraham Lincoln, October 30, 1862, Lincoln MSS.

With the appointment of Justice Davis, President Lincoln had finally filled the three vacancies on the Supreme Court, and on October 30 he allotted the Justices to their circuits.[36] More common procedure and more courteous policy would have been to permit allotment to await action of the Chief Justice and the membership of the Court upon reassembling in December. Furthermore, David Davis was assigned to a circuit before the Senate confirmed his nomination.

Praise for the appointment was both general and hearty. Typical of press reaction was the editorial comment of the Washington *National Intelligencer* which heaped praise upon Lincoln as well as Davis and said, "Our worthy President has made a wise selection in the appointment." It declared that Davis was a fine lawyer as well as an honorable, able, warm-hearted man who had no selfish motives.[37] And Lincoln was told that Davis was devoted to him and would be invaluable as an adviser.[38]

Upon the reassembling of Congress, President Lincoln sent the Davis nomination to the Senate on December 1. It was read and referred to the committee on the judiciary on December 3 and was reported favorably on December 5, with confirmation coming three days later.

The day that Lincoln sent the nomination of Davis to the Senate the Supreme Court reassembled for its December Term. "The United States Supreme Court commenced their term today— [reported the Baltimore *Sun*] present, Justices Wayne, Grier, Clifford, Swayne, and Miller—the Chief Justice, Taney, and three official Justices being absent." The *Sun* added that reports had circulated that the Justices, "in deference to the wishes of the new members of the Court" might not wear the robes of office, but "The Justices appeared, as usual, in their gowns." [39] The members of Lincoln's Supreme Court would remain warriors in black robes whether the new members wished to or not.

In making the Davis appointment, the President demonstrated an independence of mind that would not bend no matter what the supplications of the politicians were. The appointment of Swayne came first because Swayne fulfilled the circuit needs in relation to Ohio. The appointment of Miller came immediately following circuit reorganization because political considerations dictated the choice. The appointment of Davis lagged because Lincoln was having almost insurmountable difficulty in evaluating the demands of friendship, personal indebtedness, and political sagacity.

[36] New York *World*, October 31, 1862, p. 1; Washington *National Intelligencer*, October 30, 1862, p. 3.

[37] Editorial, Washington *National Intelligencer*, November 10, 1862, p. 3.

[38] John M. Palmer to Abraham Lincoln, November 26, 1862, Lincoln MSS.

[39] Baltimore *Sun*, December 2, 1862, p. 4.

The man who was most responsible for the success of Davis was Leonard Swett, a fact of which Davis was well aware.[40] Many years later Swett recounted the whole story in a letter to William H. Herndon, a onetime law partner of Lincoln, at the time that Herndon was preparing a life of the President. Swett might have embellished the story and the intervening years might have impaired his ability to recreate the details, but essentially it is correct as the Robert Todd Lincoln collection and other sources demonstrate.

Swett related that while the decision pended, reports trickled into Bloomington that gave some clue to the President's intentions. Swett revealed that the Davis group believed that Browning, with his advantageous position in the United States Senate, might be able to sweep Lincoln off his feet.

Finally word came that Lincoln had said essentially, "I do not know what I may do when the time comes, but there has never been a day when if I had to act I should not have appointed Browning." Lincoln's statement resulted in a meeting of Swett, Orme, and Davis. The three agreed that the statement was "too Lincolnian to be mistaken," and that the appointment of Davis was doomed.

Swett decided upon immediate action. As he described the scene to Herndon, he said to Davis and Orme, "The appointment is gone and I am going to pack my carpet-sack for Washington. . . . Lincoln is being swept off his feet . . . and I will have the luxury of one more talk with him before he acts." So Leonard Swett went to Washington.

He gained access to the President and spent a whole forenoon with him. Swett told Lincoln that "If Judge Davis . . . had not lived, and all other things had been as they were, I believe you would not now be sitting where you are." To which Lincoln replied, "Yes, that is so." Swett said that "it is a common law of mankind" to repay debts and added, "The Czar Nicholas was once attacked by an assassin; a kindly hand warded off the blow and saved his life. The Czar hunted out the owner of that hand and strewed his pathway with flowers through life."

According to Swett's account, leaving the President he proceeded to Willard's Hotel. A new thought occurred to him, and he wrote the President a note, and proceeded to the Executive Mansion to deliver it. Gaining access again, he read the letter to the President and placed it on his desk.

This letter of August 15, 1861, now to be found in the Robert Todd Lincoln collection, is the letter in which Swett told Lincoln that if Davis were appointed, Lincoln's Illinois friends would ask for nothing more. Swett stated that Lincoln's reply was, "If you mean that among friends as it reads I will take it and make the appointment." And Swett

[40] David Davis to William W. Orme, February 16, 1862, Orme MSS.

told Herndon that the appointment was made within a fortnight.[41] Actually, when Swett reminisced and attempted to recount these events twenty-six years later, he erred in declaring that Lincoln made the appointment immediately following the interview. Nevertheless, it was Leonard Swett who exerted himself the most in behalf of Davis.

As Justice Davis entered upon his new duties, he had mixed feelings. Relating events to Orme he wrote, "I was confirmed yesterday and shall get my commission and take my seat tomorrow, and the black gown. By the way, Judge Clifford is a larger man than I am." Davis admitted his apprehension to Orme, stating, "I dread going on the Bench. I wish I had your advice and counsel." [42]

Whether he enjoyed his duties or not, he was soon engrossed by them. And within a short time he began to feel more comfortable in his new role. "I never had to work so hard in my life—I feel [he wrote back to Bloomington] as if I would get along, tho[ugh] when I first got here I w[oul]d have given any thing to have been again at home." [43] He was expressing a view that he held in common with the other new members of the Court. All three had coveted appointment, but they were struck at first by the heavy responsibility and the arduous labor involved.

Davis could not be expected to drop political activities. He retained a keen interest in the political scene as his correspondence indicates. Admonishing Orme early in 1863 that "it looks very badly—," Davis continued, "Confidentially there is not a great deal of hope here . . . the general feeling is one—that is depressing—" Orme obviously did not heed Davis's injunction to "*Burn* this letter after Swett has read it." [44]

A few days later Justice Davis observed that although men like Wade and Chase did not doubt the ultimate success of the Union, "the general feeling in the street, [and in the] Hotels . . . is depressing—" [45] Later Davis himself feared for the future of the Lincoln administration, writing, "If this war is not wound up this winter, I dread the next Presidential election." [46]

Justice Davis did not hesitate to write to Lincoln about political matters and on several occasions intervened to support certain candidates for office or to obtain political favors. On one occasion Davis passed word along to Lincoln that Illinois Know-Nothings felt resentment

[41] Leonard Swett to William H. Herndon, August 29, 1887, quoted in William H. Herndon and Jesse W. Weik, *Herndon's Lincoln, The True Story of a Great Life: The History and Personal Recollections of Abraham Lincoln* (Chicago, 1889), III, 502-04.

[42] David Davis to William W. Orme, December 9, 1862, Pratt, "David Davis," p. 98.

[43] David Davis to William W. Orme, January 7, 1863, Orme MSS.

[44] David Davis to William W. Orme, February 3, 1863, *ibid.*

[45] David Davis to William W. Orme, February 9, 1863, *ibid.*

[46] David Davis to William W. Orme, August 18, 1863, *ibid.*

against the administration because Lincoln failed to grant them proper reward for support.[47] On other occasions Justice Davis transmitted to Lincoln the thoughts and desires of Thurlow Weed, prominent Albany politician and journalist, who once lamented, "*why* the President prefers his Enemies over his Friends, in this State, is a Problem too deep for my solution." [48]

At times Justice Davis brought friends to see the President, wrote him notes of congratulations, asked for political favors, and gave Lincoln advice—sometimes unsolicited and undesired. When Lincoln named former Governor Dennison of Ohio to be Postmaster General, Justice Davis congratulated Lincoln, saying that Dennison is "honorable, high-minded, pure, & dignified." [49] When the district judgeship in Indianapolis became vacant, Davis advised the appointment of David McDonald and concluded, "Excuse these suggestions." [50]

Justice Davis often was upset by the reluctance of Lincoln to pursue certain policies that he advised. "Mr. Lincoln annoys me more than I can express, [Davis wrote Orme] by his persistence in letting things take their course, without effort or organization when a combined organization in the Treasury Dept. is in antagonism—" [51] Yet, when the Republican convention of 1864 met, Davis was devoted to the cause of Lincoln. He wrote Lincoln that it had been his intention to go to Baltimore to the convention "but since the New York and Ohio conventions the necessity of doing so is foreclosed—" [52]

Thus was Justice Davis entwined with politics and the Lincoln administration. It is not surprising that his was so for Davis belonged intimately to the Illinois days of Lincoln. He would have found it very difficult to break away completely with the past just because he was a member of the Supreme Court. To have forced judicial seclusion upon Davis would have been a penalty too severe to be countenanced. As it was, a few years after the war Justice Davis stepped down from the Court to renew the political activity which was his lifeblood.

[47] David Davis to Abraham Lincoln, July 28, 1863, Lincoln MSS.
[48] Thurlow Weed to David Davis, April 11, 1864, *ibid*.
[49] David Davis to Abraham Lincoln, October 4, 1864, *ibid*.
[50] *Ibid*.
[51] David Davis to William W. Orme, March 30, 1864, Orme MSS.
[52] David Davis to Abraham Lincoln, June 2, 1864, Lincoln MSS.

CHAPTER SEVEN

A Packed Court

COURT OF TEN

Following President Lincoln's December message, 1861, on the state of the Union, the administration had determined to move slowly in relation to the Supreme Court. Even the bold thrust against the Court by Senator John P. Hale and the loud blasting of the Court by the press did not force the hand of the administration. It is true that the President had said, "Let the Supreme Court be of convenient number in every event," but he was not ready to reveal any further thought or action concerning the number of members of the Court.

But the year 1862 saw Lincoln bring the Supreme Court up to its legal size, and the year 1862 saw many other events—events that were filled with gloom and foreboding for the nation. It saw a war going very badly after initial victories early in the year in the Henry-Donelson-Shiloh campaign. It saw General George B. McClellan on the Peninsula facing Richmond, never taking it, yet fighting desperately in the battles of the peninsular campaign. It saw Lincoln order the removal of McClellan's army from the Peninsula. It saw McClellan removed from the command and replaced by General John Pope who failed in the second battle of Bull Run (Manassas). It saw Lincoln restore McClellan to his command after the second disaster at Bull Run, realizing that the cause of the Union "was critical in the extreme." [1] It saw General Robert E. Lee invade the North, although McClellan stopped him near Sharpsburg (Antietam) but then permitted him to retreat back across the Potomac. It saw Jeb Stuart for a second time make a full circuit around the army of McClellan, and it saw McClellan removed for a second time and replaced by General Ambrose E. Burnside, who came to frightful disaster at Fredericksburg.

But the year 1862 saw more yet. It saw an ever increasing demand for action against slavery. It saw Northern discontent grow ominously. It saw Lincoln grasp at Antietam to enunciate the Emancipation Proclamation though ensuing military events made prospects for actual emancipation very poor. It saw a congressional election that weakened the administration's hands because victories on the battlefield were not

[1] James G. Randall, *The Civil War and Reconstruction* (Boston, 1937 and 1953), p. 306.

attained. It saw the Radicals and the Moderates precipitate additiona.
problems for Lincoln in the form of the cabinet crisis.

And the year 1862 saw the Supreme Court moving ever closer toward
a consideration, as the result of prize cases in the lower courts, of cases
involving the legality of important acts of the Lincoln administration.
Cases involving habeas corpus and arbitrary arrest as well as the Emancipation Proclamation loomed upon the horizon, too. The first important
Supreme Court decisions of a war-related nature were to be anticipated.

Against this background and with the disasters of 1862 fresh in its
memory, the administration was ready to move further in its contest
with the federal judiciary. The administration would await no debacle,
no breath-taking defeat at the hands of the Supreme Court. It could
ill afford such additional calamity. It would move to make such defeat
less likely. Lincoln had suffered much already. It would be folly to permit
Supreme Court decisions to add to the travail.

President Lincoln and the Republicans were now to decide, concerning
the size of the Supreme Court, that the number "ten" was much more
"convenient" than the number "nine." Scarcely had 1862 ended before
the move to increase the size of the Supreme Court began. Under the
leadership of Representative James F. Wilson the committee on the
judiciary reported to the House a bill to create a tenth circuit consisting
of California and Oregon. A tenth circuit meant a tenth Justice. It was
prudence that dictated a packed Court, and President Lincoln was willing
to increase the size of the Court in order to strengthen the position of
those Justices who would view with favor the acts that the administration
deemed necessary.

Admittedly this was only moderate packing of the Court, but the tenth
Justice in addition to the three other Lincoln appointees and other
friendly Justices on the bench would provide an adequate margin of
safety. Furthermore, a Justice to serve a circuit consisting of California
and Oregon could easily be justified on the basis of the intricacies of
California land law and the large number of cases heard.

So it was that in the same days that the *Prize Cases* were being considered by the Court that Congress went about the task of creating a
tenth circuit and a tenth Justice. The Court could not fail to see the
implications. To pack it just at this time was a sharp warning that its
size, its powers, and its role rested upon the will of the Congress and the
President. The *Prize Cases*, which were argued before the Supreme Court
from February 10 to February 25, 1863, gave the administration a desire
to act with dispatch. (The *Prize Cases* are discussed in Chapter 9.) The
move to provide a tenth Justice, although it originated in the House,
first gained momentum in the Senate. On February 20, 1863, Milton S.
Latham of California introduced into the Senate a bill to provide for a

circuit consisting of California and Oregon. The bill was referred to the committee on the judiciary, and Senator Trumbull reported it favorably three days later—the administration was demonstrating speedy action. On February 26, the Senate, sitting as the Committee of the Whole, considered the proposal.

The most important provision of the bill that was reported by the committee on the judiciary was *"That the Supreme Court of the United States shall hereafter consist of a Chief Justice and nine associate justices,* any six of whom shall constitute a quorum; and for this purpose there shall be appointed one additional justice . . . with the like powers, and to take the same oaths, perform the same duties, and be entitled to the same salary as the other associate justices."[2] There was no delay. The Senate, deeming that swift action was necessary, passed the bill the same day that it took up consideration of it.

Action concerning the tenth Justice took place in the House only a few days later, on March 2. Here again there was no delay. With its rules suspended, the House, also deeming action to be imperative, concurred in the Senate's action. The bill was enrolled and signed by Speaker Galusha A. Grow on March 3, and sent to President Lincoln who approved it the same day, exactly one week before the decision in the *Prize Cases* was announced.

In addition to providing a tenth Justice who was to be assigned to the Tenth Circuit, the act provided for certain additional improvements for California and Oregon. The special system of circuit courts which had been provided for the area in 1855 was abolished. For the future the act provided, "there shall . . . be circuit courts held for the districts of the States of California and Oregon by the Chief Justice, or one of the associate justices . . . assigned or allotted to the circuit to which such districts may respectively belong."[3] It was stated also that all legal actions pending which were of circuit court jurisdiction were to be transferred to the newly established circuit court at San Francisco, Los Angeles, or Portland. And lastly, the act directed that the Justice of the Tenth Circuit was to receive, in addition to his regular salary, one thousand dollars for traveling expenses each year he attended sessions of the Supreme Court. As a part of the process of perfecting the circuit system, President Lincoln at a later date signed a bill adding Nevada to the Tenth Circuit.[4]

These same days saw two other enactments that concerned the federal judiciary. One was passage of a law that looked toward greater efficiency in the circuit courts. The other, a move to satisfy the demands of Indiana,

---

[2] *Cong. Globe*, 37th Cong., 3rd sess., p. 1300. My italics.

[3] 12 Stat. 794.

[4] *Cong. Globe*, 38th Cong., 2nd sess., p. 1155.

Michigan, and Wisconsin, all of which were dissatisfied with the circuit in which they had been placed.

The act to give greater efficiency to the judicial system, signed by President Lincoln the same day he signed the bill creating a Tenth Circuit, provided that a Justice could be assisted in his circuit by the Justice of another circuit if disability, absence, or accumulation of business made such procedure desirable.[5]

Modification of the circuits resulted from the dissatisfaction with which Indiana, Michigan, and Wisconsin viewed the act of July 15, 1862. Senator Trumbull explained to the Senate on January 19, 1863, that the senators from Indiana and Michigan asked that the Seventh Circuit (composed of Ohio and Indiana) and the Eighth Circuit (composed of Michigan, Wisconsin, and Illinois) be altered so that the Seventh would consist of Ohio and Michigan and the Eighth would consist of Illinois, Indiana, and Wisconsin.[6] John A. Bingham informed the House of Representatives that the bill would have no effect but to alter the Seventh and Eighth Circuits, that there was no objection to it in the Senate or House, and that "I am informed by one of the judges of the Supreme Court that its immediate passage is necessary to the administration of justice." [7]

There being no opposition to the change of these two circuits, the bill was passed by the Congress and signed by President Lincoln on January 28, 1863. A bill to place Wisconsin in the Ninth Circuit with Missouri, Iowa, Kansas, and Minnesota was introduced in the House by Albert G. Porter of Indiana on February 4. It was accepted promptly by the Congress and was signed by President Lincoln on February 9. The states were yet seeking what they deemed the magical circuit in which to be placed, but the process was vastly simplified because appointments to the Supreme Court were not involved.

The Thirty-Seventh Congress, which ended its days in March, 1863, had dealt notably with problems of the federal judiciary. It had reorganized the circuit system, it had confirmed the filling of three long-standing vacancies on the Supreme Court, it had considered proposals to abolish the Court, and finally, it had packed the Court by creating a tenth Justice.

Many factors must be considered in explaining the reasons for adding a tenth Justice to the bench. The main motive was to make the Supreme Court "safe." But blending themselves with that motivation are several other considerations. Consequently, it is easy to be blinded to the imperative necessity that the Supreme Court be made "safe." That there were

[5] *Ibid.*, 37th Cong., 2nd sess., appendix, p. 221.
[6] *Ibid.*, 37th Cong., 3rd sess., p. 393.
[7] *Ibid.*, p. 519.

several other considerations made it all the easier to comply with the urgent need that existed and all the easier to obscure the basic motivation.

To add a tenth Justice from California did satisfy the conspicuous need for a Justice who understood the complicated land title cases that were appealed to the Court from California.[8] To create a circuit for the Far West would serve to stimulate loyalty of the West to the Union.[9] But the contemporary press did not overlook the basic motive in providing a tenth Justice. In commenting on the creation of a tenth justiceship, the New York *Times* said with understanding, "This judge will be assigned to the Circuits on the Pacific Coast. He, of course, adds one to the number which will speedily remove the control of the Supreme Court from the Taney school." [10]

The need to pack the Court was not overlooked by Wait Talcott, formerly a member of Congress from Illinois, who asked Senator Trumbull, "How many judges are there & how do they stand & what are their names & what states [are they] from?" The same interrogator of Trumbull asked, "How would the Supreme Court decide in regard to the [Emancipation] Proclamation, if it gets before them?" Trumbull was informed that some new states should be added while the Republicans were in control. "Can't you by doing so [Talcott asked Trumbull] make a necessity for another Judge, & put in one that will be true & help keep the power of the Court right?" [11]

Keep the power of the Court "right." That was the strongest motivation for adding a tenth Justice to the Supreme Court during the Civil War. Senator Garrett Davis of Kentucky stated on the floor of the Senate on January 14, 1868, that the Radicals forced the creation of the tenth justiceship.[12] But Lincoln had fought the Radicals on many points. If they alone had sought a tenth justiceship, the unanimity demonstrated in its creation would have been lacking. The move to add a tenth Justice to the Court was a carefully planned step of the administration. Once the decision was made it moved with swiftness and zest and Union men in general concurred.

The *Prize Cases*, decided the same day Lincoln's appointment to the tenth seat was confirmed, demonstrated dramatically that the administration's margin of safety on the Taney Court was sorely slim. It was a question whether "the conduct of the war might be at least inadvertently sabotaged by judges who were more deeply devoted either to the South

[8] Carl B. Swisher, *Stephen J. Field: Craftsman of the Law* (Washington, 1930), p. 111.

[9] Swisher, *Roger B. Taney*, pp. 562-63.

[10] New York *Times*, March 4, 1863, p. 1.

[11] Wait Talcott to Lyman Trumbull, February 1, 1863, Trumbull MSS.

[12] *Cong. Globe*, 40th Cong., 2nd sess., p. 498.

or to their conceptions of the law than to the immediate needs of the government." [13] It was recognition of this fact that dictated that the Court be enlarged.

The power of the government to defend itself would be questioned again before the Supreme Court, and a tenth Justice would at least make certain "that questions of the power of government to suppress rebellion would not come before a Court too hopelessly weighted on the side of the old-line Democratic view of public policy." [14] The Supreme Court had to be removed as a factor potentially dangerous to the Union. A Congress and a President that had experienced the debacles of 1862 would not stand idly by to experience disaster at the hands of the Supreme Court.

A CALIFORNIAN CALLED

Stephen Johnson Field, whom Lincoln appointed to fill the tenth justiceship, was a distinguished Californian. Born in Connecticut in 1816, he was one of a family of ten. He, along with his brothers David Dudley, Cyrus West, and Henry Martyn, was destined for fame. As a youth of thirteen, Stephen went to the Levant with a sister and her husband, the Reverend Joseph Brewer (parents of the future Supreme Court Justice David J. Brewer). Following his return to this country, he was graduated from Williams College in 1837, and entered the office of his brother David in New York City to study law. He was admitted to the bar in 1841 and joined his brother in a partnership that lasted until 1848.

In November, 1849, he sailed for California. Field settled in Marysville, bought sixty-five lots (on paper) and assisted in forming a local government. Here he served as *alcalde* and was elected to the California legislature in 1850. As a member he was active in drafting the civil and criminal practices for the state. After returning to the practice of law at Marysville he was elected to the California supreme court in September, 1857.

This court had been struggling for a number of years with land title cases: there were forged and overlapping grants as well as conflicts between the common law and Spanish land law. The treaty of Guadaloupe Hidalgo with Mexico in 1848 had confirmed existing grants, but it had to be ascertained precisely what existing grants included. Judge Field set for himself the task of bringing order out of chaos. As a member of the California supreme court, he wrote decisions in broad terms in order to establish principles that could be applied generally, hoping that less litigation finally would arise.

When the Civil War came, as a Democrat who had no sympathy for Southern principles, Field joined the Union party in California and

---

[13] Swisher, *Stephen J. Field*, pp. 115-16.

[14] Fairman, *Mr. Justice Miller*, p. 60.

demonstrated his deep-seated loyalty. His appointment to fill the tenth seat upon the Supreme Court was urged upon President Lincoln by the whole California congressional delegation.[15] It might well have eased Lincoln's conscience that such a Union man—a former Democrat—was available for appointment to the tenth seat on the Supreme bench.

Field played a significant role in keeping California loyal to the Union,[16] and he had given fine expression to that loyalty when, on the occasion of the completion of the telegraph line connecting the Pacific coast with the Atlantic, he telegraphed President Lincoln on October 25, 1861, "the people of California desire to congratulate you upon the completion of the great work. They believe that it will be the means of strengthening the attachment which bind both East & West to the Union." Significantly, Field concluded, "they desire in this first message across the continent to express their loyalty to that Union & their determination to stand by the Government in this its day of trial[.] They regard that Government with affection & will adhere to it under all fortunes[.]" [17]

Field's strong Unionist position, his contribution to California legal practices, his knowledge of land title cases, and the support of California's congressional delegation as well as that of Governor Leland Stanford made him the most logical choice to fill the tenth justiceship.[18]

David Dudley Field, who had been active in bringing about Lincoln's nomination in 1860 and who gave Lincoln advice and counsel throughout the war, played a prominent role in securing the tenth justiceship for his brother.[19]

Henry M. Field, another brother, has recorded the steps taken to secure Lincoln's choice of Stephen. Henry Field related that disputed land titles in California were proving so troublesome to the United States Supreme Court that the Justices "themselves were confused by the contradictory opinions." As a consequence, he continued, it was determined to add a tenth Justice to the Court, one who would have a knowledge of California land law and one who could help the rest of the Justices out of their dilemma. The senators and representatives of

---

[15] Charles Warren, *The Supreme Court in United States History*, new and rev. ed. (Boston, 1928), II, 380.

[16] Swisher, *Roger B. Taney*, pp. 555-56.

[17] Stephen J. Field to Abraham Lincoln, October 25, 1861, Lincoln MSS.

[18] Swisher, *Stephen J. Field*, p. 116.

[19] There appears in the Robert Todd Lincoln Collection a telegram dated February 25, 1860, addressed to Lincoln in care of David Dudley Field in New York City. See Horace White to Abraham Lincoln, February 25, 1860, Lincoln MSS. This was when Lincoln was in New York to speak at Cooper Institute. Horace Greeley and David Dudley Field, both early supporters of Lincoln in New York, accompanied Lincoln to the platform on that occasion.

California and Oregon "went in a body to President Lincoln [Field declared] to ask for the appointment of Mr. Stephen J. Field, then Chief Justice of California, whose name they presented, not as their first choice, but as their only choice."

While the nomination was pending John A. C. Gray, prominent New York merchant and railroad enterpriser, gained access to Lincoln and spoke to him in behalf of Judge Field. Lincoln agreed that Field was eminently qualified for the appointment. Lincoln, said Henry Field, asked Gray one question, " 'Does David want his brother to have it?' 'Yes,' said Mr. Gray. 'Then he shall have it,' was the instant reply, and the nomination was sent in that afternoon, and confirmed by the Senate unanimously." [20]

In one regard the selection of Field was peculiar. In all his Supreme Court appointments Lincoln was cautious to appoint men to the Court who were fully sympathetic with the measures the administration devised to win the war and who had given no indication of opposition to the drastic policies which were considered necessary. And yet, in July, 1862, as chief justice of the supreme court of California, Stephen J. Field had written an opinion holding that the Legal Tender Act was not applicable in the payment of state and county taxes in California.[21] As a Supreme Court Justice, however, Field did support the administration when the Legal Tender Act was challenged during the war, but later he ruled consistently against its constitutionality.

President Lincoln nominated Field to the Supreme Court on March 6, 1863, three days after the act creating the tenth justiceship had received presidential signature. Secretary of the Navy Gideon Welles recorded in his diary, "Appointments considered yesterday and to-day. Generally conceded that Field . . . was the man for the Supreme Court." [22] The nomination was read and referred to the Senate committee on the judiciary on the seventh; confirmation came on the tenth.[23] Field requested that he be permitted to delay taking the oath until May 20, 1863. Shortly thereafter, by order of President Lincoln, he was allotted the Tenth Circuit.[24]

---

[20] Henry M. Field, *The Life of David Dudley Field* (New York, 1898), pp. 195-96, note.

[21] 20 Cal. 350. See also Joseph Ellison, "The Currency Question on the Pacific Coast during the Civil War," *Mississippi Valley Historical Review*, June, 1929, XVI, 52.

[22] John T. Morse, Jr., *Diary of Gideon Welles, Secretary of the Navy Under Lincoln and Johnson* (Cambridge, 1911), I, 245 (March 6, 1863). Cited hereafter as Welles, *Diary*.

[23] Nomination of Stephen J. Field to the Supreme Court, March 6, 1863, Papers of the Attorneys General.

[24] 67 U.S. 8; T. J. Coffey to William T. Carroll, June 12, 1863, Attorney General's Letter Books.

The nomination of a former Democrat undoubtedly pained the Radicals, but Lincoln gained some satisfaction in elevating to the Court a former Democrat who from the beginning of the war was exclusively a Union man. Stephen J. Field, at this juncture forty-seven years old, added vigor and energy to the high Court. And he did not cause the administration any regrets in the future.

Newspapers reacted very favorably to the appointment. "He is a brother of David Dudley and Cyrus W. Field of New York, [stated the Washington *Morning Chronicle*] who are well known for their ability, integrity, and patriotism. No better appointment, we feel sure, could have been made." [25] The Sacramento *Union*, declaring that the California bar as well as the California congressional delegation strongly endorsed the appointment, predicted: "He will prove a valuable acquisition to the bench of the Supreme Court. . . ." On the basic problems of the day it found Field "as sound as could be wished" and "unconditionally for the Union." [26]

The new Justice, for his introduction to Washington, was provided with a letter written by former congressman Thompson Campbell of Illinois, who had been a friend of Lincoln in Springfield. Campbell wrote to Representative Washburne of Illinois, "This letter will be handed to you by my friend Judge Field, whose acquaintance I wish you to make, as he is a gentleman whose political opinions on the great questions of the day are in perfect harmony with your own." Campbell informed Washburne that with conditions as they were Justice Field would make a notable contribution in Washington. [27]

Stephen J. Field had the very unusual experience of having (within a fortnight) been tendered by President Lincoln, first, the office of circuit judge for California and second, the office of Supreme Court Justice.

In April, 1862, M. Hall McAllister, who was judge of the circuit court for California, which had been created in 1855, upon the approval of President Lincoln was granted a six months leave of absence because of illness. [28] Two months earlier, Governor Stanford had telegraphed Lincoln, "Should a vacancy occur in the office of U.S. Circuit Judge for California myself & Friends wish to be consulted about the appointment." [29] In January, 1863, McAllister resigned the post.

The California senators, Milton S. Latham and James A. McDougall, immediately recommended Field. "I . . . [stated] that I could not accept

[25] Editorial, Washington *Morning Chronicle*, April 3, 1863, p. 2.

[26] Washington *Morning Chronicle*, April 3, 1863, p. 2, quoting the Sacramento *Union*.

[27] Thompson Campbell to Elihu B. Washburne, October 22, 1863, Washburne MSS.

[28] *H.R. Exec. Doc. No. 129*, 37th Cong., 2nd sess., p. 2.

[29] Leland Stanford to Abraham Lincoln, February 25, 1862, Lincoln MSS.

the place, [Justice Field later related in his *Reminiscences*] that I preferred to remain Chief Justice of the Supreme Court of the State than to be a judge of an inferior federal court, but that if a new justice were added to the Supreme Court of the United States, I would accept the office if tendered to me."

Despite the fact that Field had stated his position frankly, the two senators persisted and President Lincoln nominated Field for the California circuit judgeship on February 23, the appointment having the unanimous support of California's congressmen. In his *Reminiscences* Justice Field explained that Latham and McDougall later told him that they urged his appointment as circuit judge in the belief that a tenth Supreme Court justiceship would soon be created and that "if I were circuit judge it would more likely be tendered to me than to any one else."

While the nomination of Field as circuit judge was pending before the Senate, however, Congress created the tenth justiceship, and the act that created it abolished the circuit system that California had had since 1855. Consequently, as Justice Field explained, "the entire delegation from the Pacific States united in recommending my appointment to the new office. The delegation at that time consisted of four Senators and four members of the House, of whom five were Democrats and three Republicans. . . ." Field added that Pacific interests and western land titles differed so greatly from those of the East that "it was deemed important to have some one familiar with them on the Supreme Bench of the United States."

Field delayed taking the oath of office because at the time he was appointed "many important cases" were pending before the supreme court of California. If Field left the California bench at once, some of the cases would have had to be reargued. But by May 20 the cases were disposed of and "it was the birthday of my father. I thought it would be gratifying to him to know that on the eighty-second anniversary of his birth his son had become a Justice of the Supreme Court of the United States." [30] Quite in harmony with his training as the son of a "Congregational minister in Puritan New England," [31] Justice Field promptly deposited with the sub-treasurer at San Francisco, to the credit of the United States, that portion of his salary which covered the period from March 10 to May 20 and which was sent to him in error.

On the occasion of his resignation from the Supreme Court in 1897 after more than thirty-four years of service, Justice Field reviewed the conditions that led to his appointment and stated that when Congress

---

[30] These reminiscences are to be found in Stephen J. Field, *Personal Reminiscences of Early Days in California, with Other Sketches* (published privately, 1893), pp. 140-42.

[31] Swisher, *Stephen J. Field*, p. 2.

created the tenth seat it was "with the intention that it should be filled by some one familiar with . . . [the] conflicting titles and with the mining laws of the coast." The choice fell upon him, he declared, because he had "framed the principal of these laws." [32]

This is the story of the creation of the tenth justiceship of the Supreme Court and the man that Lincoln named to fill it. But the passion and drama that were involved in enlarging the Court are to be found elsewhere than in its official record. In good legal taste—though lacking the human touch—it was recorded in the *United States Reports* that "An Act of Congress having been passed authorizing a tenth judge, the Honorable Stephen J. Field was appointed." [33]

The *United States Reports* are formal and correct, but courts and cases involve men and the affairs of men. In this instance, the creation of a tenth justiceship, the formal statement in the *Reports* cannot disavow that the Court was packed—packed, albeit, to save it, to save the Constitution, and to save the Union.

---

[32] 168 U.S. 715.

[33] 67 U.S., memoranda, 2.

CHAPTER EIGHT

Taney and His Brethren

ADMIRABLE RESTRAINT

With the selection of Stephen J. Field, Lincoln had made his final appointment to the Court while it was headed by Chief Justice Taney. It is now appropriate to examine the relationships that existed between the Lincoln appointees and the pre-Lincoln members. In addition, it is pertinent to look at Attorney General Bates's attitude toward the Justices and to discuss the staff and bar of the Court.

Mutual respect, freedom from bitterness, even a spirit of camaraderie, characterized the relations of Chief Justice Taney and the nine Associate Justices. Here were ten men of varying political backgrounds, outlooks, and attachments. They were men who would be called upon to settle legal controversies arising out of the war—controversies for which there would be no precedents upon which to base opinions. Yet they were to accomplish the unexpected. No small part of the credit for this must be allotted to Chief Justice Taney, James M. Wayne, who was presiding Justice during Taney's lengthy absences, and John Catron, who presided if both Taney and Wayne were absent. Their restraint in dealing with the membership set the pace and established the pattern.

The comradeship of the Justices, despite the strongly antithetical political views of several of them, grew partly out of their numerous off-the-bench contacts, but it resulted mostly from the mutual respect that they developed toward each other. These Justices were involved in battle just as were the armies, but their battlefield was the courtroom and the conference table, and when their arguments were adjourned so was their bitterness.

Visits by members of the Court to Chief Justice Taney, whose age impaired his activity, reveal the relationships that existed among them. Bates recorded in his diary that when the Court was ready to adjourn in March, 1862, "Taney requested the judges severally, to call to see him at his house" before they departed from Washington. Bates declared that Taney "took an affectionate leave of each one, and told several of them, especially Nelson, that he did not expect to see them again. That he had a pre sentiment [sic] that he should die very soon." Bates stated that Justice Nelson remarked that Taney would not "live many weeks," and naturally, Bates pondered as to a successor.[1]

---

[1] Bates, *Diary*, p. 243 (March 24, 1862).

Toward the Lincoln appointees Chief Justice Taney maintained an attitude of friendliness and restraint, and despite political differences and his absences, Taney's hand was firmly felt. Concerning the new Justice Miller, Taney wrote to Justice Clifford, "I saw Judge Miller our new brother a few days ago.—He called as he was good enough to say to pay his respects to me & to ask me to administer the oath of office—which I did—" Attorney General Bates presented the new Justice to Taney upon that occasion. In concluding his comments, Taney said, "It was the first time I had seen him, & his appearance & manner made a very favorable impression on me—" [2]

It had been feared that a clash between Taney and Miller was inevitable because their views were incompatible, Miller having been an ardent opponent of slavery. But no clash came. Relations between the two became cordial, and at the end of the first term that Miller attended the Chief Justice took him by the hand and stated, "My brother Miller, I am an old and broken man. I may not be here when you return. I cannot let you go without expressing to you my great gratification that you have come among us." Taney admitted that he had feared a collision with Miller, but "On the other hand, this has proved one of the pleasantest terms that I have ever attended. I owe it greatly to your courtesy. Your learning, zeal, and powers of mind assure me that you will maintain and advance the high traditions of the Court." [3]

Justice Miller, too, revealed what he once thought of Chief Justice Taney and how his opinion changed. He told a friend that when he went to Washington he had never seen Taney, but he remembered that Taney "had attempted to throttle the Bank of the United States, and I hated him for it." Miller said that he remembered that Taney took his "seat on the Bench, as I believed, in reward for what he had done in that connection and I hated him for that." The new Justice said, too, that he recalled that Taney was "the chief spokesman for the Court in the Dred Scott case, and I hated him for that."

But Miller developed high regard for Taney. "I realized that my feelings toward him [wrote Justice Miller] were but the suggestions of the worst elements of . . . [my] nature; for before the first term of my service in the Court had passed I more than liked him, I loved him." And Miller came to offer some defense of Taney, stating that despite all "that has been said of that great, good man, I stand always ready to say that conscience was his guide, and sense of duty his principle." [4]

[2] Roger B. Taney to Nathan Clifford, August 2, 1862, Clifford MSS.

[3] Remarks of J. M. Woolworth, member of the Supreme Court bar, on November 14, 1890, at the memorial service for Justice Miller held in the United States circuit court at Omaha, *Proceedings of the Bench and Bar of the Supreme Court of the United States in Memoriam Samuel F. Miller* (Washington, 1891), addenda, 60-61.

[4] Remarks of H. E. Davis, member of the Supreme Court bar, on December 6, 1890, at the memorial services for Justice Miller held by the Supreme Court, *ibid.*, 17.

The manuscript minutes of the Supreme Court establish that only on five occasions were Chief Justice Taney and the nine Associate Justices able to meet together. Illness strengthened the Republican hold upon the Court because Taney was able to attend few sessions in 1863 and 1864 and others among the aged Democratic Justices were ill, too.[5] But despite his lengthy absences, Taney's influence was strongly felt.

On March 17, 1864, Taney's eighty-seventh birthday, members of the Court and several members of the Supreme Court bar visited the Chief Justice to pay their respects. Taney's attendance during the term then in session had been extremely irregular, and it was assumed correctly that this would be his last birthday.

The Washington *National Intelligencer* considered Taney's birthday an event of public interest. Declaring that Taney was "Detained at his home more by recent indisposition . . . than by the infirmities of age," it announced that the members of the Court visited him "to pay their respects officially to their Chief, and at the same time to tender him personally their congratulations on the returning anniversary of his birthday." The *Intelligencer* informed its readers that the presiding Justice, James M. Wayne, instructed a member of the bar to curtail arguments at an early hour so that members of the Court and the bar could visit Taney at his residence "where . . . all who called were received with urbanity and affability which characterize the distinguished and venerable jurist in his intercourse with society."

Chief Justice Taney, according to the *Intelligencer*, expressed the hope that he would soon be able to resume his judicial duties and "is now prevented from doing so only by the prudential restrictions which his physician thinks it proper to impose at this season, so trying to delicate constitutions by its frequent and sudden changes of temperature." And the *Intelligencer* found that although the Chief Justice was somewhat frail as the result of illness and advanced age, "his mind is as vigorous and his memory as vivid and tenacious as at any period of his long and laborious career." [6]

Thus it was that an official relationship of cordiality was maintained among members of the Taney Court. There was a mutual respect among its members even including Lincoln's appointees. There was, in addition, mutual respect between certain administration leaders and the Court, although the prevalent attitude of administration leaders toward several of the pre-Lincoln Justices was one of contempt. That Attorney General

---

[5] Minutes of the United States Supreme Court, December 7, 1863 to April 18, 1864. The Court technically consisted of ten until July 23, 1866, when its number was reduced during the days of Reconstruction, but its ten members never again met together after December 11, 1863.

[6] Washington *National Intelligencer*, March 18, 1864, p. 3.

Bates did not join in this attitude is evidenced by an entry in his diary shortly before Taney's death, "This day *Chief Justice* Taney (as he promised last week) sent me his photograph picture . . . [inscribed] in his own hand writing. The chirography, both on the card and on the envelope, is remarkably good, for a man of his age—88." [7] Basic differences always existed within the Court, and the Justices fought momentous judicial battles, but the enmity that was engendered was mitigated by the repression of resentments.

GREGARIOUS COURT

Justices during the Civil War enjoyed many off-the-bench contacts, contacts that were conducive to an atmosphere of friendliness and brotherliness. Oddly enough, it was their circuit duties that contributed to these social relations. Because most of the Justices maintained no permanent residence in Washington, circuit duties requiring their absence from the city many months of the year, the majority of them lived in a Washington hotel or boarding house. As it happened, several boarded at the same residence year after year.

Chief Justice Taney maintained his permanent residence at Twenty-three Indiana Avenue, in Washington, and Justice Wayne lived at Two Franklin Place. Justice Nelson lived at the National Hotel in 1863 and at Willard's Hotel in 1864. Justice Miller lived at the National Hotel in 1863. In 1864 Justice Grier and Justice Clifford lived at Mrs. Taylor's, at the corner of Third and C Streets. A popular boarding house during the war, Morison's, at Twenty-five, Four-and-a-half Street, West, attracted a number of the Justices. Here for a time lived Grier, Clifford, Catron, Miller, Swayne, and Davis. Justice Davis, referring to his living quarters in a letter written a month after he entered upon his duties, said, "I made a mistake in my quarters and have changed them to where the Judges are." Davis originally stayed at Morison's, but he moved to the National Hotel where Swayne, Miller, Clifford, and Nelson lived at that time. [8]

There is ample evidence of warm friendship between Justices who differed as to the war, and opposed each other when war-related problems were heard. Justice Clifford, one of the inveterate fishermen of the Court, graciously sent his brother Justices bountiful gifts of his catch. On one

[7] Bates, *Diary*, p. 400 (August 18, 1864).

[8] William H. Boyd, compiler, *Boyd's Washington and Georgetown Directory,* . . . *1860* (Washington, 1860), *passim;* Thomas Hutchinson, compiler, *Boyd's Washington and Georgetown Directory,* . . . *1862* (Washington, 1862), *passim;* Thomas Hutchinson, compiler, *Boyd's Washington and Georgetown Directory,* . . . *1863* (Washington, 1863), *passim;* Andrew Boyd, compiler, *Boyd's Washington and Georgetown Directory,* . . . *1864* (Washington, 1864), *passim.* See also the *Congressional Directory,* 38th Congress, 1st Session, (Washington, 1864), p. 35.

occasion, Justice Grier wrote him, "the fish you were so Kind as to send me was received at my house. Fearing it would spoil by an attempt to send it further . . . [Grier was at Bedford Springs, Pennsylvania at the time] they salted it up—" Grier said that he regretted that he had not been at home to enjoy the gift "*fully*—but it will be good even when *salted* & will *preserve* at least the kind remembrance of myself and each member of my family, which they already entertain for the donor—" [9]

Clifford sent fish to Chief Justice Taney, too, and Taney wrote him this somewhat amusing although almost solemn acknowledgment, "It came this morning—but I am sorry to say, the time consumed in its voyage, was more than it could bear in this hot weather . . . I need not say that I owe & return you as many thanks for your kind recollection of me—as if the fish had come in prime order." [10]

Several Justices often dined together or attended dinner parties together where most of the guests were leaders of the government. Justice Davis extended an invitation to such a gathering when he wrote to Joseph Holt of Kentucky, "The Judges at this House [Morison's] give a dinner tomorrow at 5 . . . precisely, to their brethren & a few friends. I am privileged to write you—I trust that you will not fail to come—The Company will be agreeable—" [11]

Bates carefully recorded in his diary details of a dinner party that he attended in company with several Justices. The dinner was given by John V. S. L. Pruyn, Democratic member of Congress from New York. "I did not know Mr. P.[ruyn] before, [Bates wrote] and, from what I heard of him, expected a *political* dinner, but was agreeably disappointed in finding it *legal* only—4 Justices of the S[upreme] C[ourt,] 3 Senators[,] and 2 or 3 members of the House." [12]

Senator Orville H. Browning, whose aspirations to join the Court have already been examined, often mixed socially with its members. On one occasion he recorded in his diary, "At 5 P.M. dined at Judge Wayne's with Judge Nelson, Senator Foster, Mr. Blatchford of New York, and Mr. Peachy of California." [13] On another occasion, interestingly enough not long before the Supreme Court handed down its decision in the *Prize Cases*, Browning attended another dinner replete with Court members. "Went to dinner at 5 P.M. [he wrote] in company with Hon[orable] Mr. Ewing of Ohio, with Judges Catron, Wayne, Greer, [*sic*] Swain, [*sic*] Davis, Clifford & Miller of the Supreme Court." In the company also were

[9] Robert C. Grier to Nathan Clifford, July 24, 1861, Clifford MSS.

[10] Roger B. Taney to Nathan Clifford, August 2, 1862, *ibid*.

[11] David Davis to Joseph Holt, December 30, 1862, Holt MSS., Library of Congress.

[12] Bates, *Diary*, 346 (March 19, 1864).

[13] Theodore C. Pease and James G. Randall, eds., *The Diary of Orville Hickman Browning*, (*Collections of the Illinois State Historical Library*, vol. XX), vol. I (Springfield, 1925), I, 523 (January 10, 1862). Cited hereafter as Browning, *Diary*.

William H. Seward, Joseph Holt, former Supreme Court Justice Benjamin R. Curtis, James M. Carlisle, Edward Bates, and Jeremiah S. Black.[14]

BATES OF MISSOURI

The member of the Lincoln administration who was most closely associated with the Taney Court was Attorney General Edward Bates, who served Lincoln almost until the war ended. Bates developed sympathy for the Court and came to find danger in many of the policies adopted by Lincoln. The repeal of the Missouri Compromise in 1854 and an antipathy toward slavery had drawn Bates into the Republican party and in Missouri he developed into one of the most prominent Republicans. Since he was a leader of a strong segment of the party and a citizen of a border state, Lincoln had invited him into the cabinet. But as a member, Bates resisted the ever increasing pressures of the Radicals.

A letter which Bates wrote Lincoln in 1862 on the occasion of enlarging the United States court of claims may be taken as typical of Bates's views on judicial appointments. Informing Lincoln that a bill providing for additional judges was pending, he stated that "Those two places are eagerly sought for, and already, the friends of different gentlemen are active in getting influential persons committed to their respective favorites." Bates told Lincoln that he had no persons in mind and counseled that the seats, if created, should be filled without haste. (Lincoln ultimately appointed David Wilmot of Pennsylvania and Ebenezer Peck of Illinois). With indirect though obvious reference to the two vacancies existing at that time on the bench of the Supreme Court, Bates added, "Such places are not rewards or provisions for even very meritorious friends, but trusts of the highest importance, deeply affecting the general interest." [15]

As Attorney General, Bates was criticized for not personally arguing cases that were brought before the Supreme Court. Perhaps the sharpest criticism was made by the New York *World*, a newspaper which fastened upon Bates responsibility for arbitrary arrests. "The great mining, prize, and tax cases of the late session . . . [the *World* pointed out] have made the name of Mr. Bates conspicuous, perhaps illustrious even, by its invisibility and impenetrable obscurity." [16]

Bates, himself, was aware of the validity of this criticism. The Fossat case, argued in the spring of 1864, was the first important case that Bates personally handled before the Supreme Court. In his diary he recorded that he argued the case before presiding Justice Wayne and that "I do believe that my leaving most of the cases to be argued by *retained* counsel,

---

[14] *Ibid.*, I, 606 (December 31, 1862).

[15] Edward Bates to Abraham Lincoln, April 17, 1862, Lincoln MSS.

[16] Editorial, New York *World*, March 20, 1863, p. 4.

had spread pretty widely at the bar and perhaps to some members of the Court, the belief that I was unable or afraid to encounter the leading members of the bar." It was Bates's conclusion "that this case has dispelled that illusion both at Bench and Bar." [17]

When the Court ruled against him, Bates was highly agitated. He did not restrain his criticism and wrote in his diary that "I was surprised at the judgment, and confidentially believe that it is dangerously erroneous, in several particulars—" [18] Suddenly his criticism of the Taney Court and the federal judiciary knew no bounds. Of the Court upon which now were seated four Lincoln appointees, he wrote, "Every day I am pained (sometimes shamed and disgusted) at witnessing the proceedings in this highest of all courts—both the substance and the mode—" He concluded that the Court decided cases purely on transient reasons rather than in harmony with precedent, charging "the scales of justice rise and sink by some . . . capricious will." Pertaining to cases involving California lands, Bates lamented, "At this term [the December Term, 1863] two cases have been decided differently upon the very same grounds. One claim was rejected for a lack of Registry—that seeming to be the only ground—and another claim was confirmed in spite of that objection!!"

Once having given vent to his feelings, Bates went from one criticism of the federal judiciary to another. He found that looseness and irregularity in the lower courts were permitted and encouraged by the Supreme Court; he charged that no one could know the true record of a case appealed from the lower courts because "it is so hidden and smothered with *hotch potch* matter." [19] All of this criticism, of course, Bates confined to the secret pages of his diary. Some of it was valid criticism, but Bates, as Lincoln's chief officer of the law, should have had the resourcefulness to evolve policies to correct the abuses if they existed. Responsibility in these matters rested chiefly upon his shoulders. In condemning conditions in the federal judiciary Bates was condemning himself.

He believed his office to be a legal office rather than a political one, and he felt his duty "above all other ministers of State was to uphold the Law, and to resist all encroachments, from whatever quarter, of mere will and power, upon the province of the law." Not only was he critical of the Taney Court, at times he was critical of the administration as well. He found it increasingly difficult to uphold the law in this troublous

---

[17] Bates, *Diary*, p. 342 (March 2, 1864). The Fossat case provoked Bates to write in his diary his honest opinion of Justice Grier. Caleb Cushing, one of the lawyers engaged in the case, had aroused the disgust of the Court. Concerning the incident, Bates wrote, "Judge Grier said to me, in a loud whisper, that every body in ten feet, must have heard—'Ef you speak, give that damned Yankee hell.' I need not say that I was disgusted at his grossness; but Mr. Justice Grier is a natural-born vulgarian, and, by long habit, course and harsh." *Ibid.*, p. 340 (February 26, 1864).

[18] *Ibid.*, p. 354 (April 5, 1864).

[19] *Ibid.*, pp. 356-57 (April 10, 1864).

time. Exercise of arbitrary power was to become more and more distasteful to him. "I am often mortified [wrote Bates in his diary] at being obliged to witness such encroachments, without the power to resist successfully. Still, I remonstrate, and make a 'continual claim' for the right." [20]

STAFF AND BAR

The Supreme Court during the Civil War, in addition to its membership and the Attorney General, was served by a staff consisting of a reporter, a clerk, a marshal and a crier. Changes in the staff of the Taney Court were frequent during the war. In some instances these changes came in the normal course of events, but in at least one instance change resulted from the conflict in which the nation was engaged. Consequently, Chief Justice Taney and the Justices had to turn frequently to the subject of the Court's staff.

Chief Justice Taney announced when the Court assembled for the December Term, 1861, that the Reporter, Benjamin C. Howard, who had served for almost twenty years, had resigned on September 13, 1861.[21] The national tumult was only emphasized by the fact that Howard resigned to run, as an opponent of the Union, in his native Maryland as Democratic candidate for governor.

The vacancy was filled by the appointment of Jeremiah S. Black.[22] The Court could not long function without a reporter, whose annual salary was $1,300, because it was his duty to prepare and publish an adequate record of each case that was heard. Black remained the reporter for a little over two years and during his tenure prepared two volumes of *United States Reports*. Then he resigned to devote himself to private law practice, being motivated by the need for greater income and by the volume of cases involving California land titles, cases well known to him because of his experience in Buchanan's cabinet.

When his desire to resign was known, Chief Justice Taney canvassed the Court to learn the wishes of the majority in regard to a replacement. To Justice Clifford, Taney wrote that he hoped that care would be taken in selecting a successor who was well fitted. Taney expressed fear, alluding to Black, that a person who had been active politically might find the work "plodding." [23] Black's resignation was accepted in March, 1864, while the December Term, 1863, was in progress. It was understood that he would assist in preparing for publication the cases heard during his

---

[20] *Ibid.*, 350 (March 22, 1864).

[21] Washington *National Intelligencer*, December 5, 1861, p. 3; Swisher, *Roger B. Taney*, p. 561; Minutes of the United States Supreme Court, December 4, 1861.

[22] Washington *National Intelligencer*, December 17, 1861, p. 3; Minutes of the United States Supreme Court, December 16, 1861, and December 17, 1861.

[23] Roger B. Taney to Nathan Clifford, February 11, 1864, Clifford MSS.

tenure; any other arrangement, it seemed, would put an intolerable burden upon his successor.

The vacancy was filled by the appointment of John William Wallace of Pennsylvania, a legal scholar and law librarian.[24] Since Black did not bother to find time to assist the new reporter, it was necessary for Congress to extend the time limit on publication of the reports of the term.[25]

In the preface of the first volume that he edited, Wallace explained the burdensome task to which he found himself assigned. He emphasized that with the exception of a half dozen cases, he had not heard the arguments that he was reporting. At one point he planned to issue the volume without his name attached to it but realized that an "unacknowledged book, was distasteful wherever mentioned." He declared his heartfelt appreciation for the assistance given him by Justice Field, who helped with California land cases, and Justice Wayne, who presided over the Court in the absence of Taney. Wallace concluded that the volume was prepared under such unfortunate circumstances that "if I shall find any one whose estimate of it . . . is lower than mine, I promise him . . . that I will exchange my opinion . . . for his." [26]

Shortly before the volume was published the Washington *Morning Chronicle* stated in an editorial that it believed that Wallace would prove to be an excellent reporter. But it expressed the hope that he would not burden the reader with elaborate details in patent cases or detailed maps in land cases.[27] In the first volume that he edited Wallace departed vastly from custom. A case involving fraud, *Parker v. Phetteplace*, called to his mind Shakespearean lines, and he proceeded to quote them at great length in a footnote! [28] Nonetheless, he was to provide the Court with reports of excellent quality for many years, ultimately preparing twenty-three volumes of the *United States Reports*.

In the summer of 1863 the Clerk, William T. Carroll, who had served since 1827, died. The office was a valuable one and was sought energetically. Its duties included making a "true and faithful record of all the orders, judgments, decrees and proceedings of the Court.[29] It was the estimate of the New York *Times* that fees accruing from the office amounted to $20,000 a year.[30]

[24] Minutes of the United States Supreme Court, March 23, 1864.

[25] *Cong. Globe*, 38th Cong., 1st sess., p. 1842; Washington *Morning Chronicle*, April 6, 1864, p. 2.

[26] 68 U.S., preface, xiii.

[27] Editorial, Washington *Morning Chronicle*, January 25, 1865, p. 2.

[28] 68 U.S. 687.

[29] Samuel T. Spear, *The Law of the Federal Judiciary: A Treatise on the Provisions of the Constitution, the Laws of Congress, and the Judicial Decisions Relating to the Jurisdiction and Pleading in the Federal Courts* (New York, 1883), p. 399.

[30] New York *Times*, December 8, 1863, p. 1.

Justice Davis immediately wrote his friend William Orme, "Mr. Carroll of Washington is dead—His place is valuable & applicants press for his place—" [31] Later Davis wrote Orme "Nothing w[oul]d delight me so much as to see you Cl[er]k of the Sup[reme] Court—but candidates are thick as blackberries, & I am of the opinion that Mr. Middleton the Deputy clerk, will be appointed—" [32] Davis was correct. Upon the reassembling of the Court for the December Term, 1863, Daniel W. Middleton was appointed.[33] He was to serve in this capacity for almost twenty years.

The Court was served by two other functionaries. One was a marshal, the other, a crier. During these years the Court had no marshal who served it exclusively. The marshal of the District of Columbia had the additional responsibility of carrying out for the Court the serving, executing, and processing of all its orders and decrees. On July 26, 1861, Lincoln appointed Ward H. Lamon, with whom he had once been associated in the practice of law, to be marshal. The post carried a yearly remuneration of two hundred dollars plus fees. The crier, whose duties consisted of proclaiming the orders of the Court and announcing that it was in session or that it had adjourned, was a minor functionary.

Not a part of the staff of the Court, but attached to it was the Supreme Court bar. Although theoretically parties to cases could plead their own cases, in reality litigants were represented by lawyers who could qualify as members of the bar of the Court. To be admitted a lawyer had to practice for three years in the supreme court of the state in which he held citizenship and had to have good private and professional reputation.

Leading members of the bar who were active in cases heard during the war—the bar at this time was distinguished—included Edwin M. Stanton, Montgomery Blair, John J. Crittenden, Reverdy Johnson, James M. Carlisle, Richard H. Dana, Jr., Benjamin R. Curtis, Thomas Ewing, Henry Stanbery, Jeremiah S. Black, Daniel Lord, Orville H. Browning, David Dudley Field, Samuel W. Fuller, Alphonso Taft, John P. Usher, William M. Evarts, William H. Seward, Thomas A. Jenckes, Elihu B. Washburne, Richard Olney, Thomas A. Hendricks, Benjamin F. Butler, Lyman Trumbull, and Titian J. Coffey.

---

[31] David Davis to William W. Orme, July 29, 1863, Orme MSS.

[32] David Davis to William W. Orme, September 1, 1863, *ibid.*

[33] Minutes of the United States Supreme Court, December 7, 1863.

CHAPTER NINE

Their Gravest Decision

INSURRECTION OR WAR

Almost two years elapsed after the beginning of the war before a basic war-related case came before the Supreme Court. When the Court finally faced a case of importance related to the war, however, it was confronted by a decision so momentous that it must be deemed the most significant decision the Court handed down during the conflict.

From the beginning the Lincoln administration maintained that the conflict was insurrection rather than war. Admission that war existed would be an invitation to foreign powers to recognize and assist the Confederacy. One of the necessities of the South, if it were to succeed, was to obtain this aid and recognition. Among Lincoln's foremost desires was his wish to prevent the Confederacy from being accepted by foreign nations as a sovereign and independent state.

The President, realizing the immediate necessity of preventing the South from having access to foreign markets, instituted by proclamations on April 19, and April 27, 1861, blockade of the entire coastline of the Confederacy. The blockade was a military necessity, yet it invited complications. Instituting a blockade implied action against another sovereign power; consequently the President's proclamation granted the South belligerent status and was an acknowledgment that war existed between two sovereign powers. Although the Lincoln administration denied this because it wished to do all it could to prevent foreign recognition of the Confederacy, such was the accepted custom of international law.

Since Lincoln's action was taken without congressional authorization, on July 13, 1861, the Congress empowered the President, whenever he deemed it necessary, to declare ports closed where the authority of federal customs collectors was challenged. Therefore the question was whether to continue the blockade or to inaugurate a closed-port system. In order to help him arrive at the proper decision, Lincoln asked Secretary of the Navy Gideon Welles to examine the questions involved and submit an opinion. On August 6 Welles provided the President with a twelve-page letter covering the subject.

Welles emphasized that whether the blockade continued or the Southern ports were declared closed, armed squadrons would be required to patrol the Southern coasts. He made it clear to the President, however, that naval policy should conform with federal position. If the Southerners were deemed merely to usurp Union authority, a closed-port system was proper. Welles stated that in general the attitude of the federal government was that the South was usurping authority, and he questioned the advisability of making an exception to that policy by applying a blockade.

He reminded Lincoln that there was question as to the legality of blockade and warned that if it were not upheld by the courts, the United States would have to pay a vast sum for seizing cargoes, breaking up voyages, and selling vessels as prize. Resistance to blockade by litigation in the courts, the Secretary of Navy pointed out, would even serve to promote sympathy between the Confederacy and other powers.

The closing of ports, Welles maintained, involved domestic questions solely. He believed that to close the ports would be to institute policy that was "clear, distinct, honorable, and legally and morally impregnable." And he believed, too, that the policy of blockade was not only faulty but would fail to be sustained in the federal courts. He admitted that blockade was used when the conflict began, but he stated that the makeshift policies of the early days of the war need not be retained. He recommended that the administration alter its policy to conform with the wishes of Congress.[1]

Welles was correct in believing that danger rested in the policy instituted by Lincoln and continued, despite congressional legislation providing for a closed-port system. Nevertheless the administration rejected his advice and took the chance that it might have to face momentous consequences. There was the strong possibility that the legality of a blockade based solely upon presidential authority might be denied by the United States Supreme Court. Although the Congress, by the act of July 13, 1861, recognized that insurrection existed, whether the blockade from April 19 to July 13 could be sustained before the Court was questionable.

Friends of the administration were well aware of the fact that it might meet an adverse decision on this matter. It was no coincidence that the same days that the Court was hearing the *Prize Cases*, which involved vessels that were seized for violation of the blockade, the Congress and the President were cooperating to create a tenth circuit and a tenth Justice. This was a direct threat and a direct challenge to the Supreme Court.

Issues in the *Prize Cases* struck at the very foundation of Lincoln's policies. The Supreme Court could not have been called upon to give a more momentous decision in relation to the war. An adverse decision by the Court concerning the legality of blockade from April 19 to July

---

[1] Gideon Welles to Abraham Lincoln. August 6, 1861, Lincoln MSS.

13 would reflect upon all acts Lincoln had taken before the assembling of Congress on July 4 and upon Lincoln's concept of executive powers in wartime.

The government was at the mercy of the Justices in this matter. If the Court ruled that the conflict was insurrection rather than war, then the seizure of vessels by blockading units was illegal, and foreign trade was thwarted illegally. If the Supreme Court ruled that it was really war, this would indicate that through blockade the United States had given the Confederacy recognition, and foreign powers would be within their rights to do the same. On the other hand, if the Court ruled that no war existed either before or after the action of Congress on July 13, blockade of the enemy would be illegal. Under such circumstances ability of the Union to suppress the South would be doubtful. Any one of these prospects was gloomy.[2]

Only if the attorneys managing the cases in behalf of the government could devise a satisfactory argument, and only if the majority of the Court upheld the administration, would the decision be one beneficial to the Union. There was more at stake than the question of the legality of Lincoln's policy of blockade established in the absence of Congress and without its approval: a decision by the Court upholding legality of the blockade would *ipso facto* establish that war actually existed. And although the administration hoped to sustain the legality of the blockade, it had to deny that war existed or face foreign assistance to the South. With this prospect it is not surprising that the Congress added a tenth Justice to the Supreme Court. Under the circumstances it is surprising that Congress delayed until the crisis was upon the administration, and that Congress limited itself to just one addition to the high bench.

In view of the military and naval situation at the beginning of the war, naval blockade of the entire Southern coastline was a gigantic enterprise. It could be made effective only as the naval strength of the Union increased. It involved blockading over 3,500 miles of seacoast in which there were numbers of rivers, bays, harbors, inlets, sounds, and passes.[3]

One of the earliest challenges of Lincoln's policy resulted from the seizure in May, 1861, of the British schooner *The Tropic Wind* while trying to run the blockade of Virginia ports. Legality of the seizure was questioned before the United States circuit court for the District of Columbia, chief justice James Dunlop presiding. He upheld the seizure of the vessel. This decision at least set up a precedent, and even the New York *World* supported the view that the blockade was valid. The decision, the *World* declared, was firmly supported by past decisions of the Supreme Court.[4]

---

[2] Swisher, *Roger B. Taney*, pp. 563-64.

[3] Washington *National Intelligencer*, June 3, 1863, p. 3.

[4] New York *World*, June 22, 1861, p. 4.

On July 13, 1861, Congress expressly granted to the President the power to close Southern ports and to seize vessels which evaded his order.[5] And on August 6 the President signed a resolution of the Congress which declared:

That all the acts, proclamations, and orders of the President . . . after the fourth of March, eighteen hundred and sixty-one, respecting the army and navy of the United States, and calling out or relating to the militia or volunteers from the States, are hereby approved and in all respects legalized and made valid, to the same extent and with the same effect as if they had been issued and done under the previous express authority and direction of the Congress. . . .[6]

But even this legislation did not clear up the question of whether, when blockade existed, war existed. If blockade existed, the law of war applied; if neutral vessels were seized, the law of war applied.

Additional challenge of Lincoln's policy was made. Owners of vessels that were seized brought suit to secure return of their property. They questioned authority of the President to institute the blockade; they challenged the right of Congress, since no war was declared, to authorize closed ports. They posed a serious threat to Union efforts to combat the Confederacy without granting the South recognition.[7]

Leaders of the administration viewed with apprehension the probability that problems of prize would have to be taken to the Supreme Court. As the year 1861 came to a close, the need for clarification became pressing. But William M. Evarts, a New York lawyer who had assisted Lincoln in naval matters at the beginning of the war, advised Attorney General Bates to move slowly in bringing prize cases before the Court. "I respectfully submit to your consideration [wrote Evarts, who later served as a government lawyer in the *Prize Cases*] whether it will be advisable for the Government to call on the argument of these causes . . . until the bench shall be filled by appointment to the vacancies." [8]

Attorney General Bates felt the pressure of lawyers who represented clients whose property had been seized. These lawyers recognized that it was to their advantage to press for an early hearing before the Supreme Court. Lincoln's appointees could be expected to support his policies. When Lincoln made his first appointment to the Court and other appointments were expected quickly, demands for action were thrust upon Bates.[9]

Consequently, plans were made to try the cases in March, 1862. Assistant Attorney General Titian J. Coffey wrote William T. Carroll, clerk

[5] 12 Stat. 255-58.

[6] *Ibid.*, 326.

[7] Louis B. Boudin, *Government by Judiciary* (New York, 1932), II, 38.

[8] William M. Evarts to Edward Bates, December 27, 1861, Papers of the Attorneys General.

[9] Bates, *Diary*, p. 231 (February 14, 1862).

of the Court, "Please send . . . [me] printed copies of the record in any
. . . of the *prize cases* which may have reached the Supreme Court. It is
the purpose of the Attorney General to have them all argued together as
early in March as may be." [10]

But plans were changed. It was decided to delay the *Prize Cases*. Bates
informed Evarts that some of the Justices did not desire to hear the cases
of prize out of turn and that whether argued or not the cases would not
be decided until the following term. Bates explained, also, that the Court
would not hear cases out of their regular order unless the government requested it on the basis of public safety. The pressures the lawyers exerted
upon Bates disturbed him, however, and he wrote to Evarts, "I am urged
in several quarters to ask for a special term. You can oblige me by giving
your advice upon that point." [11]

For the administration it would have been a grievous error of strategy
to bring the *Prize Cases* before the Supreme Court in March, 1862. At
that date only one Lincoln appointee sat upon the Court. Two vacancies
existed. Bates apparently had anticipated a full Court by March, 1862. As
it was Congress continued to wrangle over circuit reorganization. So
Bates delayed. The consequence was that the *Prize Cases* were not heard
until the following year.

The delay undoubtedly saved the administration from defeat. The full
Court, on which there were three appointees of Lincoln, sustained the
government by the barest majority—a vote of five to four. Appointees
of Lincoln made up three of the five who upheld him. Prior to the three
appointments the vote would have been four to two against Lincoln's
acts. Delay on the part of Lincoln's Attorney General turned defeat into
victory.

DANA'S FORMULA

Since there were a number of cases of prize pending before the Supreme
Court, Attorney General Bates received permission to have the cases
argued *en bloc*. Bates, who found himself under the pressure of heavy responsibilities, did not have time to prepare the cases so the government
was represented by other counsel.[12] Arguments began on February 10,
1863, and proceeded until February 25. Large audiences attended the
Court to hear the arguments. The momentous nature of the issues provoked an intense interest in the proceedings.[13]

---

[10] Titian J. Coffey to William T. Carroll, February 15, 1862, Attorney General's
Letter Books.

[11] Edward Bates to William M. Evarts, March 11, 1862, *ibid*.

[12] Editorial, New York *World*, February 19, 1863, p. 4.

[13] New York *World*, February 13, 1863, p. 4.

Four cases were involved in the litigation. Richard H. Dana, Jr., whom Lincoln had appointed district attorney for Massachusetts, represented the government in the case of *The Brig Amy Warwick;* Edward Bangs of Massachusetts represented the claimants. Charles Eames, who served as legal counselor for the Navy Department during the Civil War, represented the government in the case of *The Schooner Crenshaw;* the firm of Daniel Lord, Charles Edwards, and C. Donahue, represented the claimants. William M. Evarts and Charles B. Sedgwick of New York represented the government in the case of *The Barque Hiawatha;* Charles Edwards represented the claimants. And Charles Eames represented the government in the case of *The Schooner Brilliante;* James M. Carlisle of Washington represented the claimants.

Dana had conducted the case of *The Brig Amy Warwick* in the district court at Boston, and Attorney General Bates invited him to conduct the case on appeal before the Supreme Court. The brilliant performance of Dana probably saved the government from defeat that would have been catastrophic.

Dana kept his friend, Thornton K. Lothrop, the assistant federal district attorney for Massachusetts, informed as to the progress of the arguments before the Court and his reactions to the proceedings. Following his argument, Dana wrote that he was well satisfied and that "The compliments I have received from the judges and audience and counsel are quite too flattering to be put on paper. They seem to think the philosophy of the law of prize has been developed for the first time in its bearing on the present question." [14] A few days later Dana again wrote Lothrop. He said that he had won "Grier's heart" and that Attorney General Bates appeared to be overcome with emotion. As to Grier, Dana added, "He pats me on the shoulder and says I have cleared up all his doubts, and that it is the best argument he has heard for five years, etc." [15]

One unfortunate circumstance developed while the cases were being argued. Charles Eames, who had been designated as the chief counsel representing the government, aroused the resentment of some of the members of the Court, including Chief Justice Taney. Lincoln-appointee Justice Swayne visited Bates the day after arguments were completed to tell Bates of the feelings of the Justices. Swayne said that Eames had made himself obnoxious, that his arguments were poor, that he harmed the government's cause, and that he acted "like a harlequin" and turned the trial into a farce. Bates feared that the Court's attitude toward Eames

---

[14] Richard H. Dana, Jr., to Thornton K. Lothrop, February 18, 1863, quoted in Charles Francis Adams, *Richard Henry Dana: A Biography*, 3rd rev. ed. (Cambridge, 1891), II, 270.

[15] Richard H. Dana, Jr. to Thornton K. Lothrop, February 23, 1863, *ibid.*

might jeopardize the government's position. "This is all very unjust, [Bates concluded] not to say c[r]uel, and shews [*sic*] a degree of passion and prejudice not very creditable to that high court." [16]

The four vessels which were involved in the appeal were brought into port under the President's proclamations of blockade. All were condemned as prize in Unites States district court proceedings. The claimants of the vessels appealed the condemnation decisions to the Supreme Court. The same legal principles were involved in all four instances.

The Brig Amy Warwick was from Richmond, Virginia, and was owned by William Currie, George W. Allen, and Abraham Warwick. It had voyaged from New York to Richmond and then departed for Rio de Janeiro where it took on five thousand bags of coffee to be delivered to Baltimore, Philadelphia, or New York, depending upon orders to be given to its master upon arrival at Hampton Roads. It was captured off Cape Henry on July 10, 1861. Its master, whose vessel was flying the American flag at the time of seizure, was unaware that a conflict was in progress between the Union and the South. The brig was taken to Boston and condemned as prize. Its owners denied hostility to the United States and appealed on the basis that its master did not know of conflict or blockade.

District Attorney Dana devised the formula that recruited for the government the support of two Democratic Justices.[17] He declared that one major question existed: "At the time of the capture, was it competent for the President to treat as prize of war property found on the high seas, for the sole reason that it belonged to persons residing and doing business in Richmond, Virginia?"

The question he propounded to the Court he answered with irrefutable logic. He argued that it did not matter whether the owners took part in the war, whether they were loyal to the enemy, whether they were by birth or naturalization citizens of the enemy state, whether they were subjects of a neutral state, whether they were citizens of the United States, whether the goods would aid the enemy, or whether the vessel at the time of seizure was on a voyage to or from the enemy. Dana set up a general rule covering all seizures at sea. *"If the power* [declared Dana] *with which you are at war has such interest in its transit, arrival, or existence, as to make its capture one of the fair modes of coercion, you may take it."*

That no declaration of war had been made did not influence the situa-

---

[16] Bates, *Diary*, pp. 281-82 (February 23, 1863).

[17] This discussion of the arguments in the case of *The Brig Amy Warwick* and the case of *The Brilliante* is based upon 67 U.S. 636-62. In the official reports of the Supreme Court only Dana's argument, presenting the government's case, and Carlisle's argument, presenting the case for the claimants, were published. The Lawyers' Edition of the *United States Reports* includes the arguments of Evarts and Lord as well. It is a special annotated edition of the cases heard by the Supreme Court. Often it provides information that does not appear in the official reports.

tion, maintained Dana. He pointed out that it is not necessary for Congress to declare war before the President can exercise war powers, asserting, "War is a *state of things,* and not an act of legislative will." He argued that if a war is sprung upon the United States, the President has the authority to "repel war with war. . . ."

Dana asserted that the act of August 6, 1861, retroactively recognizing the validity of presidential acts to suppress the rebellion, was not necessary. Congress was aware at the time it passed the act, Dana pointed out, that the President had exercised "as of right, full belligerent power to capture at sea on all the recognized grounds of war—contraband, breach of blockade, an enemy property. . . ."

That was the formula of Richard Dana, Jr. The conflict was war—war with all the rights of war accruing to the Union. It was the responsibility of the President—with the Congress in session or in recess—to take steps necessary to maintain the authority of the United States. Belligerent rights on the part of the United States, furthermore, did not infer that belligerent rights would accrue, *ipso facto,* to the Confederacy. The rights of a sovereign nation differ from those of an area in insurrection.

The most impressive argument in behalf of the claimants was made by James M. Carlisle in the case of *The Schooner Brilliante.* Carlisle had served as legal adviser to the British legation in Washington and frequently represented foreigners in the courts of the United States. The Mexican vessel, *The Brilliante,* was owned by Raphael Preciat and Julian Gual, one of whom was a naturalized American citizen and the other a Mexican citizen. Its cargo consisted of flour belonging to the owners of the vessel and two other Mexican citizens. The vessel had gone from Campeche to New Orleans, where it took on the cargo which was to be taken to Sisal and Campeche, ports of Mexico. While on its voyage home, *The Brilliante* anchored at Biloxi Bay, intending to communicate with the blockading fleet to get permission to proceed to sea. While at anchor, it was seized, taken to Key West, and condemned as prize.

The vessel was seized on June 23, 1861. The principal owner, Raphael Preciat, at the time of the seizure was United States consul at the port of Campeche. Carlisle argued that there was no intention of actual breach of blockade. He pointed out that the vessel anchored at Biloxi Bay voluntarily to obtain a permit to leave. If it could not obtain permission, Preciat was going to use a letter that he had obtained from the commander of one of the blockading vessels to forward *The Brilliante* to Mobile where he wished to pick up his son who attended school. *The Brilliante* asked for permission to depart at Biloxi Bay because the crew mutinied and refused to go to Mobile.

Carlisle declared that the claimant, although sailing from New Orleans, had the right to expect that he would be permitted to depart. He questioned the power of Lincoln to institute a blockade because "insurrection is not war; and invasion is not war." He argued that blockade cannot exist unless there is war, that Congress alone can put the United States into war, and that acts passed by Congress subsequent to the seizures did not retroactively validate Lincoln's acts. The seizure of *The Brilliante* was made, Carlisle maintained, "during that period when the President, casting about among doubtful expedients, had used the navy . . . '*in the nature* of a blockade.' It is denied that during this period there was *WAR*, or that the rights and obligations of war, either under the municipal or international law, had arisen."

Carlisle attacked the concept that the President, when the circumstances demanded it, could exercise emergency powers. "To suppose that this Court [Carlisle stated] would desire argument against such a notion, would be offensive. It comes to the plea of necessity. The Constitution knows no such word." Carlisle denied that the framers of the Constitution "contemplated and tacitly provided" that in an emergency the President should become a dictator.

The Carlisle arguments demonstrated what was at stake in these proceedings. The concept of the role of the government in this emergency was at issue. Lincoln's interpretation of the presidency in wartime was questioned. The ability of the federal government to sustain itself against challenge was at stake.

Two other vessels were involved in the *Prize Cases*. One was *The Schooner Crenshaw*, owned by partners, one of whom lived in the North and the other, in the South. The vessel was captured at the mouth of the James River on May 17, 1861. It was bound for Liverpool with tobacco from Richmond, and the claimants asserted that they had had no adequate notice of the blockade. They were represented by Charles Edwards, who was counsel for the British consulate in New York City for some twenty-five years. "If a partner at the South is doing a public wrong [Edwards argued], his body may have to suffer; but where he has linked himself in mercantile matters with partners at the North, natural equity, if it chooses to affect his partnership standing at all, should vest in the northern loyal partner the whole assets." [18]

The other vessel was *The Barque Hiawatha*, a British vessel. It was on a voyage from Richmond to Liverpool, its cargo consisting mainly of tobacco. It left Richmond on May 17, 1861, was seized as prize, taken to New York City, and condemned in the United States district court. The

---

[18] Brief of Charles Edwards in the *Crenshaw Case* of the *Prize Cases*, p. 4, Records and Briefs of the United States Supreme Court, 1863, Law Division, Library of Congress. The Records and Briefs include the complete records of the cases as well as all of the briefs submitted to the Court. They are printed but not circulated publicly. The limited material published in the official reports is selected from the Records and Briefs.

owners of *The Hiawatha*, Miller, Massman, and Company, denied through Edwards, who served as their counsel, that sufficient notice of the blockade had been given.

Many years after the war Thornton K. Lothrop described the dangers that Dana faced in the *Prize Cases*. If the Court ruled that no war existed, Lothrop explained, the blockade would be illegal; if the Court ruled that the state of rebellion had emerged into a state of war, foreign powers would interpret this as justification to recognize the Confederacy.[19] Either eventuality would prolong the conflict and jeopardize the Union. Dana's task consisted of developing arguments to convince the Court that it was proper for the federal government to enjoy all of the rights of belligerency without at the same time granting those rights to the Confederacy.

The day before the Supreme Court handed down its decision Dana, in a spirit of uneasy anticipation, poured out his feelings in a letter to Charles Francis Adams, United States Minister to England. "So the judiciary [Dana wrote] is actually, after a war of twenty-three months' duration, to decide whether the government has the legal capacity to exert these war powers." He lamented that the fact the Supreme Court was faced with such a decision demonstrated the weakness of a "written Constitution."

A comprehension of all the issues involved was demonstrated by Dana in this letter to Adams: "Contemplate, my dear sir, the possibility of a Supreme Court deciding that this blockade is illegal! What a position it would put us in before the world whose commerce we have been illegally prohibiting, whom we have unlawfully subjected to a cotton famine and domestic dangers and distress for two years!"

Dana proceeded to assure Adams that he anticipated a favorable ruling; it was the mere possibility of an adverse one that made the system, in his opinion, absurd. He declared that a year earlier, when the blockade was new and before Lincoln had appointed three Justices, an adverse ruling would have been probable. He said to Adams, "The bare contemplation of such a possibility makes us pause in our boastful assertion that our written Constitution is clearly adapted to all exigencies, the last, best gift to man." [20]

THE JUSTICES SPEAK

A throng attended the Supreme Court proceedings on March 10, 1863. Lawyers and spectators were attracted from throughout the land. It was widely recognized that the nation was at the crossroads awaiting a

---

[19] Thornton K. Lothrop to Charles F. Adams, August 25, 1890, quoted in Adams, II, 398-99.

[20] Richard H. Dana, Jr. to Charles F. Adams, March 9, 1863, *ibid.*, II, 267.

momentous ruling.[21] The entire membership of the Court participated in hearing the *Prize Cases*. On this day, however, only the Associate Justices were present. Chief Justice Taney was absent—absent because of illness or ill will or both. And Justice Catron, "apparently indisposed, retired from the bench before the reading was concluded." [22]

Justice Robert C. Grier spoke for the majority. He was joined by the three Lincoln appointees—Swayne, Miller, and Davis—and the loyal and devoted Justice James M. Wayne of Georgia. The opinion of Justice Grier and the majority gave the administration a great victory.[23] Grier stated that two questions had to be answered in determining whether the claimants had any legal foundation for their appeal: 1. Did the President have the right to institute blockade of the Southern ports? 2. What is included in the term "enemies' property?"

Justice Grier dealt with the first question at great length; the second, he dealt with briefly. He ruled that there could be no successful challenge of the President's authority to inaugurate blockade, and he declared that a state of war existed when Lincoln issued the proclamation of blockade. Grier examined the problem of what war is and when it is that war exists. He eliminated the contention that war exists only by declaration. "War has been well defined [Justice Grier stated] to be 'That state in which a nation prosecutes its right by force.'" Such prosecution of war need not involve declaration of war at all, he concluded.

In one of the outstanding passages in his opinion, Grier declared:

A civil war is never solemnly declared; it becomes such by its accidents—the number, power, and organization of the persons who originate and carry it on. When the party in rebellion occupy and hold in a hostile manner a certain portion of territory; have declared their independence; have cast off their allegiance, have organized armies; have commenced hostilities against their former sovereign, the world acknowledges them as belligerents, and the contest a *war*. They claim to be in arms to establish their liberty and independence, in order to become a sovereign State, while the sovereign party treats them as insurgents and rebels who owe allegiance, and who should be punished with death for their treason.

Justice Grier maintained that parties in a civil war find it necessary to concede belligerent rights to each other because the concession of such rights tends to lessen the cruelties and miseries of war. Consequently, he stated, "They exchange prisoners, and adopt other courtesies and rules common to public or national wars." If this procedure is not followed, Grier argued, retaliation by each contestant would be shocking.

Grier wrote that the true test of whether civil war exists is to deter-

---

[21] New York *World*, March 11, 1863, p. 1.

[22] New York *Tribune*, March 11, 1863, p. 1.

[23] This discussion of the majority opinion of the *Prize Cases* is based upon 67 U.S. 665-82.

mine whether "the regular course of justice was interrupted by revolt, rebellion, or insurrection." When interference with civil courts exists, the Supreme Court ruled, civil war exists, and the government may prosecute it as if a foreign foe were invading the country.

Although the Constitution confers on Congress the right to declare war, Grier pointed out, it is impossible for Congress to declare war upon one or several of the states. When an emergency such as insurrection occurs, the President has the responsibility of repelling the invasion and suppressing the insurrection. Whether it is domestic or foreign challenge, war exists even though the declaration of it is only "unilateral," said Justice Grier.

The majority of the Court ruled that the conflict between the North and the South was war—war despite the fact that there was no declaration of war. "The President [affirmed Grier] was bound to meet it in the shape it presented itself, without waiting for Congress to baptize it with a name; and no name given to it by him could change the fact." The Justice declared, furthermore, that although it was deemed an insurrection by the Union it was war, nevertheless, "It is not necessary that the independence of the revolted province or State be acknowledged in order to constitute it a party belligerent in a war according to the law of nations." England, through its proclamation of neutrality, he stated, acknowledged that war existed, as did others.

The Court rejected the arguments of the claimants, characterizing them as adroit but inaccurate. Justice Grier crushed their contentions, declaring that the Court recognized as did the whole world that the civil war in progress was "the greatest civil war known in the history of the human race. . . ." He declared, "to affect a technical ignorance of the existence of war" would be to "cripple the arm of the Government and paralyze its power by subtle definitions and ingenious sophisms." Grier cast out the theory set up by the claimants that the Southerners were not "*enemies*" because they were "*traitors*" and that the conflict was not "*war*" because it was "*insurrection.*"

The Court held that the President's acts were legally correct on the basis of presidential power alone. The President had the power to institute blockade of the South which neutral powers were obliged to recognize; the conflict was insurrection *and* war; the Southerners were traitors *and* enemies.

Having disposed of the first question, Justice Grier turned to the second question, that of "enemies' property." This he disposed of promptly. He ruled that all persons residing within the territory of the Confederacy were liable to treatment as enemies and their property was subject to seizure as "enemies' property." Grier held that the personal allegiance of the owner did not alone determine the status of property.

Involvement in illegal traffic was a factor that condemned property and made it "enemies' property."

With these principles as the guiding factors Grier was ready to apply them to the cases before the Supreme Court. He asserted that at the time of the capture of *The Amy Warwick* all of its claimants were residents of Virginia so the brig was legal prize. *The Hiawatha* was condemned as prize because it left Virginia on May 18, 1861, although the fifteen days of grace that had been granted by the proclamations expired on May 15. Grier ruled that a vessel in a blockaded port is "presumed to have notice of blockade as soon as it commences. This is a settled rule of the law of nations." *The Brilliante* was condemned because it tried to escape through the blockade. *The Crenshaw* was condemned because it attempted to run the blockade. All property on board *The Crenshaw* was condemned as "enemies' property" except tobacco belonging to Irwin and Company which was bought and paid for before the war began.

The decision of the Supreme Court reinvigorated a nation that had seen much tragedy and defeat for two long years. A defeat at the hands of the Court at this time would have shattered the morale of the Union. Grier, Wayne, Swayne, Miller, Davis—these were the men whose devotion to the Union succored it during this time of unparalleled challenge.

VIGOROUS DISSENT

Four Justices—Nelson, Taney, Catron, and Clifford—ruled against the government in the *Prize Cases*. They concluded that until Congress took action to recognize the existence of insurrection, as it did on July 13, 1861, the conflict was not legally war but merely a "personal war" of President Lincoln. Dana won even these four over to the view that after July 13 the conflict between the Union and the Confederacy was war. But they saw fit to deny the validity of Lincoln's acts in the period from the beginning of the conflict in April until Congress recognized on July 13, 1861, that insurrection existed. It was the opinion of the minority that even if the federal government faced dissolution, the President had to await congressional approval of measures of war. Did it not occur to the minority that a foreign invasion or a domestic insurrection might make it impossible to call the Congress together?

Justice Nelson delivered the minority opinion, stating that he spoke for Chief Justice Taney and Justice Catron as well as himself. Justice Clifford, although he announced that he, too, dissented, did not join in the dissenting opinion and did not submit a dissenting opinion of his own.[24]

Justice Nelson examined two questions in arriving at his decision:

---

[24] This discussion of the dissenting opinion of the *Prize Cases* is based upon 67 U.S. 683-99.

1. Was adequate warning given to vessels that were seized? 2. Did a status of war actually exist?

As to the first question, Justice Nelson dealt with it briefly. He pointed out that on the last day of grace, May 15, 1861, *The Hiawatha* was ready to depart but no tug was available. Under the terms of the President's proclamation, furthermore, a first warning, written into a ship's papers, was required. He rejected the contention that a warning is dispensed with in a case where the master of a vessel has previous knowledge that blockade exists. Nelson concluded that the proclamations, themselves, provided for warning that was not given. He held that only on the second attempt to run the blockade could vessels be seized and held as prize.

Next Justice Nelson examined the question of whether war existed before Congress authorized the President to close ports in insurrectionary areas. He concluded that at the time *The Hiawatha* was seized war did not exist because the law-making body of the government had not recognized the existence of war. "No power short of this [Nelson maintained] can change the legal status of the Government or the relation of its citizens from that of peace to a state of war. . . ."

The minority admitted that acts of 1795 and 1807 gave the President power to protect the United States, but it denied that under these acts the President could wage war against a state of the Union or confiscate the property of citizens of a state. Until Congress takes action, wrote Justice Nelson, "no citizen of the State can be punished in his person or property, unless he has committeed some offense against a law of Congress passed before the act was committed, which made it a crime, and defined the punishment." Until Congress acted, it was a "personal war" of President Lincoln, maintained the minority, because the President cannot recognize or declare a civil war.

The opinions in the *Prize Cases* cleared up basic questions in relation to the conflict. The Supreme Court reached a crisis in hearing these cases. It engaged in its most vital struggle of the period of the war. Upon its decision hinged the fate of Lincoln's endeavors to combat the foe. In its broadest implications the ruling supported Lincoln's claim to emergency powers for the President. By implication the Court sustained in the *Prize Cases* the contention of Lincoln that vast wartime power existed and could be legally exercised. The decision gave promise that any future challenge of Lincoln's powers would be similarly pushed aside.

Some of the press saw in the decision a significant turning point. As the New York *Times* expressed it: "It is our firm conviction that the Supreme Court would [now] indorse the constitutional validity of every important act of the Executive or of Congress thus far in the rebellion. If this is a wrong conviction, we care not how soon we are rid of it by the actual test." [25] But the New York *World* commented, "The reasoning of the minority seems to be decidedly the stronger, and more accordant with the spirit as well as letter of the Constitution. . . ." [26]

The Supreme Court had met its gravest hurdle. Fate played its part in the decision, however. Without vacancies that enabled Lincoln to place Republicans upon the Court, the policies of the administration would not have been sustained unless Congress had added a number of seats to the Court. Had no vacancies existed for Lincoln to fill, it is a foregone conclusion that that would have ensued. As it was, Congress gave blunt warning by providing for one addition.

These warriors of the Court held in their hands "the fate of our nation." The future of the country depended no less upon them than "upon the gathering of armies and fitting out of fleets." Here was the supreme crisis "in jurisprudence as well as in war." [27] Despite Dana's lamentation to his friend concerning a "written Constitution," the federal system had met and passed its most critical test.

---

[25] Editorial, New York *Times*, March 13, 1863, p. 4.

[26] Editorial, New York *World*, May 15, 1863, p. 4.

[27] Hampton L. Carson, *The History of the Supreme Court of the United States with Biographies of all the Chief and Associate Justices* (Philadelphia, 1902), II, 382.

CHAPTER TEN

Malice Aforethought

JUSTIFICATION BY EMERGENCY

One of the most painful subjects to the chief law-enforcement officials of the Lincoln administration was the matter of arbitrary arrest. The policy of President Lincoln was established in the Merryman case at the beginning of the war, and he did not alter it. Consequently, the problem would not quiet itself, and those who maintained that a government of laws was paramount to maintenance of the Union, fought Lincoln's policy throughout the war.

Chief Justice Taney, who made his position clear in the case of John Merryman, enunciated a view that was widely accepted even by men who deemed themselves friends of the Union. The problem boiled down to this: should the federal government be entitled to employ all possible means to secure Union authority or should the confining bounds of legality be permitted to endanger the very existence of the Federal Union?

President Lincoln maintained that the security of the Union was paramount and throughout the war directed military commanders in threatened areas to refuse to recognize the privilege of habeas corpus, time-honored in nations of Anglo-Saxon tradition. He did not establish that policy without misgivings, but he set up a rule to cover all contingencies and one that was unchangeable.

Lincoln was no dictator, but he exercised the powers of the presidency more boldly than any other American president. He seized powers and exercised extra-legal authority for the sole purpose of sustaining the normal, legal authority of the government of the United States. Such powers were released from his grasp the moment the Union was no longer benefited by their exercise. Lincoln did order that troublemakers be seized, but they were released and forgotten once their capacity to harm the Union was at an end.

Lincoln provided only one vindication of his policy: necessity justified the exercise of arbitrary power by the President. No stronger vindication of Lincoln's policy could have existed. If the federal government were to be denied the right to sustain itself when an emergency engulfed it, the Constitution had within it the seeds of its own destruction. Senator James R. Doolittle of Wisconsin reflected the administration's view accurately when he asked of the Senate: "Suppose a civil war arises, and

Congress is driven out of the capital, what then is to be done? Where is the power to suspend your *habeas corpus?*" In civil war, Senator Doolittle affirmed, it "is the part of the executive business with which the President is clothed, to judge when the courts may safely . . . sit, issue their process and try offenders." [1]

At the time that Senator Doolittle expressed his views, Senator Lyman Trumbull joined the debate to state that he believed that the attack against arbitrary arrest was unfortunate and that nothing could be gained by it. "I claim [declared Trumbull] that we will put down rebellion and preserve the Constitution; we will not violate the Constitution nor attempt to overthrow it. . . ." In this early senatorial debate on arbitrary arrest— congressional debate on the subject never ceased throughout the war— Trumbull finally asked Senator Orville H. Browning, who criticized Lincoln's denial of the writ, "Does my colleague want the country to believe that Congress is making war on the President?" [2]

The administration at an early date after the controversy over Merryman took pains to explain not only its position but also the significance of arbitrary arrest. A proclamation of amnesty to political or state prisoners was issued by Secretary Stanton on February 14, 1862, by order of the President. [3] This proclamation granted amnesty to such prisoners who were no longer deemed dangerous. It was stated, however, that in the confusions and perplexities of the early days of the war harsh methods were inevitable, the war itself being without precedent in American experience. "Every department of the Government [it lamented] was paralyzed by treason."

Disaster was so complete, continued the proclamation, that Congress "had not anticipated and so had not provided for the emergency." It was as a consequence that responsibility for action, Lincoln believed, rested in the hands of the Chief Executive, whose failure to cope with the crisis would have been a breach of his solemn oath. In this proclamation the administration criticized the federal courts particularly, stating, "The judicial machinery seemed as if it had been designed not to sustain the Government, but to embarrass and betray it." In no statement did the administration express better the contempt it felt for the judicial authorities who sought to thwart Union efforts as Civil War opened.

The administration emphasized that doubt began to exist in many quarters "whether the Federal Government which one year before had been thought a model worthy of universal acceptance had indeed the ability to defend and maintain itself." But it was explained that at least the executive branch did not fail to meet the needs of the occasion. And

[1] *Cong. Globe*, 37th Cong., 2nd sess., p. 96.

[2] *Ibid.*, p. 98.

[3] *Offic. Rec.*, ser. II, vol. 2, 221-23.

as the emergency intensified, "the President felt it his duty to employ with energy the extraordinary powers which the Constitution confides to him in cases of insurrection."

Executive direction instituted sweeping policies and activities. The President "called into the field" whatever military and naval forces he deemed necessary. The President "directed measures to prevent" the use of post offices for correspondence contributing to the rebellion. The President "subjected passengers to and from foreign countries" to newly devised passport controls. The President "instituted a blockade." And the President suspended the writ of habeas corpus in areas that were disturbed.

All of these acts were in response to need that was urgent. They were taken under the authority of the President and by his direction. Without them the cause of the Union would have been more desperate than it was. If a man of less courage had held the presidency when action was the crying need, the American Union might have perished. But Lincoln took the steps he deemed necessary. Lincoln's justification was the stark reality of the destruction that awaited unless action was prompt.

In granting amnesty in February, 1862, the administration believed that circumstances had changed and that "Apprehensions of public danger and facilities for treasonable practices have diminished with the passions which prompted heedless persons to adopt them." In fact, it inferred that the insurrection was declining. Since it was the desire of the President to return to normality, he was granting amnesty, and prisoners were given the right to be paroled if they would swear not to give aid to the Confederacy.

But after initial successes, the year 1862 brought disasters. It is not surprising that Lincoln found it desirable to return to a rigorous policy on arbitrary arrest. Two days after he issued the preliminary emancipation proclamation on September 22, the President found it necessary to suspend the writ of habeas corpus. The new directive explained that the ordinary processes of law were deemed inadequate to restrain disloyal persons and that, therefore, anyone within the United States who discouraged enlistment, resisted the draft, or aided the Confederacy would be seized and punished by military authorities. The order directed, furthermore, that in all such instances of arrest the privilege of habeas corpus would go unrecognized.[4]

From the beginning of the war Lincoln's policy on arbitrary arrest had provoked widespread criticism. Even the proclamation of amnesty had not quieted the furor. But the sweeping order of September, 1862, set off a greater controversy than had yet been seen because it was all-encompassing in its assertion of presidential power.

---

[4] *Works*, V, 436-37 (September 24, 1862); Randall, *Constitutional Problems*, 151-52.

The Washington *Morning Chronicle* expressed an attitude that was typical of those elements that were favorable to the administration. Declaring that the troublemakers were justifiably imprisoned, this newspaper stated, "We believe it was necessary in some cases, and that in most of the other cases no real harm or injustice had been done." [5] It maintained that, after all, if a man is caught "in a room of thieves it would ill become him to put on airs when the police insisted on searching his pockets." [6]

Horace Binney, distinguished member of the Pennsylvania bar, supported the administration with reasoning that was widely accepted. He maintained that in a rebellion judicial officers can function only imperfectly, and "It is not a season of the judicial trial of all persons who are implicated in the rebellion." Binney attributed to the President all power necessary to combat rebellion and argued that "the obvious and just deductions from these observations" is that within Executive hands rests the power to suspend the writ of habeas corpus. Unless the President exercised these powers, Binney warned, "the very arms of the Government might be baffled and its worst enemies escape." [7]

Criticisms of the manner in which the administration handled habeas corpus were widespread. Much of it came from those whose loyalty to the Union was slight, indeed. On the other hand, much opposition came from those who were honestly devoted to the Union but refused to agree that it was the right of the executive to deal arbitrarily with the almost sacred writ of habeas corpus.

Professor Joel Parker of the Cambridge Law School expressed his views —they were widely shared—in a letter to the editor of the Washington *National Intelligencer*. "Dear Sir: Will you permit me to say [stormed the Professor] that the sooner the Republican party cuts itself loose from all unconstitutional projects . . . the sooner it will begin to provide for its own salvation." [8]

Lincoln's proclamation of suspension in September, 1862, incensed the New York *World* which had continuously challenged Lincoln on his extra-legal activities. It charged that he suspended the writ although Chief Justices Story, Marshall, and Taney all declared that Congress alone possessed the power to do so. [9] As bad as the sedition laws of John Adams were, the *World* pointed out, trial by jury yet existed. "We have to go [said the *World*] to the worst despotisms of foreign lands . . .

[5] Editorial, Washington *Morning Chronicle*, December 1, 1862, p. 2.

[6] *Ibid.*, December 12, 1862, p. 2.

[7] Horace Binney, "The Privilege of the Writ of Habeas Corpus under the Constitution," *Fahnestock Pamphlets*, vol. XXXIX, no. 2 (Philadelphia, 1862), 46-47.

[8] Washington *National Intelligencer*, May 17, 1862, p. 3.

[9] Editorial, New York *World*, September 8, 1862, p. 4.

to find any such system of arbitrary imprisonment as has prevailed for the last year under this free American republic." [10]

Another noteworthy attack upon Lincoln's seizure of arbitrary powers was made by Senator Garrett Davis of Kentucky, who labeled Lincoln's war department a "lawless organization" and charged that Lincoln and his associates were only pretending to desire restoration of the Constitution.[11] Charles A. Wickliffe, also from Kentucky, opposed Lincoln's policies and asserted in the House of Representatives, "I deny that because war exists with eleven States the President has the right to suspend the *habeas corpus* in the States of Pennsylvania, Indiana, Ohio, or other states." [12]

Friend and foe of Lincoln would not let the habeas corpus issue quiet itself; in fact, it could not quiet itself. By its nature it struck at the heart of the controversy over federal power to resist treasonable aggression. Lincoln interpreted his responsibilities as dictating that he, in his executive capacity, had inherently the power to take any necessary steps to preserve the Union. He interpreted his responsibilities as absolutely independent of congressional action.

There was only one way to clarify presidential powers: let the Supreme Court examine and define them. But Lincoln dared not submit the question of presidential power to the Court, for he feared that it would rule that no special wartime power to suspend the writ of habeas corpus was granted to the Chief Executive by the Constitution. Consequently, the administration's policy was to evade the Court. Lincoln knew that if it ruled against him the cause of the Union would become even more desperate than it was; therefore effort was made to avert giving the Court an opportunity to adjudicate this momentous question.

Avoid the Court

Opposition newspapers such as the New York *World* called upon the administration—challenged it— to take the issue of arbitrary arrest to the Supreme Court. The *World* declared that only the Court could give a "binding decision" relative to "the question of the extraordinary arrests, made since the commencement of the war. . . ." [13]

Secretary of War Edwin M. Stanton finally came to the conclusion that it would be wise to test arbitrary arrest before the Supreme Court, but Attorney General Bates stayed his hand. He counseled Stanton in a letter which today is one of the most significant revelations of the ad-

[10] *Ibid.*, September 11, 1862, p. 4.
[11] *Cong. Globe*, 37th Cong., 3rd sess., p. 533.
[12] *Ibid.*, p. 1105.
[13] Editorial, New York *World*, April 17, 1862, p. 4.

ministration's attitude toward the Supreme Court and of the fears that the administration harbored.

Bates warned Stanton to stay away from the Supreme Court. Declaring that he learned that Stanton contemplated taking to the Court a Wisconsin case involving the writ of habeas corpus, the Attorney General stated that he believed it would be "extremely impolitic" to engage in such a battle.

Bates stated frankly that if the question of the privilege of habeas corpus were brought before the Court, he feared that it would rule against the administration. "It will be conceded [he told Stanton] that in the present condition . . . a decision of that court against the power of the President to arrest and hold without trial, disloyal persons, would inflict upon the Administration a serious injury."

Bates asked Stanton to contemplate what would happen if the Court, "*invoked by the Executive* to sustain these arrests should pronounce them illegal." He stated that such a decision would paralyze the administration and would animate the enemy more "than the worst defeat our armies have yet sustained." The Attorney General argued that the administration should not face such peril unless it became imperatively necessary to do so.

Bates discounted the possibility that the Court would rule favorably to the administration. He said that if it were thought that the policy of the executive needed vindication by the Supreme Court, "it is all important to know first that it will receive that vindication. . . . I confess to you frankly, that, knowing as we do, the antecedents and present proclivities of the majority of that Court (and I speak of them with entire respect) I can anticipate no such results." It is significant that Bates expressed these views after Lincoln had appointed three Justices, but before the Republicans had packed the Court.

Bates said that both Chief Justice Taney and Justice Clifford would undoubtedly rule against the government. The rest of the Democrats on the Court probably would do the same. This was no indication that the majority of the Court was disloyal, Bates added. "Many loyal men deny this power to the President [Stanton was told] and, however confident *we* may be that he possesses it, it is no imputation on the loyalty of the majority of the Court to presume that on this point they agree with their political school."

Bates would not desist. He piled argument upon argument. He said that the decision the administration had to make was whether the Union could be furthered better without the Supreme Court decision than "with decision *against* the power assumed by the President. . . ." If the Court ruled against the power, Bates asked, could the administration, since it sought the decision, fail to obey it? He believed that the administration would be less constrained to recognize an adverse ruling if a person who was seized appealed to the Court and it supported him.[14]

Attorney General Bates understood the members of the Taney Court. In his analysis of the situation he had the advantage of association with Justices who could inform him, unofficially of course, what the general feeling was. Bates's advice to the Secretary of War was sound. What he proposed to Stanton, furthermore, became basic policy; the administration did not press before the Supreme Court cases which almost certainly would be decided adversely. It became the resolve of the administration to do what it deemed necessary and to prevent interference by denying, wherever possible, an opportunity to the Court to hand down a decision in a doubtful case. The result was that the administration received vast criticism for acts of questionable constitutionality, but it preferred to incur that criticism rather than risk defeat. Actually this was tacit admission that certain deeds transcended the Constitution. But Lincoln dared not do otherwise.

The fact that the Court could not easily interfere with Lincoln because his measures often had results that could not be undone was recognized by many observers of the press. "Suppose [editorialized the New York *Times*] we believe the admission of Western Virginia, and the suspension of the habeas corpus to be unconstitutional, the interference with the treasonable Press unwise, the Proclamation ill-advised. These things are now *faits accomplis* for good or for ill." [15] This was deliberate on the part of Lincoln; often when he acted there was no way to recall the action. He presented Congress with innumerable *faits accomplis;* it was his determination to confront the Court in the same way.

TANEY AND LINCOLN DISAGREE

Arbitrary arrest was not the only fundamental issue on which the President and the Chief Justice took opposing stands. On another important issue of the day—the manner in which to build up the military forces of the United States—Lincoln and Taney held widely divergent views, too.

Up to this point in its history, the United States had never adopted a conscription system that was based upon federal law. Its armed forces had always been expanded by voluntary means. Although some states had had experience with conscription during the Revolution, opposition to a conscription system based upon federal authority made itself felt both at the time of the War of 1812 and the Mexican War. When the Lincoln administration proposed a federal conscription law during the Civil War,

[14] Edward Bates to Edwin M. Stanton, January 31, 1863, Stanton MSS.
[15] Editorial, New York *Times*, March 1, 1863, p. 4.

a violent controversy resulted. Again the Chief Executive justified his position on the basis of the national emergency. Again the Chief Justice did not let the plea of necessity sway his thinking.

Both the President and the Chief Justice prepared statements justifying themselves. Lincoln's views were expressed in a letter to Governor Horatio Seymour of New York, and Taney's views were expressed in an undelivered opinion holding the draft unconstitutional. The President composed his thoughts during the heat of the controversy over the constitutionality of conscription. The Chief Justice probably devoted himself, while at home ill during the summer or winter of 1863, to the preparation of an opinion concerning conscription. Whether his health would have permitted his attendance in Court if this problem had come before it, of course has to remain uncertain.

In order to win the war the Union had to devise a more suitable means of raising armies than to rely upon troops raised by the states or by volunteering for service in the federal forces. To satisfy a need that was urgent, the Congress enacted on March 3, 1863, a conscription act, the provisions of which were faulty in many respects but were probably the best that could be attained at the time. The law provided for drafting all males, twenty to forty-five, except that certain federal and state officials were exempt, as were the son of a dependent widow, the only son of infirm parents, and the mentally and physically unfit. The original act made no provision for conscientious objectors. A drafted man could pay three hundred dollars in lieu of service, or even hire a substitute, and those provisions gave the conscientious objectors as well as others a way out.

For many reasons—certainly there were flaws in the system that had been adopted—opposition to conscription flared dangerously in parts of the North. The most serious complications were the draft riots in New York City in the summer of 1863. The situation was so serious that Lincoln temporarily suspended the draft in that area, and when it was resumed the quotas were reduced.

President Lincoln stated his position clearly in correspondence with Governor Seymour.[16] He rejected Seymour's appeal that the draft be suspended permanently in New York and emphasized that he could not delay enforcement of the draft while a test of its constitutionality was brought before the Supreme Court. He said that appeal to the Court would consume time that could not be spared. But that argument is hardly convincing. The draft could have been enforced while a case was brought before the Court. Was there a fear in Lincoln's mind that the Taney Court, if given an opportunity, would rule against the constitutionality of conscription?

---

[16] Abraham Lincoln to Horatio Seymour, August 7, 1863, *Works*, VI, 369-70.

Lincoln argued that the enemy lost no time and brooked no argument. He pointed out that if the Union re-experimented with volunteering and also delayed for appeal to the Supreme Court the Southerners would outstrip Northern efforts to put armies in the field. He concluded by stating to Governor Seymour something of his philosophy in dealing with the problems presented to the executive by this unprecedented conflict. "My purpose [stated Lincoln] is to be in my action, just and constitutional; and yet practical, in performing the important duty, with which I am charged, of maintaining the unity, and the free principles of our common country."

Over in the Taney residence the Chief Justice, with hours of inactivity enforced upon him by prolonged illness, also did some thinking about the constitutionality of conscription. Taking pen in hand, Taney determined to establish that conscription was merely another example of usurpation by the occupant of the Executive Mansion.

The Chief Justice titled his opinion "Thoughts on the Conscription Law of the U. States—Rough Draft Requiring Revision." The opinion was never used. The Supreme Court did not hand down during the Civil War any decision on conscription, but Taney prepared it to have at least a rough draft ready in case an occasion for its use presented itself.

He maintained that since the federal government possessed delegated powers it remained to be demonstrated whether "the power exercised in passing the Conscription Act . . . has been delegated to the Federal Government." Taney argued that no such delegation of power had been made. He saw an additional flaw in conscription: the federal government, by conscripting state officials, could at will disorganize state governments. Under the law, Taney asserted, the only state officials exempted were governors of states, and he declared, "if they had not been specially exempted, [they] might be forced into the army, and find themselves standing by the side of their generals and Judges as privates in the ranks and commanded and disciplined by officers appointed by a different sovereignty."

He denied that emergency could justify conscription on the part of the federal government since the Constitution defined the power of the national government just as fully in war as in peace. Of the federal courts in wartime, Taney declared, "They can never be called on to execute or enforce unconstitutional laws—or recognize as justifiable assumptions of power which the constitution has not conferred."

In conclusion he wrote, "For the reasons above stated, I am of opinion that this Act of Congress is unconstitutional and void,—and confers no lawful authority on the persons appointed to execute it." [17] That these

---

[17] Roger B. Taney, "Thoughts on the Conscription Law of the U. States,—Rough Draft Requiring Revision," copied from the unpublished manuscript in his own handwriting by M. L. York for George Bancroft, May 7, 1886, Taney MSS., N.Y. Pub. Lib.

words did not ring in the ears of Abraham Lincoln resulted from the fact that this opinion of the Chief Justice was of no practical consequence unless it was handed down as the majority opinion of the Supreme Court. And Lincoln had no intention of assisting the Court in having an opportunity to rule on the problem of conscription.

While the draft crisis raged in New York City the New York *Tribune* and the New York *World* engaged in a verbal war over the legality of conscription and the proper method for the Lincoln administration to adopt to build up the armed forces. The *Tribune* argued that conscription was legal under the necessary and proper clause of the Constitution and stated, "All this talk about the necessity of the General Government calling on the States for their quota is the mere clap trap of the politicians." [18] With equal venom the *World* struck back, "The *Tribune's* plea of necessity is a singing of the old song. It is the stereotyped Republican excuse for violations of the Constitution. The unconstitutional emancipation of slaves was *necessary* as a war measure. The paper legal tender was *necessary* to the support of the government. The conscription is necessary to fill up our armies." [19] The *World* declared that it hoped, furthermore, that if the Supreme Court had an opportunity to rule on conscription, the Lincoln administration would abide by the decision rather than ignore judicial process as it did in other instances. [20]

TANEY BROODS

Roger B. Taney, who never concluded that it was the role of the judiciary to be quiescent during the Civil War, brooded over what he considered to be the effrontery of the administration in another instance and gave vent to his feelings. This time the controversy concerned application of a wartime income tax to the salaries of the judges of the federal courts.

The income tax, provided by an act of August 5, 1861, levied three per cent on incomes over eight hundred dollars yearly. The Chief Justice made it clear that he considered the act unconstitutional in so far as it applied to the judicial officers of the United States. He protested to Secretary of the Treasury Chase in a letter of February 16, 1863, and ordered that the protest, since it was ignored by the Secretary, be entered in the minutes of the Supreme Court for March 10, 1863.

In this controversy the Chief Justice did not restrain his criticism of the administration and did not hesitate to lecture Chase for dereliction of duty. Taney informed Chase that the Treasury had seen fit to deduct three per cent from the salaries of the Justices. He declared that it was

---

[18] Editorial, New York *Tribune*, July 22, 1863, p. 4.

[19] Editorial, New York *World*, July 23, 1863, p. 4.

[20] *Ibid.*, August 1, 1863, p. 4.

his duty as Chief Justice to protest since the Constitution itself states that the compensation of judges "shall not be diminished during their continuance in office." He maintained that if Congress could diminish the salaries of federal judges by a tax of three per cent, the salaries could "in the same way be reduced from time to time at the pleasure of the legislature."

He reminded Chase that the judiciary, as one of the three branches of the federal government, is of such a character that it must be maintained completely independent of the other branches. It was with this in view that the framers of the Constitution provided that Congress could not reduce the salary of a federal judge during his tenure.

With unassailable argument Taney declared, "Language could not be more plain than that used in the Constitution. It is, moreover, one of its most important and essential provisions." The safeguards of the citizen, continued the Chief Justice, are of little value in times of excitement unless all means to influence the judiciary are withstood. He added that if the question could have been decided in a judicial proceeding, he would not have troubled Chase with a letter, "But all of the judges of the courts of the United States have an interest in the question, and could not therefore with propriety undertake to hear and decide it."

Taney feared that taxing the salaries of judges might be looked upon as a precedent establishing the right of Congress at will to reduce their salaries. Since the policy removed the judiciary from its rightful independent position, Taney declared that he must not "by any act or word of mine leave it to be supposed that I acquiesce. . . ." It was in this spirit that he presented Chase "this respectful but firm and decided remonstrance," requesting him to place the letter in the public files of the treasury department "as the evidence that I have done everything in my power to preserve and maintain the judicial department in the position and rank in the government which the Constitution has assigned to it." [21]

Secretary Chase sent Taney's letter to Attorney General Bates and Bates marked it, "No reply." Consequently, after delay of almost a month, the Chief Justice ordered the letter copied into the minutes of the Supreme Court so that his protest would be a matter of public record.[22]

Taney was not alone in considering the income tax on Justice's salaries to be a flagrant violation of the Constitution. With biting sarcasm Justice Grier wrote Chase, "If it should be decided in favor of the constitution the sum now theretofore retained might be added to the next quarter. My drafts on Phila[delphia] for family expenses are about *to be protested*

[21] Roger B. Taney to Salmon P. Chase, February 16, 1863, written into the Minutes of the United States Supreme Court for March 10, 1863, at the direction of Chief Justice Taney. The letter was printed in 39 L. Ed., 1156-57 as an appendix to the income tax cases heard by the Supreme Court in the October Term, 1894.

[22] Swisher, *Roger B. Taney*, p. 569.

—Why may I not have the 97 per cent now 'pendanti lite,' as to the balance?" [23] But the administration refused to heed the two Justices. Their position, however, was vindicated after the war when Secretary of the Treasury George S. Boutwell ruled in 1872 that taxing salaries of Supreme Court Justices was unconstitutional.

The conflict over the income tax demonstrated again the tension that characterized relations between the administration and the Taney Court. Although Lincoln did not wish to destroy the Court, he was not adverse to denying it little courtesies and recognitions, the granting of which would have done much to improve relations with it.

The Court's situation remained precarious. The Chief Justice had no intention of permitting its normal role to be disturbed, but the administration, as Attorney General Bates revealed to Stanton, intended to avoid the Court unless there was no alternative but to face it. Chance dictated that Taney would be confronted by Lincoln when old age and illness interfered with service on the bench. And Taney never met a more forceful adversary. Nonetheless, the Chief Justice persisted to the end in endeavoring to retain for the Court the role prescribed for it under the constitutional system of the United States.

---

[23] Robert C. Grier to Salmon P. Chase, January 30, 1863, Chase MSS., Library of Congress.

CHAPTER ELEVEN

Threats and Threats Again

FURIOUS DISSATISFACTIONS

The Supreme Court was now to be subjected to the second concerted effort during the Civil War to destroy or modify it. It began to appear probable that cases involving arbitrary arrest, legal tender, and the Emancipation Proclamation would be appealed, and those who were afraid of the Court hoped to alter it before interference with the administration resulted. The controversy over arbitrary arrest raged furiously; Congress even entered it to strengthen the President's position. Fears that the Court might interfere with the Legal Tender Act and the Emancipation Proclamation precipitated the new attack, which came in the form of proposals to pack the Court again or force aged Democratic Justices off the bench through retirement.

Following the President's order of September 24, 1862, suspending the writ of habeas corpus, the protest was so loud that Congress determined upon clarification. And so it enacted into law, March 3, 1863, special power for the President to suspend the privilege of habeas corpus anywhere in the United States.[1] The act was passed to relieve the President of embarrassment and to assert congressional authority as well.

Even this legislation did not provide the solution. It left too many questions unanswered. Had Lincoln acted legally prior to its enactment? Had Lincoln grasped power arbitrarily? Had Congress needlessly granted the President a power he had exercised almost from the time that the rebellion began? Concerning all of these questions, uncertainties yet remained.

The controversy continued because the administration proceeded essentially as it had before the law was enacted. Prior to the act Lincoln had ordered persons held at his own pleasure, and he continued to do so. Under the new law, however, an exact procedure was dictated. Federal judges were to be provided by the Secretary of War or the Secretary of State with lists of political prisoners and future custody depended upon indictment by a grand jury. If names were not listed with a federal judge, he was free to discharge any prisoner on a writ of habeas corpus, providing the prisoner took an oath of allegiance to the United States. Under

---

[1] 12 Stat. 755-58.

the act power was placed in judicial hands rather than in the hands of the President.

Lincoln did not comply with the requirements of the act and did not alter his procedure to conform with it. He would not bow to the congressional dictum that suspension of the writ was solely a congressional power. That legislative action on the writ of habeas corpus served to increase the difficulties is indicated by an entry in the diary of Edward Bates in September, 1863. He recorded that the cabinet met on September 14 to canvass the problem of the increase of habeas corpus writs and that "The Pres[iden]t was great[ly] moved—more angry than I ever saw him—"

The cabinet discussed what policy should be adopted to enforce suspension of the writ under the authority of the Congress and the President. Attorney General Bates argued that no judge had the right to interfere with the President's power to withhold habeas corpus, and he suggested that the administration act on the defensive, that it "inform the judge who issued the writ, of the cause of imprisonment, refuse to deliver the body, and retain possession by force, if need be." [2]

The day following this cabinet meeting a new proclamation was issued by the President—a proclamation suspending the writ under the authority of the newly passed statute of March 3, 1863.[3] Although this proclamation was a recapitulation, it was in accordance with congressional authorization. The administration had concluded that opposition might be brought to an end if the President issued a proclamation citing his authority.

The view that congressional procedure, as dictated by law, would be less arbitrary than the President's fiat was not shared by the New York *World*. It commented in an editorial titled "The Complete Overthrow of Public Liberties," that enactment of the law suspending the privilege of habeas corpus was "the darkest hour since the outbreak of the rebellion." It charged that Congress had completed the process of "laying the country prostrate and helpless at the feet of one man." In a spirit of foreboding it concluded, "The ninety days during which Congress has now been in session are the last ninety days of American freedom." [4]

The New York *Times* had already warned that arbitrary arrest should be limited to "extreme and very peculiar cases." Recognizing that the Congress was acquiescing in the administration's policy, it called upon Lincoln to use his powers sparingly and judiciously "in States like our own, almost universally loyal. . . ." [5]

Objections to arbitrary arrest continued to be presented to administra-

[2] Bates, *Diary*, pp. 306-07 (September 14, 1863).

[3] *Works*, VI, 451-52 (September 15, 1863).

[4] Editorial, New York *World*, March 3, 1863, p. 4.

[5] Editorial, New York *Times*, November 20, 1862, p. 4.

tion leaders both before and after Congress took a hand in the matter. It was not only the general public that was aroused. Opposition to summary action by the military provoked leaders within the administration itself. And some of these leaders, despite all the loyalty that they could muster toward the Lincoln administration, at times were provoked to express their opposition to the denial of "public liberties."

Letters of protest from the general public naturally made their way to those officials concerned with military arrest. On July 17, 1862, Congress created the office of Judge Advocate General for the purpose of providing supervision of all proceedings of courts-martial and military commission,[6] and shortly thereafter Lincoln appointed Joseph Holt of Kentucky to fill the post. Holt had served Buchanan as Postmaster General and later as Secretary of War. When the conflict began he played an important role in winning Kentucky to the cause of the Union.

Holt was told, "I do very much fear that the matter of military arrests are managed very injudiciously.—too many . . . people are taken up: too many agents are entrusted with such authority—and some of them wholly unfit—" [7] Another correspondent of Joseph Holt expressed himself more forcefully, writing that Lincoln "may drive the ship of state on shoals of *proclamations*, or snaps of 'Habeas Corpus.' In short he may render the vessel (the constitution) a wreck during his brief pilotage;— but with very good intentions!" [8]

On the other hand a letter written to Governor James F. Robinson of Kentucky supported the arrests, justifying them because it was felt that the courts moved too slowly to cope with those who sought to undermine the Union. Robinson was told, "It must be made respectable and a good thing to be loyal, and disgraceful and dangerous to be disloyal. It is the rebels that must fear, and not the loyal." [9] That letter, with its sound philosophy, was referred by Governor Robinson to Judge Advocate General Holt in the hope that it would be of value to the administration.

The divergent points of view that were expressed are demonstrated, too, by additional letters. "May I ask you in the name of *humanity*, [read one letter that finally was turned over to Holt] to use your influence to have me a hearing. Two months have Elapsed—and no notice of what I am accused or of my accusers." [10] But to balance that letter there was another which approved of the seizure of "sundry notorious rebel Southern sympathizers" in St. Louis and informed Holt

[6] 12 Stat. 598.

[7] J. B. Temple to Joseph Holt, July 28, 1862, Holt MSS.

[8] Hugh Campbell to Joseph Holt, November 15, 1862, *ibid.*

[9] G. Granger to James F. Robinson, November 22, 1862, *ibid.*

[10] Samuel Ford to William P. Wood, May 1, 1863, *ibid.*

that the arrests received "the commendation and decided aproval [*sic*] of every truly loyal man in this part of our country." [11]

On one occasion Judge Advocate General Holt, himself, intervened with Stanton to obtain the release of witnesses who were being held for what seemed an excessive length of time. The persons were witnesses who were held along with Colonel Thomas Zarvona who was charged with piracy. They had been taken to Fort McHenry in July, 1861, but the trial was long delayed by the illness of Chief Justice Taney. Holt asked that they be released on their own recognizance to appear when Zarvona's trial took place. "The imprisonment [Holt wrote Stanton] of a witness for so long a period of time and under such circumstances is without a precedent and should not be long permitted." Holt added that he believed it would be "an act of simple justice" to provide the witnesses with reasonable compensation "for the time which they have lost by the confinement to which they have been subjected." [12]

In view of the continuous furor aroused by arbitrary arrest Lincoln at last felt obliged to enunciate his views again. He chose to make the occasion of his statement the reply to a letter from Erastus Corning, prominent businessman and politician of New York, and other Democrats who were meeting in Albany. The President asserted that although resolutions adopted at Albany stated that he was responsible for unconstitutional policies, the policies that had been adopted were based upon powers that were inherent in the Constitution. Lincoln declared that at the beginning of the war Southern sympathizers pervaded many departments of the government. All of these sympathizers, the President pointed out, were loud in their devotion to "Liberty of speech," "Liberty of the press," and "*Habeas Corpus*." It was their purpose, he informed Corning, to agitate so that normal rights and privileges under the Constitution would not be denied, the result being that they could "keep on foot amongst us a most efficient corps of spies, informers, supplyers and aiders and abettors of their cause in a thousand ways." Lincoln charged that they sought to use the rights and privileges of the Constitution in order to undermine the authority of the Federal Union.

The President maintained that it was because energetic action was not taken early enough that the cause of the Union became so desperate. He pointed out that such men as General Robert E. Lee, General Joseph E. Johnston, General Simon B. Buckner, and Commodore Franklin Buchanan "were all within the power of the government since the rebellion began, and were nearly as well known to be traitors then as now. Unquestionably if we had seized and held them, the insurgent cause would be much weaker. But no one of them had then committed any crime defined in

[11] Wallace Sigerson to Joseph Holt, May 9, 1863, *ibid*.

[12] Joseph Holt to Edwin M. Stanton, March 18, 1863, *Offic. Rec.*, ser. II, vol. II, 409.

the law." The President maintained that if any of them had been arrested, release could have been obtained through habeas corpus if the writ were permitted to operate. "In view of these and similar cases, [Lincoln added] I think the time not unlikely to come when I shall be blamed for having made too few arrests rather than too many."

Lincoln rejected the contention that military arrests could be justified in localities in which there was insurrection but not in areas where there was relative peace. Significantly philosophizing upon the whole issue, the President told Corning, "I concede that the class of arrests complained of, can be constitutional only when, in cases of Rebellion or Invasion, the public Safety may require them; and I insist that in such cases they are constitutional *wherever* the public safety does require them. . . ." [18]

Newspaper reaction to Lincoln's latest justification of arbitrary arrest was largely favorable. The New York *Tribune* commented editorially, "we think the President's vindication of the *right* to arrest Rebel sympathizers in every part of the country is most triumphant. His elucidation of the constitutional sanction of such right, in times like the present, has never been surpassed in clearness and force." [14] The New York *Times* stated that although Lincoln abided by the Constitution, it was clear that he regarded "the public safety" as the supreme law of the land. [15] It was Lincoln's sincerity in the Corning letter that impressed the Washington *National Intelligencer*, which declared that a perusal of the letter would establish for every person a feeling "of the . . . purity of his intentions." [16] But the New York *World*, delaying its comments for a few days, issued another blast of condemnation against Lincoln and the arbitrary methods that he employed. [17]

Only a few weeks later, again employing the technique of answering individuals who addressed resolutions of a public meeting to him, the President penned to Ohio Democrats a justification of his acts. If, as some leaders of the administration feared, the Supreme Court was to hear and decide the question of arbitrary arrest, at least Lincoln would have his views on record, views elaborately drawn and carefully enunciated.

Lincoln wrote Matthew Birchard, prominent Ohio jurist and Democratic leader, and others who sent him resolutions of the Ohio Democratic state convention that their statements were clothed in such phraseology as to make it appear that he sought "arbitrary personal prerogative."

---

[18] The letter of Abraham Lincoln to Erastus Corning, June 12, 1863, is to be found in *Works*, VI, 260-69.

[14] Editorial, New York *Tribune*, June 15, 1863, p. 4.

[15] Editorial, New York *Times*, June 15, 1863, p. 4.

[16] Editorial, Washington *National Intelligencer*, June 16, 1863, p. 3.

[17] Editorial, New York *World*, June 18, 1863, p. 4.

Lincoln declared that when the public safety demands that certain steps
be taken, it is the President as Commander-in-Chief of the armed forces
who has both the power and responsibility to take action. He pointed
out, too, that if a President abuses his power, "he is in . . . [the people's]
hands, to be dealt with by all the modes they have reserved to themselves
in the constitution." [18]

It is not surprising that the controversy over arbitrary arrest lasted
as long as the war raged. Lincoln continued, whenever he deemed it
necessary, to see to it that arbitrary arrests were made when circumstances justified them. Dissatisfaction was so widespread that it could not
fail to result in demands for clarification of arbitrary arrest. Such clarification could come only at the hands of the Supreme Court, and fears were
prevalent among Republicans that the Court might see fit to interfere.
As a consequence, the Supreme Court faced new denunciations and new
threats.

THE COURT AGAIN IN PERIL

With Lincoln believing it necessary repeatedly to justify his position
on arbitrary arrest, it is understandable that his followers began to fear
that the Supreme Court might thwart him. Although the Washington
Morning Chronicle observed that "The Supreme Court is unimpaired in
its functions, and every loyal man in the Union, from the President
downwards, would most cheerfully submit to any decision it might pronounce," [19] demands to pack the Court began to manifest themselves
again. Many who did not consider additional packing desirable suggested
that a retirement plan be provided for aged Justices. There was no
altruism in the proposal: retirement of Supreme Court Justices would
give opportunity to add friends of Lincoln to the Court. Although renewed plans to pack the Court and plans to provide a retirement system
were considered, the Radicals were not to succeed in their efforts.

Many fears were hovering over the administration in 1863 in relation
to the Supreme Court in addition to the question of arbitrary arrest.
What would the Court conclude if it were given opportunity to review
the Emancipation Proclamation? Would the Court sustain the administration in the issuance of the legal tender notes? It was questions such as
these that provoked renewed demands to assault the Court.

A controversy was raging in the press over the constitutionality of
emancipation by presidential decree. The New York *World* charged that
Lincoln "snubbed" and "insulted" the judiciary and demanded to know
whether the Republican party "contemplated the possibility of a review

---

[18] The letter of Abraham Lincoln to Matthew Birchard, June 29, 1863, is to be
found in *Works*, VI, 300-306.

[19] Editorial, Washington *Morning Chronicle*, October 5, 1863, p. 2.

of Mr. Lincoln's proceedings by the Supreme Court." It lamented that it felt that only when peace was restored would the Court "be reinstated in its august prerogative of annulling the unconstitutional acts of other departments of the government."[20]

The New York *Times* expressed the view that constitutionally the President would have been wiser to bring emancipation about through a military order rather than a proclamation. It predicted challenge of the proclamation in the courts and in regard to emancipation stated, "it is a matter of utmost importance to the President, to the slaves, and to the country, that it should come in a form to be sustained. It must be a legal and a constitutional act, in form as well as in substance." [21]

Lincoln, himself, could find no justification for emancipation except military necessity. In his annual message of December 8, 1863, he stated that as a civil act the government of the United States "had no lawful power to effect emancipation in any State." He added that for a long time he had hoped that the insurrection could be put down without the need of "resorting to it as a military measure." But when the necessity presented itself Lincoln recognized that "the crisis of the contest" was at hand and proclaimed emancipation in insurrectionary areas.[22]

The ever-watchful New York *World* warned editorially on January 5, 1864, that a move to pack the Supreme Court had arrived. The Court had begun a term in which war-related problems would loom large. The *World* admonished Democrats in the Congress "to keep a sleepless eye on the plot that is hatching to destroy the independence of the Supreme Court, by the creation of new abolition judges to outvote the present members of the court and overthrow long-settled constructions of the Constitution which are as old as the government itself." [23]

The full extent of the hatred felt toward Chief Justice Taney and the fear that the Court might upset policies of the administration were expressed by the Washington *National Intelligencer* which quoted Wendell Phillips, a leading abolitionist from Massachusetts, who had declared in a speech in New York City in December, 1863,

The [emancipation] proclamation of 1863 was to be filtered through the secessionist heart of a man whose body was in Baltimore and whose soul was in Richmond. It was to pass the ordeal of the bench of Judges who made the Dred Scott decision, and announced that a negro has no rights that a white man is bound to respect. It was to pass the ordeal of a bench of Judges the majority of whom came out of the wickedness of Buchanan and Polk and Franklin Pierce—the only two of whom who refused to concur in the Dred

---

[20] Editorial, New York *World*, November 21, 1862, p. 4.

[21] Editorial, New York *Times*, January 3, 1863, p. 4.

[22] Lincoln's annual message of December 8, 1863, is to be found in *Works*, VIII, 36-53.

[23] Editorial, New York *World*, January 5, 1864, p. 4.

Scott decision being no longer in the Court. God help the negro who depended upon Roger B. Taney for his liberty. The Supreme Court was the point where our democratic system touchest nearest to despotism.[24]

It was the New York *Tribune* that piously devoted itself to the renewed effort to pack the Supreme Court. It justified its attitude by declaring that there was a need for more Justices so that the work of the Court could be transacted more efficiently. It is true that the Justices were overworked, but it is likewise true that a Court of ten was sufficient in number. By one step—a simple one at that—Congress could have eased the burdens of the Justices. Circuit duties for the Justices should have been ended. But Republicans who were so concerned about the Court neither contemplated nor suggested that.

Instead, the *Tribune*, with obvious hypocrisy, proposed to reorganize the circuits and increase the number of Justices. In its latest plan to pack the Court it suggested the creation of a new southern circuit (New Orleans and the surrounding area) as well as two new circuits for the Northeast. This would result in a Supreme Court of thirteen. The *Tribune* justified its proposal on the basis of increased population. Indeed, it made an effort to relate the size of the Court to the size of the population of the land. "If this Court needed eight judges a quarter of a century ago [explained the *Tribune*], it certainly needs thirteen now; for, its ordinary business has more than doubled during that period, while the present war has already added largely to its labors." And the *Tribune* suggested additional justification. It pointed out that ultimately problems growing out of the war would be brought before the Court and that even a Court of thirteen would find itself overburdened.[25]

A letter written at this time to Secretary of the Treasury Chase by Lorenzo Sherwood indicates that the proposal to increase the size of the Court was being considered in very high quarters. Sherwood wrote to remind Chase of their discussion of the need for "one or more additional circuit courts." And Chase was informed, "Since the matter was mentioned between us I find that it had already been discussed to some extent by others. I believe that when this subject is properly reflected on by our friends in Congress there will be little hesitation as to the adoption of the measure." [26]

The New York *World* set out to combat the proposal to increase the Court. It argued that the Court already was larger than it would have been if purely judicial considerations had determined its size, pointing

---

[24] Editorial, Washington *National Intelligencer*, December 29, 1863, p. 3.

[25] Editorial, New York *Tribune*, December 31, 1863, p. 4.

[26] Lorenzo Sherwood to Salmon P. Chase, January 6, 1864, Chase MSS., Library of Congress.

out that a large Court would become deliberative rather than judicial. It stated that to increase the Court or introduce a retirement plan would be comparable to swamping the British House of Lords. It criticized those who endeavored to tamper with the Court and concluded: "The Constitution is practically what the Supreme Court construes it to be. Make a majority of the judges the creatures of the President, and he will dictate its decisions." [27]

The renewed attack took its most ominous form when the Court actually turned its attention to cases questioning the legality of legal tender and the constitutionality of arbitrary arrest. Again it was John P. Hale who spearheaded the assault, declaring to the Senate: "I will take this occasion to say that in my humble judgment if there was a single, palpable, obvious duty that the Republican party owed to themselves, owed to the country, owed to humanity, owed to God when they came into power, it was to drive a plowshare from turret to foundation stone of the Supreme Court of the United States. They should have done it."

Hale deplored the fact that the Lincoln administration had seen fit to "build up and patch up" the Supreme Court by appointments to fill vacancies. He stated again his opinion that the Taney Court should have been dissolved. Hale declared that the Republicans had "failed in that most obvious duty" and explained that as a protest against this piecemeal policy, "I voted when I was in the Senate (for I believe one of them was passed upon when I was not present) against the confirmation of every one of Lincoln's appointees. . . ."

Hale proceeded to denounce the Court even though there were four appointees of Lincoln upon it, and he even criticized the decision of the Court in the *Prize Cases*, declaring, "one of the first acts of these new judges that you were in such a hurry to place on the bench of the Supreme Court was to decide that we were not at war." He concluded, "when we had an opportunity to throw off this old man of the sea [the Supreme Court] after it had fastened . . . upon the country some of the most odious and damnable doctrines that disgrace our history, we failed to improve it, and we have now got to hug it just as long as we exist; and God only knows how long that will be. I hope for some time to come." [28]

It remained for the New York *World*, which had warned of the impending attack, to answer Senator Hale. And it did so with skill. After finding Hale very ungrateful to a Court that sustained his views, the *World* declared, "Now, let us whisper a word to Senator Hale. The

[27] Editorial, New York *World*, January 4, 1864, p. 4.

[28] Hale's renewed attack upon the Supreme Court is to be found in the *Cong. Globe*, 38th Cong., 1st sess., p. 753.

readiest and cheapest engine of despotism in the world is a packed Court.
. . . The whole temper of your party is wound up to asserting that packing a court is honest." [29]

With the Court over which he presided again subject to denunciation, the aged Chief Justice found his animosity toward the administration renewed. Despite his infirmities and discomforts, the Chief Justice brooded over the turn of events and expressed his feelings to his associates. He wrote an intimate friend both of his illness and his fears for the Court. Reflecting upon his infirmities, Taney said, "my walking days are over; and I feel that I am sick enough for a hospital. . . ." As to his view of the political developments of the day, Taney had much to say. Expressing hope that he would "linger along to the next term of the Supreme Court," Taney wrote, "Very different, however, that Court will now be. . . . Nor do I see any ground for hope that it will ever again be restored to the authority and rank which the Constitution intended to confer upon it." He concluded, "We can pray for better times, and submit with resignation to the chastisements which it may please God to inflict upon us." [30]

BAIT TO THE AGED

Although the renewed efforts by Hale and the Radicals to destroy or pack the Court did not succeed, an indirect effort to secure new Justices was made by proposals to set up a retirement plan for the Court. Retirement appeared to many as the most feasible means of getting rid of aged Democratic Justices.

In various quarters the most fascinating subject upon which to speculate during the war was the possible decease of certain superannuated members of the Court. The anticipation with which departures were awaited reveals the malice that rested in the hearts of the enemies of the Court. Those who were vengeful grasped every bit of news about the illnesses of Democratic Justices with undisguised relish.

On one occasion an article that appeared in the press circulated a statement declaring that Chief Justice Taney was ninety-four years old. Taney acknowledged receipt of a copy of the article by writing a friend, "I thank you for your note which I received today enclosing an editorial . . . from the New York Daily News." Taney proceeded to state that if he really were ninety-four years old, he feared "the public could hardly be persuaded that I was any longer fit for the headship of the Court—" [31] Even Chief Justice Taney realized that there was an age beyond which he could no longer continue to serve.

[29] Editorial, New York *World*, March 11, 1864, p. 6.

[30] Roger B. Taney to D. M. Perine, August 6, 1863, quoted in Samuel Tyler, *Memoir of Roger Brooke Taney*, p. 454.

[31] Roger B. Taney to G. S. S. Davis, July 11, 1863, Davis MSS., N.Y. Hist. Soc.

In view of the hatreds engendered by some of the pre-Lincoln members of the Court, it is interesting to examine the ages of the Justices at the time that Lincoln became President and the ages of the appointees he named. Before Lincoln added men of comparative youth to the Court, it is true that the Court consisted of old men.

The average age of the Justices toward the end of the Buchanan administration was sixty-nine. Shortly after the resignation of Justice Campbell, the average age of the members had advanced to seventy-one. Once Lincoln began to make appointments the average age dropped, and, in fact, dropped each year of Lincoln's presidency thereafter. In 1862 the average age was sixty-five; in 1863, sixty-four; in 1864, sixty-two. Three of Lincoln's appointees were under fifty at the time of their appointment (Miller, 46; Davis, 47; Field, 47), and the other two were under sixty (Chase, 56; Swayne, 58). (The appointment of Chase as Chief Justice is dealt with in Chapter 16.) The average age of Lincoln's appointees at the time of their appointment was fifty-one.

There is irony in criticism of the sexagenarians, septuagenarians, and the octogenarian Lincoln found on the Court when he became President. Republicans could call them worn out and disapprove of them. But it was long service that had aged a Taney who came to the Court as a man of fifty-nine, a Wayne who came as a man of forty-five, a Catron who came as a man of fifty-one, a Grier who came as a man of fifty-two, and a Nelson who came as a man of fifty-three.

In 1863 Taney was in the eighties, Catron, Wayne, and Nelson were in the seventies, Grier was sixty-nine, and Clifford was sixty. Several of them, furthermore, suffered from recurring illness. It is not surprising, therefore, that since so many feared what the Court would rule in war-related cases pending before it, a move was made in the Congress in December, 1863, to offer retirement to Justices who were deemed past an age suitable for service. Resignation, of course, provided an answer, but the Justices would not resign. They were largely unable to relinquish the salary that was provided, and none intended—barring death—to permit Lincoln and the Republicans to name his successor.

In part to relieve the Justices of financial disability in resigning and in part to lure Democratic Justices from the Court, James Harlan of Iowa introduced a retirement plan into the Senate.[32] The terms of the plan were simple: a Justice who had attained the age of seventy and who had served up to fifteen years was to be allotted a pension of $4,000 annually upon retirement; fifteen to twenty years of service qualified a Justice for $4,500 annual pension; twenty to twenty-five years, $5,000; twenty-five to thirty years, $5,500; over thirty years, full salary. During the war years the annual salary of a Justice was $6,000; the salary of the Chief Justice

---

[32] *Cong. Globe*, 38th Cong., 1st sess., p. 42.

was $6,500. Any Justice could take advantage of retirement by asking the President to place him on the retirement list. The resulting vacancy was to be filled by the President in the usual manner.

Attorney General Bates recorded in his diary: "The principle is right, but the details all wrong. 70 years is no proper time; for a Judge may be much younger than that, yet, mentally or physically incapable of the duties, and still too poor to give up his salary." Bates preferred outright resignation with pension for "worn out Judges." [33]

The retirement plan was not given serious consideration by the Senate. On January 25, 1864, Senator Lafayette S. Foster of the committee on the judiciary reported the bill adversely. Without any explanation he stated that the bill should not pass.[34] Although Senator Henry B. Anthony of Rhode Island attempted to give the bill new life a few months later, the effort to provide a retirement system for the Justices failed.[35]

If it had been demonstrated that it was necessary for the war effort, such beneficient legislation as a retirement plan could have been expected. Otherwise, the Court would continue to be menaced and threatened but would not be provided with a system of retirement. As a matter of fact, no retirement plan was provided for Supreme Court Justices until additional controversy had developed over the Court in Reconstruction days and in the days of Franklin D. Roosevelt. And in both instances motives were dictated not by magnanimity but by the desire to lure from the Court Justices whose attitudes were feared or whose decisions were opposed.

Lincoln and the Congress decided against packing the Court or attempting to lure Democrats off the bench. But the Court was threatened as it was just prior to its ruling in the *Prize Cases.* The Court demonstrated in these days, however, that it was safely dominated by Unionist sentiments as indicated by the cautious decisions it handed down in the legal tender case on December 21, 1863, and the Vallandigham case on February 15, 1864, cases which are now to be considered.

---

[33] Bates, *Diary*, p. 322 (December 19, 1863).

[34] *Cong. Globe*, 38th Cong., 1st sess., p. 319.

[35] *Ibid.*, p. 1416.

CHAPTER TWELVE

Other Battles in Ermine

SIDE-STEPPING LEGAL TENDER

While the Supreme Court was being subjected to the renewed threats of the Radicals, it was hearing arguments in two cases of primary importance. In these cases the administration found its policies sustained, the Court upholding decisions of lower federal courts by announcing that it lacked jurisdiction. In both instances the strong possibility existed that if the Court had seen fit to review the decisions, the administration would have suffered defeat. But self-denial had become a means for the friends of Lincoln on the Court to prevent interference with the administration. And the Radicals in the Congress were standing in the distance to do the Court harm if the administration were not sustained.

One of the subjects upon which the Court was invited to rule during the December Term, 1863, involved the issuance of unsecured paper money. As a matter of public necessity the Lincoln administration reluctantly decided to resort to such money in order to bolster Union finances. After it was made clear that Secretary of the Treasury Chase thought that it was necessary, Congress enacted the Legal Tender Act on February 25, 1862. It authorized the Treasury to issue $150,000,000 of non-interest-bearing notes which were declared legal tender for all debts of a public or private nature (with the exception of duties on imports and interest on the public debt). Ultimately some $432,000,000 in greenbacks, as these notes were commonly called, were issued.

While the decision to issue the greenbacks was still pending, the New York *World* stated: "We hold that the Constitution does not contain a single word which affirmatively gives even a shadow of authority to the government to force its paper obligations as 'money' upon the people." It predicted that the Supreme Court would still be able to "throw its protecting mantle over that vast field of private rights" even if Congress "in the madness of the hour" saw fit to approve the pending bill.[1]

Despite opposition, necessity prevailed as it always did during the Lincoln administration. The only hope of the opponents of the act was that the Supreme Court might have an opportunity to declare it unconstitutional. When challenge was made in the courts of New York, the

---

[1] Editorial, New York *World*, January 27, 1862, p. 4.

World predicted, "Whatever our . . . courts may do, there is no question but that the Supreme Court of the United States, when the matter comes before them, must decide the act of Congress void because of its constitutionality." [2]

The validity of the Legal Tender Act was involved in a case known as *James J. Roosevelt v. Lewis H. Meyer* which arose in the New York courts. In a ruling on June 3, 1863, the supreme court of New York denied Congress the right to issue paper money without adequate security to support it. The New York *Tribune* announced at once that appeal would be made to the highest court of the state, the court of errors and appeals, "there to be heard and decided by loyal, impartial, and incorruptible judges, and of its ultimate rightful disposition there is no reason to entertain a single fear." [3] The New York *World* maintained, however, that the question of legal tender would have to be decided ultimately by the United States Supreme Court because legal tender clearly "[is] repugnant to the Constitution." [4]

On September 29, 1863, the New York court of errors and appeals handed down a ruling on legal tender in the case of *The Metropolitan Bank v. H. H. Van Dyck*. The appeal court, which ruled that Congress had the power to enact legal tender, thus reversed the decision of the supreme court of New York in the case involving Roosevelt and Meyer.[5] The *Tribune*, sighing with relief, stated, "the Law is sustained, and all is well," [6] but the *World* again challenged the Republicans to take the problem of legal tender to the United States Supreme Court for final adjudication.[7]

Appeal to the Supreme Court was made in the case of Roosevelt and Meyer. Arguments took place before it on December 18, 1863. The decision was handed down on December 21. Involved in the case was the question whether Roosevelt was obliged to accept legal tender notes in payment of $8,171 which Meyer owed him. Roosevelt refused to accept anything except gold and sought a writ of error under section twenty-five of the Judiciary Act of 1789.

R. W. Roelker, the attorney acting in behalf of Meyer, moved that the request be denied on the ground that the Supreme Court had no jurisdiction because the highest court of a state had decided in favor of an act of Congress. "In order to give jurisdiction to this court, [Roelker argued] it must appear by the record that one of the questions stated in the 25th section of the Act of 1789 did arise in the court below, and that

---

[2] *Ibid.*, November 20, 1862, p. 4.
[3] Editorial, New York *Tribune*, June 4, 1863, p. 4.
[4] Editorial, New York *World*, June 8, 1863, p. 4.
[5] New York *Times*, September 30, 1863, p. 4.
[6] Editorial, New York *Tribune*, September 30, 1863, p. 4.
[7] Editorial, New York *World*, October 23, 1863, p. 4.

a decision was actually made thereon by the same court in the manner required by the section." [8] Roelker declared that only the validity of the Legal Tender Act was questioned in this case.

Under the Judiciary Act of 1789 appeal from the highest court of a state to the Supreme Court of the United States was dependent upon the following considerations: 1. Validity of a statute of the United States must be drawn into question. 2. The appeal must be drawn on the ground that the statute is repugnant to the Constitution, laws, or treaties of the United States. 3. The decision of the state court must be against the validity of the federal statute.[9]

Scharff and Henry, the legal counsel of Roosevelt, argued that under the act of 1789 Roosevelt was entitled to an appeal to the Supreme Court because "there was drawn in question, in the court below, the true construction of certain clauses of the Constitution." They added that Roosevelt had the privilege of appeal because he was being denied rights guaranteed by the Constitution.[10]

The decision of the Court embodied fully the argument presented by Roelker. An examination of the Records and Briefs of the United States Supreme Court reveals that the opinion of the Court, handed down by Justice Wayne, not only followed Roelker's reasoning, it even took over some of the language in which Roelker phrased his argument.

Justice Wayne announced that the Justices concluded that inasmuch as the validity of the Legal Tender Act was questioned "and the judgment of the Court of Error and Appeals . . . was in favor of it, and of the right set up by the defendant, this court had no jurisdiction to reverse the judgment; that the dismissal of the case was accordingly to be directed."[11]

It is to be noted that Chief Justice Taney was absent and did not participate in this case. But the rest of the Court did participate, and even if Justice Nelson dissented, the decision was almost unanimous.[12] The Court chose to ignore Roosevelt's appeal that his constitutional rights were violated. To examine these constitutional rights might have led the Court to a decision adverse to the administration. But the majority of the Court did not desire to interfere with a measure devised by the administration to aid the war effort. Yet the Court did not choose to state that legal tender was valid. It interpreted the Judiciary Act of 1789 narrowly and gracefully side-stepped the broad issues involved.

---

[8] 17 L. Ed. 501.

[9] 1 Stat. 85-86.

[10] 17 L. Ed. 502.

[11] 68 U.S. 517.

[12] According to 68 U.S. 517, Justice Nelson dissented but filed no opinion; the report of the case in 17 L. Ed. 502 also states that Nelson dissented. The minutes of the United States Supreme Court for December 21, 1863, however, make no reference to a dissenting opinion in the case of *Roosevelt v. Meyer*.

It cannot be said that the Court did not dare to return a decision adverse to the administration. The unanimity of the decision reveals that the Court preferred to deny itself jurisdiction rather than to consider a problem that might lead to a blow against the administration. This was a negative approach to problems growing out of the war, and it was one that the Court chose to follow on other occasions.

The Washington *Morning Chronicle* posed the problem of the Court and the administration accurately when it asked: "can it be possible that this great Republic, approaching the close of a great civil conflict, with every prospect of terminating it successfully by the combined efforts of her gallant army and navy, should be denied by any tribunal to possess a power belonging to any other country, and *absolutely necessary for our very existence among the family of nations?*" [13]

Chief Justice Taney, who was confined to his home at the time that the validity of legal tender was being questioned, quite naturally turned his attention to the subject. On this subject Taney brooded as he had over conscription. Although he was too ill to attend Court when the case was heard, nonetheless, he prepared an undelivered opinion that branded legal tender unconstitutional.

Taney titled his undelivered opinion, "On Paper Money." He began his argument with an analysis of federal powers. Citing the fact that the federal government has delegated powers solely, the Chief Justice declared that Congress has no power to provide legal tender *"unless it is granted in express terms—*or is incident to some one of the powers conferred—or is a necessary and proper means of carrying it into execution."

The Chief Justice pointed out that the states themselves are prohibited from making anything other than gold or silver legal tender in payment of debt, and "the power thus denied to the State is not conferred on Congress." He said that there was no need to prohibit Congress from issuing legal tender notes because Congress had only delegated powers and issuing legal tender notes was not among them. Taney declared, "the Statesmen who framed the Constitution were aware of the temptation which all governments are under to issue paper money, rather than to impose taxes." In the Revolutionary days and later, Taney held, the evils of legal tenders issued by the states were amply demonstrated, and the framers of the Constitution found no necessity to make specific prohibition on their issuance "because no power over the contracts or debts of individuals had been conferred on the United States." [14]

Taney's views on the Legal Tender Act demonstrate again the wide, unbridgeable gap between him and Abraham Lincoln. Only illness pre-

---

[13] Editorial, Washington *Morning Chronicle*, February 10, 1865, p. 2.

[14] Roger B. Taney, "On Paper Money," copied from the unpublished manuscript in his own handwriting by M. L. York for George Bancroft, May 3, 1886, Taney MSS., N.Y. Pub. Lib.

vented Taney from expressing these views as his official opinion. But on legal tender as on conscription, the Chief Justice and the administration did not clash openly, although all the ingredients for a controversy were present. If the Chief Justice had not been absent, would he have persuaded other Justices to join him in the view that the greenbacks were unconstitutional?

Fortunately for the administration, no other case involving legal tender made its way to the Court during the war. If the Court had had to rule directly upon the subject the administration rightfully could have feared an adverse decision.[15]

VALLANDIGHAM SETS A TRAP

The December Term, 1863, which had already seen the Court refuse to interfere with legal tender, was to see the attention of the court finally directed to the subject of arbitrary arrest.

The arrest of Clement L. Vallandigham, a prominent Democratic politician from Ohio, aroused public interest more than any other arrest during the war. The bitter controversies that developed elevated it to the level of national significance. The unusual action ultimately taken by the President—banishment of Vallandigham—struck the public fancy and gained the case additional notoriety.

The controversy developed out of an order of Major General Ambrose E. Burnside, commander of the military department of Ohio, who issued a general order on April 13, 1863, stating that he would not tolerate treason in his department.

Former Representative Clement L. Vallandigham, who had served in the United States House of Representatives from 1858 until his defeat in the election of 1862, was arrested at Mount Vernon, Ohio, on May 5, 1863. He was arraigned the next day before a military commission that sat at Cincinnati. The charge was that at a public meeting at Mount Vernon, Vallandigham had declared that the "present war was a wicked, cruel, and unnecessary war, one not waged for the preservation of the Union, but for the purpose of crushing out liberty and to erect a despotism." [16]

---

[15] The Court again faced legal tender a few years after the war. In 1870, with the appointees of Lincoln sorely split, legal tender was ruled unconstitutional by Chief Justice Chase and Justices Nelson, Clifford, and Field. The minority consisted of Miller, Davis, and Swayne. There were at the time only seven members of the Court. Following the appointment of two additional Justices—legislation authorized President Grant to make these appointments—the Court reversed itself in 1871 and upheld legal tender by a vote of five to four. In this reversal the appointees of Lincoln again were split apart. The majority now consisted of Miller, Davis, and Swayne, joined by the two new appointees, William Strong of Pennsylvania and Joseph P. Bradley of New Jersey. Chase, Nelson, Clifford and Field were now in the minority.

[16] 68 U.S. 244.

Vigilant in behalf of civil liberties, the New York *World* stated promptly that it considered the detention of former Representative Vallandigham a flagrant violation of the Constitution. "If Mr. Vallandigham has committed any offense against the laws, there are in the State of Ohio [forcefully argued the *World*] several federal judges in the full, plenary, and unobstructed exercise of their functions, before whom sworn complaints could have been made and a warrant procured for his arrest." [17]

Vallandigham denied that the military commission had any authority over him, and he refused to enter any plea whatsoever. The commission directed that a plea of "not guilty" be entered so that the trial could proceed. Vallandigham was permitted to have the aid of counsel, and he was permitted to call witnesses in his behalf. On that basis the military hearing proceeded.

In Vallandigham's behalf it was argued before the commission that he had been arrested without due process of law; no warrant for his arrest had issued from any judicial officer. Since he was not a member of the armed forces, furthermore, Vallandigham denied that a military commission had jurisdiction over him. He demanded that he be tried on an indictment by a court that had competent jurisdiction.

The Judge Advocate rejected Vallandigham's claims and following presentation of the evidence against him, the commission ruled that he was guilty as charged. The sentence was that imposed was that he was "to be placed in close confinement in some fortress of the United States, to be designated by the commanding officer of this department, there to be kept during the war." [18]

President Lincoln and members of the cabinet anticipated that Vallandigham would attempt to obtain assistance from the federal courts in Ohio. Lincoln, Stanton, Chase, and Seward canvassed the situation carefully and even considered a special suspension of the privilege of the writ, but Lincoln finally informed Stanton, "Since parting with you I have seen the Secretaries of State and the Treasury, and they both think we better not issue the special suspension of the Writ of Habeas Corpus spoken of—" [19]

Concerning the prospect that a writ of habeas corpus might be obtained by Vallandigham, Lincoln proceeded to tell Stanton, "Gov. Chase thinks the case is not before Judge Swaine [*sic*], that it is before Judge Levett [*sic*], that the writ will probably not issue, whichever the application may be before; and that, in no event, will Swaine [*sic*] commit an imprudence—" The President explained why Chase did not anticipate the

---

[17] Editorial, New York *World*, May 6, 1863, p. 4.

[18] 68 U.S. 247.

[19] Abraham Lincoln to Edwin M. Stanton, May 13, 1863, Stanton MSS.

issuance of a writ: "His chief reason . . . is that he has seen in a newspaper that Judge Levett [sic] stated that Judge Swaine [sic] & he refused a similar application last year." Lincoln was not unwilling to await developments in this clash with the fiery former congressman.

Vallandigham moved swiftly to seek the protection of the civil courts. He requested the United States circuit court for the southern district of Ohio, presided over by Judge Humphrey H. Leavitt, to grant him a writ of habeas corpus. Leavitt, in denying the request, cited a decision that he and Justice Swayne had handed down in the October Term, 1862. That decision, concerning the military arrest of Bethuel Rupert, was written by Swayne. The Justice had held that military arrests were justifiable as a military necessity even in areas where martial law did not exist. And he had declared that in case of military necessity, civil courts were without authority to hear applications for a writ of habeas corpus.

In his decision Judge Leavitt maintained that "when the life of the republic is imperiled" every patriot must "concede to the Constitution" the capacity to adapt itself so as to prevent the destruction of the nation. He concluded by saying that it was no time for a member of the federal judiciary to "embarass [sic] or thwart" the Chief Executive.[20]

With that victory attained the Lincoln administration could breathe more easily. But the tempest that had been churned up by the seizure of Vallandigham would not subside. Even the friendly New York *Tribune*, despite the ruling of Judge Leavitt, called upon the administration to release Vallandigham. "We doubt that any good will result from arresting and trying such men as Vallandigham," said the *Tribune*, "and therefore hope the President may see fit to turn him loose." "We reverence Freedom of Discussion—by which we mean Freedom to uphold perverse and evil theories. . . ." the *Tribune* concluded.[21]

Many Republicans considered the seizure of Vallandigham an error. The New York *Commercial Advertiser*, a Republican newspaper, stated, "Mr. Vallandigham is a civilian, and as such, we think, has a legal right to express his opposition to the war itself, as well as the mode of conducting it, without being thereby liable to arrest." The *Advertiser* even put its position more strongly, adding, "His statements may be glaring falsehoods; his logic fallacies; his principles abhorrent, and his motives base; yet all these do not furnish a sufficient reason why he should be prohibited from uttering his views on a great public question." [22]

Such sentiments as these convinced Lincoln of the need to take action in the Vallandigham case to ease the tension. Although Vallandigham

---

[20] 28 Fed. Cas. 922.

[21] Editorial, New York *Tribune*, May 18, 1863, p. 4.

[22] New York *Commercial Advertiser* quoted by the Washington *National Intelligencer*, May 19, 1863, p. 3.

had been sentenced to confinement at Fort Warren for the duration of the war, the President on May 19, acting in his capacity as Commander-in-Chief, commuted the sentence to banishment.

The penalty ordered by the President was carried out on May 25. Vallandigham, accompanied by a military escort, proceeded toward the military lines of the Confederacy in Tennessee. Having been placed beyond the jurisdiction of the United States, Vallandigham declared in substance: "I am a citizen of the United States and loyal to them. I want you to understand that you leave here a prisoner to the Confederate authorities." [23]

Lincoln had chosen banishment for Vallandigham—a most unusual punishment at the hands of the United States— as a way out of the dilemma. His action was tacit admission that the arrest of Vallandigham, if legal, was at least inexpedient. Even banishment of Vallandigham met with considerable criticism. The Washington *National Intelligencer* spoke out forcefully, "If Mr. Vallandigham is guilty, as the President must assume he is, it only remains to say that loyal and law-abiding men have reason to complain equally of the illegal jurisdiction by which he was tried and of the illegal penalty awarded to him at the suggestion of personal caprice, where the law affixes a penalty more commensurate with the offence."[24]

The diary of Gideon Welles reveals the attitudes of leaders of the administration toward the arrest of Vallandigham as well as other arbitrary acts of Major General Burnside. Welles recorded his views frankly: "The arrest of Vallandigham and the order to suppress the circulation of the Chicago *Times* in his military district issued by General Burnside have created much feeling. It should not be otherwise. The proceedings were arbitrary and injudicious." He stated that although the acts were Burnside's, unless the administration disavowed them it had to bear the responsibility for them. "The President—and I think every member of the cabinet—[Welles continued] regrets what has been done. . . ."

Nevertheless, Welles recognized that Vallandigham and others like him sought for themselves all the benefits of the American constitutional system at the same time that they were working in behalf of its destruction. "Without the courage and manliness to go over to the public enemy, [Welles wrote] to whom they give, so far as they dare, aid and comfort, they remain here to promote discontent and disaffection." Welles concluded that despite the harm of such men as Vallandigham, disregard by military leaders of "those principles on which our government and institutions rest" was greatly to be regretted.[25]

It was during the great excitement over Vallandigham that President

---

[23] Washington *National Intelligencer*, May 27, 1863, p. 3.

[24] Editorial, Washington *National Intelligencer*, *ibid.*

[25] Welles, *Diary*, pp. 321-22 (June 3, 1863).

Lincoln wrote the letter to Erastus Corning. In this letter Lincoln made his views on Vallandigham quite clear. He explained that anyone who spoke in behalf of desertion from the army weakened the cause of the Union and that Vallandigham was arrested because he sought "to prevent the raising of troops, to encourage desertions from the army, and to have the rebellion without an adequate military force to suppress it." Lincoln declared that Vallandigham was arrested not because he voiced political opposition to the administration but because "He was warring upon the military; and this gave the military constitutional jurisdiction to lay hands upon him." Lincoln fully justified apprehension of Vallandigham as an agitator. "Must I shoot a simple-minded soldier boy who deserts, [Lincoln asked Corning] while I must not touch a hair of a wily agitator who induces him to desert?" [26]

Even the friendly press found it difficult to be carried along by Lincoln's argument in the Corning letter. The New York *Tribune* again stated that it considered the arrest inexpedient.[27] It declared later, "*It gives the Pro-Slavery Democrats the excuse they seek for opposing, embarrassing, enfeebling and paralyzing the efforts of the Government to put down the rebellion.*" [28]

The banishment of Vallandigham was inherently a weak act because his fate was dependent upon the wishes of the enemy. Lincoln's policy would have been vastly interfered with if the Confederates immediately had delivered Vallandigham back to the Union lines. At least one newspaper had speculated as to whether the South would accept him.[29] As it happened, the Confederates dealt gently with him; he was permitted to slip away and in August, 1863, he appeared in Windsor, Canada, across from Detroit.

In July, 1863, Ohio Democrats nominated Vallandigham for governor, and public demonstrations took place demanding that he be permitted to return. Vallandigham's gubernatorial campaign, however, was conducted by correspondence and by friends. A war Democrat, John Brough, running as a Republican, soundly defeated Vallandigham. But one Republican, fearful that Vallandigham would be successful, had implored Secretary Chase to return to Ohio to address a meeting of Union men in southern Ohio, writing, "This as you know, is the 'home of Vallandigham' and his friends are 'moving Heaven and Earth' to carry this County and Congressional District. We shall dispute every inch of ground, but we need help." [30]

Former Representative Vallandigham was unwilling to believe that

---

[26] Abraham Lincoln to Erastus Corning, June 12, 1863, *Works*, VI, 260-69.

[27] Editorial, New York *Tribune*, June 15, 1863, p. 4.

[28] *Ibid.*, June 16, 1863, p. 4.

[29] Washington *National Intelligencer*, May 27, 1863, p. 3.

[30] Lewis B. Gunckel to Salmon P. Chase, September 10, 1863, Chase MSS., Library of Congress.

there was no recourse from the military tribunal that tried him and the federal circuit court that refused to grant him a writ of habeas corpus. Attorney General Bates was surprised, however, when he became aware that Vallandigham was going to appeal his case. Bates wrote Stanton on January 19, 1864, telling him of a "very curious motion, in the Supreme Court." He said that the motion was expressed in four lines, asking "simply for a writ of certiorari, to be addressed to the *Judge Advocate General of the Army*, to bring up the record of the Military Commission before which he (Vallandigham) was tried."

Bates expressed the opinion that the motion was "utterly without law" and declared, "I find it hard to guess the object, or trace it to any adequate motive." He said that if Stanton wished to make any recommendations as to how to treat it he should do so "before next friday." Bates added that the move "may be only a peg on which to hang a denunciatory speech against the administration generally, & the War office in particular." [31]

But a deeper motive directed Vallandigham. Here was an opportunity to embroil the Court in the bitter controversy over arbitrary arrest. Here was an opportunity—win or lose it would arouse vast public sympathy— to force the Supreme Court to involve itself in a subject that could prove highly embarrassing to it and to the administration as well.

Argument of the case was heard on January 22, 1864. The argument of Vallandigham's counsel, George E. Pugh, formerly United States Senator from Ohio, centered around the contention that the Court had the right to review the decision of a military tribunal. The main points in Pugh's arguments were: 1. A military commission, although it has limited jurisdiction, is a court of ordinary authority. 2. A military commission has jurisdiction over cases arising in the armed forces, but it does not have jurisdiction over a citizen who is not in the armed forces. 3. Vallandigham was not charged with any crime known under the laws of the United States. 4. General Burnside enlarged upon the authority granted to him in subjecting Vallandigham to a military commission. 5. The Supreme Court, acting in its proper power, could direct that the records of a military commission be certified by the Judge Advocate General and submitted for examination.[32]

The case of the government was argued by Judge Advocate General Joseph Holt. He argued that the Supreme Court had no authority to review the proceedings of the military commission that tried Vallandigham. He stated that the Court, in such an instance, had neither original jurisdiction nor appellate jurisdiction. Holt cited cases in which precedent had been established and declared that "the appellate power of the

[31] Edward Bates to Edwin M. Stanton, January 19, 1864, Stanton MSS.
[32] 17 L. Ed. 589.

Supreme Court . . . extends only to such cases as are within the general Judiciary Act and the special Acts expressly giving appellate jurisdiction. . . ." He concluded that the Court could be called upon "with as much propriety" to issue an injunction to restrain congressional proceedings "and reverse the proceedings of the military authorities, . . . in the punishment of all military offenses. . . ." [33] With this the case of the government rested. It remained for the Court to decide.

The full membership of the Supreme Court was not present to hear the Vallandigham case. Chief Justice Taney, ailing during most of the term, was too ill to be present. Justice Miller was absent, and he took no part in the case. It thus fell to the presiding Justice, James M. Wayne, and the rest of the associates to arrive at a decision.

After the argument of the case and while the Court was formulating its decision, Justice Wayne wrote Holt, asking, "Can you . . . send to me today a . . . copy of the General Order No. 38, issued . . . on the 3 April 1863, by which a commission was organized for the trial of Mr. Vallandigham." Wayne explained that the copy might aid in "my consideration of his petition for a Writ of Certiorari." [34]

On February 15, 1864, Justice Wayne, speaking for all the Justices who participated in the case, handed down a unanimous decision against Vallandigham, although Nelson, Grier, and Field did not agree with all points made in the written opinion. The Court refused to issue a writ because it could find no authority to justify it in taking such action.

Justice Wayne ruled that General Burnside's action conformed with regulations that provided for the government of the armies, approved by the President on April 24, 1863. Under these instructions, Wayne explained, two types of military jurisdiction were recognized: 1. Jurisdiction granted by statute and under which courts-martial are held. 2. Jurisdiction derived from the law of war and under which cases not within the regulations of war are tried by military commissions. Wayne held that both jurisdictions were applicable in foreign war as well as domestic rebellion. He stated the conclusion of the Court in these terms: "Whatever may be the force of Vallandigham's protest, that he was not triable by a court of military commission, it is certain that his petition cannot be brought within the 14th section of the [judiciary] act; and further, that the court cannot, without disregarding its frequent decisions and interpretations of the Constitution in respect to its judicial power, originate a writ of certiorari to review or pronounce any opinion upon the proceedings of a military commission." [35]

The argument presented to the Court by Judge Advocate General

---

[33] *Ibid.*, 590.

[34] James M. Wayne to Joseph Holt, January 26, 1864, Holt MSS.

[35] 68 U.S. 251-52.

Holt was used so closely by Justice Wayne in formulating the decision that the similarity of the two is striking. Wayne followed Holt's reasoning and at times even borrowed Holt's phraseology.

Vallandigham had failed. He had failed to embroil the Supreme Court in a struggle with the administration. The Court, as constituted in 1864, was unwilling to quarrel with the administration although, admittedly, some of its members would have welcomed an opportunity to block Lincoln. Whatever force the Vallandigham argument had, the Court would not ensnare itself at Vallandigham's bidding.

Daniel W. Middleton, the Clerk of the Court, deemed the decision so important that he took the trouble to send a copy of it to Lincoln, stating, "Allow me the honor of presenting to you the accompanying copy of the opinion of the Supreme Court . . . delivered a few days Since, on the petition of Clement L. Vallandigham. . . ." [36]

William C. Jewett, who frequently wrote to leaders of the administration and newspapers, sent Lincoln congratulations and was unrestrained in his enthusiasm. "I congratulate you & Mr. Seward upon your now declared Constitutional military government power," he wrote. He interpreted the decision as proof that in this emergency the military power was paramount. "This secures [he continued in his enthusiasm] the Presidentcy [sic] to you during the War and waives an election[!]" [37] Lincoln must have been pained at least by the misinterpretations in the latter part of this statement.

Newspaper reaction to the decision varied depending upon political affiliation. The Washington *National Intelligencer* commented that even if "the arrest, trial, and punishment of Mr. Vallandigham were illegal, there is still no authority in the court" to alter or modify a decision of a military commission. [88] The New York *Times* said that the decision meant that "the military authority for the common defence, in time of war, inheres in the Commander-in-Chief to the exclusion of the civil authority." And the *Times* reminded its readers that since the war began "In no single instant has its [the Court's] opinion been at variance with the executive action of the President." [89]

The New York *World* promptly declared that Democratic newspapers would respect the Court's decision, stating that the demeanor of Democratic journals "will be, in this as in all other cases, respectful assent or dissent from the judgment pronounced, as a matter of reasoning; respectful obedience to the judgment pronounced as a matter of judicial law." [40]

[36] D. W. Middleton to Abraham Lincoln, March 1, 1864, Lincoln MSS.
[37] William C. Jewett to Abraham Lincoln, February 16, 1864, *ibid.*
[38] Washington *National Intelligencer*, February 17, 1864, p. 3.
[39] Editorial, New York *Times*, February 16, 1864, p. 4.
[40] Editorial, New York *World*, February 17, 1864, p. 4.

The day following the decision John W. Forney, editor of the Washington *Morning Chronicle* as well as Secretary of the United States Senate, asked Judge Advocate General Holt, "May I beg of you such an article as I may print editorially . . . in the Chronicle?" Forney, who was a close friend of Lincoln, told Holt that "The decision . . . deserves a good and able endorsement." [41] The next day the *Chronicle* commented that the Copperheads were now even without any recourse in the Supreme Court. "That venerable institution [declared the *Chronicle*] was the last sanctuary of freedom—to break up the Government—and the last hope of Copperheadism. And now even that is gone." [42]

Vallandigham had remained in his Canadian refuge, but on June 15, 1864, four months after the Court's decision, he threw caution to the winds. He suddenly turned up in Hamilton, Ohio, to address a convention of Democrats. The Lincoln administration let him go unnoticed, despite a plea to Senator John Sherman, demanding Vallandigham's rearrest. "If the Government backs down [Sherman was told] A. Lincoln will loose [*sic*] Ohio's vote . . . have the millitary [*sic*] authorities of this department to look after the scounderel [*sic*] —He is an enemy much so as Jeff Davis—" [43]

But Lincoln now adopted the policy that he, himself, believed to be the proper answer to the question posed by Vallandigham and ignored the troublemaker. To pursue him again would be more costly to the cause of the Union than to ignore him. The presidential election of 1864 was in the offing; Lincoln feared that his prospects for re-election were very poor. To challenge Vallandigham again would set off an explosion of discontent; to ignore him would force him to be consumed by his own fallacious principles. It was with wisdom that Lincoln chose no longer to enter into combat with Clement L. Vallandigham.

The Supreme Court had at least refused to interfere with the administration.[44] That brought Lincoln the victory he required. Even though it was in a sense a negative one, the important point, as far as Lincoln was concerned, was that his policies were not upset and his authority was not hampered. The Court had undoubtedly felt the pressure of the Radicals who were attacking it. That the Court might reverse itself— after the war it did so—was a problem that must have loomed in Lincoln's mind, however.

---

[41] John W. Forney to Joseph Holt, February 16, 1864, Holt MSS.

[42] Editorial, Washington *Morning Chronicle*, February 17, 1864, p. 2.

[43] T. F. Thirkield to John Sherman, June 16, 1864, John Sherman MSS., Library of Congress.

[44] James G. Randall, *Lincoln the President* (New York, 1945-53), III, 229.

CHAPTER THIRTEEN

Business as Usual

JUSTICE DESPITE WAR

Although the Taney Court heard momentous cases such as the *Prize Cases*, the legal tender case, and the Vallandigham case, non-war-related problems constituted the vast body of litigation heard by the Court during the war. Commonplace and non-commonplace cases were heard as usual. They were disposed of as usual. The Court did business as usual.

When Lincoln was inaugurated the Supreme Court was winding up its December Term, 1860—the Court adjourned on March 14, 1861— and no further meeting of the Court was scheduled until December, 1861. When the Court reassembled on December 2, it reassembled in a nation at war. Despite the civil conflict raging around it, the Supreme Court proceeded to hear cases in the manner that was prescribed by custom. An examination of the cases that came before it demonstrates that its normal, legal processes continued to function.

At least one leading newspaper of the time was deeply impressed by the uninterruption of the legal processes of the Supreme Court. "The revolutionary tempest [said the New York *World*] which has so shaken public confidence in the legislature and the executive of the nation has not yet over thrown the public faith in the integrity and dignity of the supreme judiciary. . . ." It declared that it was significant that even though the nation was torn apart by war, ordinary processes of law functioned undisturbed. "To see justice and the law dealing with great interests, dispersing powerful combinations, controlling partisan passions, and administering exact equity in the midst of a storm which threatens the very existence of the state, [the *World* continued] . . . [is a] spectacle full of encouragement to the patriot, as the reverse of the vision would be the final and darkest sign upon our national horoscope." [1]

The Supreme Court, when it met for its regular term each year on the first Monday of December, always began an exhausting session. That the Court was laden with litigation is not surprising in that "The cognizance of the court embraces litigation under all the various forms in which it is pursued in that country whence the principles of our jurisprudence are chiefly derived. It is a court of common law, of equity, and of

---

[1] Editorial, New York *World*, January 22, 1864, p. 4.

admiralty and maritime jurisdiction." [2] With both original and appellate jurisdiction, the Court was always assured of a multitude of cases. During the Civil War improvement resulted from an act of March 3, 1863, limiting appeal to the Supreme Court from the court of claims to cases involving over three thousand dollars, the appeal having to be made within ninety days. Appeal to the Supreme Court in relation to prize cases was also limited by an act of June 30, 1864, to action taken within ninety days.[3]

The *United States Reports,* in which the records of the cases heard by the Court are reported in abbreviated form, do not adequately indicate the vast amount of material with which the Court was confronted. The full record of each case is contained in the Records and Briefs of the United States Supreme Court; here are to be found all records of the cases in the lower courts as well as all briefs that are submitted. The Records and Briefs are printed but published in very limited quantity for the use of the Justices and counsel. From the Records and Briefs the main materials in a case and the main arguments of the lawyers are selected for inclusion in the official *United States Reports.* In deciding cases, of course, the Justices make full examination of the voluminous Records and Briefs. In view of these facts the number of cases heard each term and the number of opinions written by each Justice assumes new significance.

During the December Term, 1861, which ended on March 24, 1862, the Court heard over seventy cases. None of them vitally concerned the war. Almost all were simply cases involving litigation that might have been heard during any session.

Most prominent among the cases were those that involved land titles in general and California land titles in particular. As a matter of fact land cases comprised almost one-third of the whole body of cases heard during the term. In addition, cases involving right of appeal, collision at sea, contract and charter, bankruptcy, ship's cargo, bridges, patent rights, partnership, repair of a city street, ferry rights, usury, and land formed by accretion of Lake Michigan were adjudicated by the Court. These cases involved ordinary matters indeed.

But one case heard during the term merits additional consideration. It involved Nathaniel Gordon, who was charged with participation in the African slave trade. Gordon was found guilty and sentenced to death by the United States circuit court for Southern New York. Appeal was

[2] Alfred Conkling, *A Treatise on the Organization, Jurisdiction, and Practice of the Courts of the United States, with an Appendix of Practical Forms,* 4th ed., revised and enlarged (Albany, 1864), p. 80. Cited hereafter as Conkling, *A Treatise.*

[3] See 12 Stat. 766 and 13 Stat. 310.

made to the Supreme Court, and its decision was announced on February 17, 1862.

The case of Nathaniel Gordon caused the Court to restate basic rules pertaining to appeal. Chief Justice Taney declared that Gordon had been tried and sentenced by a court of competent judisdiction "from whose judgment no appeal is allowed by law, to this tribunal; for, in criminal cases, the proceedings and judgement [sic] of the Circuit Court cannot be revised or controlled here, in any form of proceeding, either by writ of error or prohibition, and consequently, we have no authority to examine them by a *certiorari*." [4]

He pointed out that the Supreme Court was requested to intervene even beyond exercising appellate jurisdiction because "the warrant is in the hands of the marshal commanding him to execute the judgment of the court." The Chief Justice stated that the Supreme Court had no appellate power to control this case and that "it would be without precedent in any judicial proceeding to prohibit a ministerial officer from performing a duty which the Circuit Court had a lawful right to command."

Aside from *Ex Parte Gordon*, the Supreme Court heard no case in the December Term, 1861, that was other than commonplace. Great judicial battles were to be waged—battles that were as important as the battles fought by the armies—but these battles awaited later terms of Court.

War and the Constitution

It was in the December Term, 1862, that the Supreme Court began to concern itself with wartime problems in which basic constitutional interpretations were involved. The term began on December 1, 1862, and ended on March 10, 1863. During the term the Supreme Court heard over forty cases, and in some of them there were problems relating to the war. This session of Court saw the Justices determine the important *Prize Cases*, which have already been examined. Although the Court heard many ordinary cases in addition, a few were filled with great public interest. About one-fourth of all the cases of the term, however, involved land titles, and again California land cases were prominent among them.

The Justices, in addition to the *Prize Cases* and land title cases, during this term adjudicated cases involving right of appeal, mortgage problems, bankruptcy, liability of cities for street repair, payment of import duties, contract, taxes imposed by states, state laws, bridge building, property rights of married women, and the city limits of San Francisco.

March 10, 1863, the last day of the term, was a momentous day for the Court. Not only did it announce the decision in the *Prize Cases*, but

4 66 U.S. 505.

it delivered important decisions relative to state taxation of United States bonds and ownership of the fabulous New Almaden quicksilver mine in California as well. It is no wonder that a throng filled the chambers on that day.

Two decisions involved effort by the commissioners of taxes and assessments of the city and county of New York to tax United States securities in which the Bank of Commerce of New York and the Bank of the Commonwealth of New York had invested a part of their capital. It is somewhat curious that during the Civil War the Supreme Court was called upon to uphold federal authority by disallowing state taxation of United States securities. The two cases provoked the Court to reassert principles similar to those established some forty years earlier in the case of *McCulloch v. Maryland.*

The unanimous decision of the Court was delivered by Justice Nelson. He applied the same rule to both cases. "That government [Justice Nelson asserted] whose powers, executive, legislative, or judicial, whether it is a government of enumerated powers like this one or not, are subject to the control of another distinct Government, cannot be sovereign or supreme, but subject and inferior to the other. This is so palpable a truth that argument would be superfluous." He pointed out that the power to borrow money is a "vital" power of government and that the sovereignty of the federal government becomes meaningless "if another government may tax it at discretion." [5] The Taney Court upheld the sovereign rights of the federal government, and the efforts in New York to tax federal securities were held unconstitutional.

Part of the throng was present to hear the decision in the New Almaden mine case. Here, too, no war-related question was involved, but interest in the decision was intense. Millions of dollars were involved, and California mining interests were keenly aroused. As the New York *Times* reported, interest was so great that many spectators had deserted the Senate and the House in order to be present in the courtroom to hear the proceedings. "The Court are fully aware [the *Times* stated] of the magnitude of the interests, and give an earnest and undivided attention to the arguments of the distinguished gentlemen engaged in the case." [6] The New York *World* was highly impressed by the fact that in the midst of civil war the Supreme Court could hear a case so laden with economic considerations and yet not be coerced by the legislative or executive branch of the government.[7]

The New Almaden decision came on the most important Supreme Court decision day of the war. Justice Swayne had hinted earlier to

[5] 17 L. Ed. 455.

[6] New York *Times*, February 1, 1863, p. 4.

[7] Editorial, New York *World*, January 22, 1864, p. 4.

Attorney General Bates that the government would win the case and that steps should be taken "to secure the interests of the Gov[ernmen]t." [8] When the decision of the Court was announced, however, the New York *Times* commented that rejection of the contentions of the claimant, Andres Castillero, came as a general surprise.[9]

Both Andres Castillero and the United States were served by outstanding counsel. Castillero's counsel included A. C. Peachy, Reverdy Johnson, Charles O'Connor, John J. Crittenden, and M. Hall McAllister. The counsel of the United States included Attorney General Edward Bates, Benjamin R. Curtis, Jeremiah S. Black, and Edwin M. Stanton.

Claims of Castillero rested upon his discovery of the mine in 1845 and steps that he took to secure title. Castillero, who formed a company to work the mine, claimed that he received juridical possession on December 3, 1845, and that the highest mining tribunal of Mexico approved it subsequently, following which the President of Mexico acceded to the grant on May 23, 1846. He was unable to gain possession, however, because war between the United States and Mexico intervened, and operations of war took place in California. Counsel argued for Castillero that "the discoverer of a mine was rewarded by an investiture, *ipso facto*, with a perpetual property and ownership of the mine, and an ascertainable amount of surface by the name of *pertenencias*, or mining spaces." [10]

But counsel for the United States argued differently. The government's counsel maintained that Castillero and the Mexican government concluded no arrangement. "It was utterly broken up [argued lawyers of the government] by the war and the military possession of the country by the United States, and was abandoned by both parties, and no right or title accrued to either party by virtue of it." The United States admitted that the mining laws of Mexico were such that Castillero could have obtained legal title, but argued that he did not complete the process and that it was impossible to do so because the Mexican War intervened.

Justice Nathan Clifford handed down the decision of the majority of the Court. The Court ruled that although Castillero had carried through part of the procedure of registering the mine under Mexican law, since all of the requirements were not fulfilled there had been no legal registration of the mine in the name of Andres Castillero.

The Supreme Court was by no means unanimous in ruling against him. Clifford was joined by Taney, Davis, Miller, Swayne, and Nelson. Taney was absent on March 10 but authorized Clifford to announce that he concurred in the majority opinion. But Justice Catron dissented in an

---

[8] Bates, *Diary*, p. 282 (February 26, 1863).

[9] New York *Times*, March 11, 1863, p. 4.

[10] This discussion of the New Almaden case is based upon 17 L. Ed. 360-448. The minutes of the United States Supreme Court for March 10, 1863, indicate that Taney subscribed to the majority opinion of the Court, however.

opinion in which he was joined by Justice Grier. And Justice Wayne, who also dissented, filed his own opinion.

Justice Catron made many forceful points in his dissent. He declared that no doubt was entertained as to Castillero's claim of discovery of the mine, that the fact of Castillero's registry of the mine was communicated to the government of the United States, that the government of Mexico recognized Castillero's claim as valid, that the proceeding had not been denounced as irregular, and that under the treaty with Mexico the United States was required "to protect all just private interests in lands in the territory acquired by it."

Justice Wayne declared in his dissenting opinion that no fraud could be demonstrated in Castillero's claim and that under the treaty with Mexico, his claim could not be denied. Wayne annexed to his opinion the opinion of Judge Ogden Hoffman, federal district judge in California, "as the best way of showing my appreciation of the law and merits of this case, and of his judicial learning and research in connection with it."

Thus a badly divided Supreme Court ruled the claim of Andres Castillero invalid, and the valuable New Almaden mine, which was important because it was the only source of mercury not controlled by the Rothschilds, became the property of the government of the United States.[11] If the vast wealth of the mine had been channeled properly into the United States Treasury, perhaps less criticism could be heaped upon the Court and the lawyers who convinced the Court that it should cast Castillero's claim aside. But the mine which was denied Castillero became the objective of a disgraceful attempt to gain for a low price from the government of the United States the most valuable quicksilver mine in the country.

Mining interests in California were up in arms over the decision. Frederick F. Low, collector at the Port of San Francisco, telegraphed Secretary of the Treasury Chase that if the federal government took steps to seize the Almaden mine, the act would play into the hands of secessionist groups in California. "The secessionists [Low warned] will seize upon it as a pretext for a general uprising I fear. See the President at once & have Gen[era]l Wright instructed by telegraph to withdraw action[.] A delay of one day in the order may be fatal." [12] A few days later Low telegraphed the President, himself, to implore that federal policy be changed. "Don't I pray you [Low begged of Lincoln] let anything be done to involve this State . . . [in] difficulty—Judge Field & Gen[era]l Wright concur with me in my views." [13]

---

[11] Leonard Ascher, "Lincoln's Administration and the New Almaden Scandal," *Pacific Historical Review*, March, 1936, V, 40.

[12] Frederick F. Low to Salmon P. Chase, July 8, 1863, Lincoln MSS.

[13] Frederick F. Low to Abraham Lincoln, July 11, 1863, *ibid.*

Finally Lincoln acted to prevent his friend and representative, Leonard Swett, from proceeding against the mine with a writ of possession, and the turmoil in California subsided. Later, Swett was instrumental in carrying through a settlement in the Almaden case that not only reflected badly upon him but upon the administration as well.

The President agreed with the decision of the Supreme Court and stated to Low in a letter of August 17, 1863, that he countermanded the order for seizure only because he did not wish to stir up complications in California. Lincoln declared that there was a general misunderstanding about the attempt to seize the Almaden mine. He explained that there was no desire to upset California mining claims, but that since the Supreme Court had ruled Castillero's claims fraudulent, steps were instituted to take possession of the mine. Lincoln asserted that there had been nothing surreptitious in obtaining his signature on the writ of possession and that "The Writ was suspended, upon urgent representations from California, simply to keep the peace." [14]

On August 31 Leonard Swett telegraphed President Lincoln that a compromise had been worked out and that "The rights and interests of the Gov[ernmen]t have been respected." [15] But Swett was serving other interests than those of the government, and the Almaden properties fell into the hands of the Quicksilver Mining Company for less than two million dollars. And later litigation before the Supreme Court saw lawyers who had argued in the New Almaden case that the quicksilver deposits were on government property argue in the Fossat case that the quicksilver deposits were on property acquired by the Quicksilver Mining Company. [16]

Leonard Swett's role in the Almaden controversy reflected badly not only upon his own personal integrity, but also upon the Lincoln administration. In this instance Lincoln's friendship was betrayed. As Leonard Ascher has stated, it was fortunate for Lincoln that the event occurred in the summer of 1863 when Gettysburg, Vicksburg, and the draft riots attracted the attention of the nation. "No satisfactory explanation of the affair was ever made; it was hushed up, [Ascher concluded]. Therefore, Messrs. Stanton, Black, Bates, Usher, Swett, and finally Lincoln could rejoice when the passage of time had caused the affair to be numbered with the forgotten scandals of the past." [17] The official biographers of Lincoln, Nicolay and Hay, treated the story of the New Almaden mine by silence—silence that is evidence of their evaluation of Leonard Swett's unethical role and of his betrayal of Lincoln.

---

[14] *Works*, VI, 394 (August 17, 1863).

[15] Leonard Swett to Abraham Lincoln, August 31, 1863, Lincoln MSS.

[16] Ascher, p. 40. For the Fossat case see 17 L. Ed. 739-55.

[17] Ascher, p. 51.

A Lack of War Cases

During the December Term, 1863, which began on December 7, 1863, and ended on April 18, 1864, the last term under the leadership of Chief Justice Taney, the Court heard over seventy cases. Of that large number, only two, *Roosevelt v. Meyer*, and *Ex Parte Vallandigham*, both of which have already been examined, were vital war-related cases. The rest of the cases were ordinary ones. About one-third involved problems of land title. Other cases concerned patent rights, mortgages and bonds and notes, bankruptcy, corporate problems, import duties, the power of a city to borrow money, tariff, collision at sea, leases, arbitration, and problems of a trust.

But in regard to one matter not related to the war, violent discord was introduced into the Court—discord between two recent appointees of Lincoln. The bitterness, which reached an intensity that is surprising, demonstrated vividly that no President can feel assurance that his appointees to the Court will work in harmony.

The controversy, which was between Justice Noah H. Swayne and Justice Samuel F. Miller, involved the power of the Supreme Court to reverse a decision of the Iowa supreme court. To reverse a state supreme court was a delicate matter in the midst of civil war and at a time when the prestige of the United States Supreme Court was low.

The case that provoked these two appointees of Lincoln to inject strong personal feelings into the proceedings, *Gelpcke v. The City of Dubuque*, "was an outgrowth of the craze for railroad extension" which at the time was causing municipalities to grant assistance in building railroads.[18] The question at stake was whether the United States Supreme Court would be bound by a decision of the supreme court of Iowa concerning the city of Dubuque's right to issue bonds to help finance a railroad. The Iowa supreme court at first upheld the legality of the bonds but finally reversed itself.

Arguing in behalf of Herman Gelpcke, who wished to have the legality of the bonds sustained, were William B. Allison and Platt Smith. They declared that opposite counsel would maintain that the United States Supreme Court must follow the most recent decision of the Iowa supreme court. "This would be correct [they admitted] if the last decision was not inconsistent with a series of decisions previously made, and on the strength of which millions of dollars have been invested by non-residents in county and city bonds of this state."[19] They demanded that faith be kept with those who had invested in the bonds.

But the defendant, the city of Dubuque, saw it differently. F. E. Bissell,

---

[18] Walter M. Rose, "Notes on the U.S. Reports," 17 L. Ed., second extra annotated ed., notes, 298.

[19] This discussion of the case *Gelpcke v. Dubuque* is based upon 17 L. Ed. 520-30.

who served as counsel for the city, argued that "In giving construction to the Constitution or law of a State, this court will follow the construction as given by the courts of the State, and will follow the latest decision of the state court rather than an earlier decision."

Noah H. Swayne delivered the decision. The Court concluded that it need not follow the latest ruling of the Iowa supreme court. Boldly Swayne declared, "It cannot be expected that this court will follow every such oscillation, from whatever cause arising, that may possibly occur." He pointed out that the Dubuque case as well as two other cases "overruling earlier adjudications, stand out, as far as we are advised, in unenviable solitude and notoriety." In denying the validity of the latest Iowa supreme court decision, Justice Swayne held that if the contract were valid when it was made, "its validity and obligation cannot be impaired by any decision of its courts altering the construction of the law."

Swayne gave the Iowa supreme court a verbal spanking. He stated that the decisions of the highest courts in the states should be uniform in interpreting state laws. "But there have been heretofore, in the judicial history of this court, [Justice Swayne proceeded] many exceptional cases. We shall never immolate truth, justice, and the law, because a tribunal has erected the altar and decreed the sacrifice." Swayne's opinion assailed the highest court of Iowa in terms that were at least unusual—at most, grossly offensive.

The Iowan on the bench of the United States Supreme Court did not remain quiet. Dissenting forcefully, Justice Miller warned that the Supreme Court was adopting a dangerously erroneous policy in not heeding the final decision of the supreme court of a state. He predicted that such a position by the Supreme Court would "bring it into direct and unseemly conflict with the judiciary of the States." He deplored the fact that the Supreme Court, in effect, was telling the federal courts in Iowa to ignore the Iowa supreme court, "and where that court has said that a statute is unconstitutional, you shall say that it is constitutional. When it says bonds are void, issued in that State, because they violate its constitution, you shall say that they are valid, because they do not violate the constitution."

Miller did not restrain his resentment at Swayne's remarks. "Is it supposed for a moment that this treatment of a decision, [he asked] accompanied by language as unsuited to the dispassionate dignity of this court, as it is disrespectful to another court of at least concurrent jurisdiction over the matter in question, will induce the Supreme Court of Iowa to conform its rulings to suit our dictations in a matter which the very frame and organization of our government places entirely under its control?"

He charged that the United States Supreme Court was usurping authority and warned that not only would the Iowa supreme court "adhere to its own opinion with more tenacity," but that this decision might lead to vast judicial conflicts between the state supreme courts and the Federal Supreme Court. He condemned Swayne's opinion as upholding usurpation that was "a step in advance of anything theretofore decided."

The controversy between Swayne and Miller was renewed a month later when a case involving Iowa in similar issues, *Myer and Stucken v. The City of Muscatine*, came before the Supreme Court. The question involved was whether a city in Iowa could borrow money for the purpose of railroad building if "its charter gives the City authority 'to borrow money for any object in its discretion.'" Swayne and Miller reaffirmed the positions they had assumed earlier.

Miller resumed the bitterness characteristic of the Dubuque decision. He wrote, "To infer . . . that the Legislature intended to make valid the bonds of the city of Muscatine, issued without any authority, is a stretch of fancy, only to be indulged in railroad bond cases, and which, it is hoped, may be confined to them as precedent." He condemned the attitude of the majority and with sweeping criticism concluded, "Yet it is by such latitudinary construction of statutes as this that it is attempted to fasten upon owners of property, who never assented to the contract, a debt of $20,000,000, involving a ruin only equaled in this country by that visited upon the guilty participants in the current rebellion." [20]

Justice Swayne's reflections upon the supreme court of Iowa did not go unanswered by Iowa's highest court. The attempt to force Iowa to recognize and accept its debt was widely resented in Iowa. Judge Joseph M. Beck of the Iowa supreme court answered Swayne in two opinions that were handed down in the next few years. In one, Judge Beck declared that the Dubuque decision was not only "remarkable for bold disregard of precedent, but it is distinguished from all other decisions of the august tribunal that rendered it, as well as from those of all other high courts in the use of language extremely disrespectful toward the Supreme Court of a State." [21]

Later, referring to the controversy, Judge Beck stated that he deplored an incident of the conflict as much "as the conflict itself." "I refer [Beck stated] to the extremely disrespectful allusion to the Supreme Court of Iowa, in the opinion of Mr. Justice SWAYNE, in *Gelpcke v. Dubuque*. In this country the bench has no patent of respect save that of public confidence, and woe is the day when one court will aid, nay originate, an attack upon the integrity and public virtue of another court. . . . To

---

[20] *Ibid.*, 568.
[21] 26 Iowa 259.

the people of Iowa, and the bar especially, is that opinion a barbed arrow that will long rankle and wound." [22]

Lincoln had not anticipated that to all the enmity and bitterness of the Taney Court there might be added differences of opinion between men that he appointed. But the December Term, 1863, demonstrated to him that very fact. It must have made Lincoln question whether any President can truly "reconstruct" the Court. It must have made him conclude that, after all, his administration had enjoyed good luck at the hands of a Supreme Court composed of Justices who were answerable to no composite authority and surely not to each other.

[22] 28 Iowa 168.

CHAPTER FOURTEEN

Dual-Role Justices

BURDENSOME DUTIES

Members of the Supreme Court were burdened for over a century with duties relative to the circuit system of the United States. As the nation expanded, as vast population developed in the Ohio valley, the Mississippi valley, and the Far West, the burdens of the Justices became greater and greater. And yet, change came slowly. Although before the Civil War circuit duties were somewhat modified, it was not until 1869 that effective improvement was initiated. Even then, circuit duties for the Supreme Court Justices continued for another forty years, but "During most of the latter part of that period . . . they were little regarded." [1]

By the time of the Civil War the federal circuit courts normally were presided over by the Justice of the Supreme Court assigned to the circuit and the judge of the district court for the district. Either jurist could preside alone, however. And in order to facilitate the hearing of cases an act of March 3, 1863, provided that a district judge could serve in a circuit court outside his district. [2]

Circuit courts had original as well as appellate jurisdiction, and federal judicial procedure was such that a Supreme Court Justice might participate in an appeal to the Supreme Court in a case in which he had ruled on circuit.

It will be remembered that President Lincoln reviewed the major problems of the federal judiciary, including the circuit system, in his first annual report to the Congress, and he suggested that circuit duties for Supreme Court Justices might be abolished. Nonetheless, no such far-reaching alteration of the federal circuit system was made during his administration.

Congress determined the time and place of sessions of the circuit courts, and changes were frequent. At times, in order to simplify the task of setting up a new circuit court, Congress provided merely that an already-created district court should exercise the jurisdiction of a circuit court as well as its own jurisdiction. In the period from 1844 to 1869 the law required, as to circuit duties for Supreme Court Justices, that "it

---

[1] John C. Rose, *Jurisdiction and Procedure of the Federal Courts,* 4th ed., revised and enlarged by Byron F. Babbitt. (Albany, 1931), p. 94.

[2] 12 Stat. 768.

shall not be the duty of the Justices . . . assigned to any circuit to attend more than one term of the circuit court within any district of such circuit in any one year." [3]

A move to improve the unwieldy circuit system came early in 1865, but it was doomed to failure. Senator Lyman Trumbull asserted in the Senate on January 17, 1865, that "The amount of business accumulating in the Supreme Court amounts almost to a denial of justice. . . ." He explained that it was proposed to change the judicial system "to a very great extent by abolishing the district courts and substituting a circuit court, having the present jurisdiction of the present district and circuit courts, and also having an intermediate court of appeals in each judicial . . . [circuit] of the United States." [4]

While the matter was pending, a typical attitude was stated editorially by the Washington *Morning Chronicle*. It expressed the fear that if Supreme Court Justices no longer had circuit duties they would suffer from loss of contact with the outside world and would be imprisoned in their libraries. Furthermore, the *Chronicle* demanded that no changes in the federal judicial system be made until restoration of the Union.[5]

It is evident that a vast modification of the circuit system was essential. But a nation in civil strife could hardly devote itself to the luxury of far-reaching change in the federal judiciary. Within a few weeks the committee on the judiciary asked to be discharged from considering the bill, and the move to improve the federal judiciary died.

CIRCUIT COMPLICATIONS

The circuit duties of a few of the members of the Taney Court— Taney, Wayne, and Catron—were hampered by the civil strife, personal illness, or unusual circumstances. Nevertheless, in general the Justices encountered almost every type of circuit case during the war. Circuit cases actually concerned the Justices with war-related problems more often than did cases of the Supreme Court. Consequently it was frequent that on circuit the Justices would first reveal their views in regard to war-related problems.[6]

---

[3] 5 Stat. 676.

[4] *Cong. Globe*, 38th Cong., 2nd sess., p. 292.

[5] Editorial, Washington *Morning Chronicle*, January 25, 1862, p. 2.

[6] Although the voluminous *Federal Cases* contains the leading decisions made by the judges of the district and circuit courts of the United States prior to 1880, it is to be noted that some cases are not included. The *Federal Cases* has to be supplemented by special compilations of decisions of particular members of the federal judiciary, contemporary law journals, newspapers of the period, textbooks, and digests. 1 Fed. Cas., preface, iii-vi.

CIRCUIT JUSTICE ROGER B. TANEY

The circuit duties of Chief Justice Taney during the war were restricted by Taney's persistent illness as well as his determination to delay the hearing of treason cases in Maryland. In addition, secession of part of his circuit limited his activities.

Circuit Justice Taney's early clash with the Lincoln adminstration, while he held circuit court in Baltimore and heard the Merryman case, has already been discussed. Following that controversy with Lincoln, Taney was disinclined to hear circuit cases that involved arrest for pro-Southern activities. Illness, which plagued Taney throughout this period, provided him with a convenient excuse to absent himself from the court at times when treason cases pended.

He succeeded in delaying treason trials in the circuit court at Baltimore during the November Term, 1861, intimating that a decision of the Supreme Court would deal with the matter.[7] Although the Court handed down no such decision, Taney obtained further delay in the spring of 1862 because he was too ill to attend circuit court.

With the November Term, 1862, scheduled, Taney deliberately took steps again to secure delay of the treason cases. He anticipated that strong pressure would be placed upon Judge William F. Giles, the United States district judge in Baltimore, to preside alone in the circuit court and hear the cases. Taney informed Giles, who had a basically friendly attitude toward the Chief Justice's position on arbitrary arrest, that he should not proceed by himself. Taney said, of course, that Giles could make up his own mind, but "In a trial before the District Judge alone, the party has not the benefit of the judgment of any Judge of the Supreme Court, and cannot have his case certified to the Supreme Court. His fate must depend upon the District Judge without appeal and without revision."[8] In harmony with the suggestion, Judge Giles postponed the treason trials until the April Term, 1863.[9]

The federal district attorney for Maryland, William Price, who was growing impatient, sought assurances that Taney would attend circuit court during the April Term, 1863. Price wrote Judge Advocate General Holt that "I have written C[hief] J[ustice] Taney to have a judge of the Supreme Court assigned for this Circuit and have not had his reply. Without such a step we will have no Court to try treason cases. The last term passed over without any trial of the kind on account of Judge Taneys [sic] illness."[10]

[7] Swisher, Roger B. Taney, p. 557-58.

[8] Roger B. Taney to William F. Giles, October 7, 1862, Chase MSS., Hist. Soc. of Pa.

[9] Washington Evening Star, November 10, 1862, p. 2.

[10] William Price to Joseph Holt, March 9, 1863, Holt MSS.

Possibly Price's demand for a Supreme Court Justice who would attend circuit court in Baltimore convinced Taney of the need to attend the April Term, 1863. At any rate the Chief Justice was present. Although war-related matters came before the Court, again he succeeded in postponing the treason trials, much to Price's dismay.

During the term the Chief Justice ruled against the government in two war-related cases and again condemned the administration's effort to exercise special wartime powers. One case involved the question of whether federal regulations controlling the internal trade of a state were valid. Circuit Justice Taney handed down a decision in this case, *Carpenter v. the United States*, denying the contention that the federal government had power to regulate the internal trade of a state in the interest of the war effort. He ruled that it was unconstitutional for Secretary of the Treasury Chase to provide that to trade in Charles County, Maryland, a citizen had to secure a federal permit. Taney said it was of no consequence constitutionally that the purpose of the regulations was to stop trading with the enemy.[11]

His decision put him back in the news. As the Washington *Morning Chronicle* pointed out, "If his latest interpretation of law is correct, the way is opened for a highly profitable trade with the rebels by all who choose to engage in it." [12] And the New York *Tribune* declared, "His motive for seeking to annull [sic] this law may be presumed to be the same which on several other occasions has led him . . . to throw the weight of his opinion . . . against all laws which strike at the Rebellion." [13]

The second case reversed a decision that had been handed down by Judge Giles. Known as *Claimants of Merchandise v. The United States,* it involved the seizure of goods destined for the enemy. Taney ruled that since the government's agents stooped to the practice of befriending the suspect's children in order to obtain evidence, it was better to return the merchandise to the owner than to support such treachery on the part of agents of the United States.[14]

Later in the year 1863 as well as in 1864 Taney's plan of avoiding treason trials was successfully continued. The Chief Justice revealed his project to Justice Nelson in the spring of 1864. "I have made up my mind [he wrote] to continue the indictments for treason whether I go to Baltimore or not. . . . It is not in the power of the Court under such circumstances, [martial law in Maryland] to give . . . [an] impartial trial —or to protect . . . [those who] should be found not guilty by the Jury—" He went on to say that a fair trial was impossible because the

---

[11] *Appleton's American Annual Cyclopedia* (New York, 1862-1903), III, 202.

[12] Editorial, Washington *Morning Chronicle*, June 26, 1863, p. 2.

[13] Editorial, New York *Tribune*, June 24, 1863, p. 4.

[14] Swisher, *Roger B. Taney*, p. 566-67.

witnesses and jurors would be fearful of saying or doing anything displeasing to the military authorities. "I will not place the judicial power [affirmed Taney] in this humiliating position—nor consent thus to degrade and disgrace it—and if the District Attorney presses the prosecutions I shall refuse to take them up[.] I shall order the cases to be continued—and shall in a written opinion place my decision upon the grounds above stated.—What do you think of it?"

And the ailing Taney, who had been informed by Nelson that he heard appeals in his office, inquired how such hearings were conducted. "Is the Circuit Court [asked Taney] kept open from day to day for that purpose? —And how, and of what day is it entered on the record?" Taney complained to Nelson of the many infirmities that plagued him and added that he felt disposed "to follow your example and require the Bar to come to me." [15]

CIRCUIT JUSTICE JAMES M. WAYNE AND
CIRCUIT JUSTICE JOHN CATRON

Justice James M. Wayne, whose circuit consisted of Southern states, during the war was unable to hold court and only resumed those duties when peace had been restored.

But John Catron played an important role as a Circuit Justice. He was involved in circuit duties in Kentucky early in the war when the state was filled with treason. During this period he was concerned with two cases of unusual interest. One case was that of former Governor Charles S. Morehead of Kentucky; the other, the case of a former United States Congressman from Kentucky, James B. Clay, a son of Henry Clay.

Former Governor Charles S. Morehead, Reuben T. Durrett, editor of the Louisville *Courier*, and Martin W. Barr, were arrested on September 19, 1861, on the charge of stirring up rebellion.[16] United States Marshal A. H. Sneed, who made the arrests, had the prisoners transferred to Indianapolis for safekeeping.

On the day of the arrest proceedings in behalf of Morehead were instituted in the circuit court in Louisville in which Circuit Justice John Catron was presiding.[17] He promptly issued a writ of habeas corpus and commanded the marshal to "bring the said Charles S. Morehead before me with the cause of his commitment. . . ." [18]

Sneed's return to the writ on September 20 was that he would produce Morehead in court by noon of the twenty-third. He failed to do so,

---

[15] Roger B. Taney to Samuel Nelson, May 8, 1864, manuscript owned by Mr. Edward S. Delaplaine of Frederick, Maryland, who supplied the author with a transcript.

[16] *Offic. Rec.*, ser. II, vol. 2, 805.

[17] Louisville *Daily Journal*, September 21, 1861, p. 3.

[18] *Offic. Rec.*, ser. II, vol. 2, 815.

however, and on the twenty-fourth he gave Catron a lengthy explanation of what had happened.

Sneed explained that when he had arrested Morehead, Durrett, and Barr, and had taken them to Indianapolis, he reported the arrests to Secretary of War Simon Cameron. And Cameron immediately directed Governor Oliver P. Morton of Indiana to "Send Governor Morehead . . . to Fort Lafayette under proper guard." [19] Military authorities took charge of the prisoners, and they were on their way to New York that night. "I never did give my consent [stated Sneed] directly or indirectly for the removal. . . ." Circuit Justice Catron took Sneed's explanation in good grace and was willing not to interpose himself. No charges, however, were voted against Morehead by grand jury sessions that met in Louisville and Frankfort shortly thereafter.

Protests against Morehead's arrest were made promptly to President Lincoln. One letter of protest bears this endorsement by the President: "Were sent to Fort Lafayette by the military authorities . . . and it would be improper for me to intervene without further knowledge of the facts than I now possess." [20]

Within two weeks Lincoln wrote to Secretary of State Seward asking him to give an interview to Samuel J. Walker, son-in-law of Morehead and "well vouched as a Union man." Lincoln informed Seward that Morehead, Durrett, and Barr should be released "when James Guthrie and James Speed [friends of Lincoln in Kentucky] think they should be." [21]

Somewhat later, Guthrie informed Lincoln that the arrest of Morehead "has not been beneficial or prejudicial to the Union cause." He stated that if Morehead would abide by Kentucky's decision to remain loyal, he should be released. And he enclosed to Lincoln a copy of General Robert J. Anderson's general order of October 7, 1861, which stated, "The commanding general learns with deep regret that arrests are being made . . . upon the slightest . . . grounds. He desires . . . [that] in all cases the evidence must be such as will convict them before a court of justice." [22]

In January, 1862, Secretary Seward gave the order to release Morehead on his promise not to enter Kentucky or take any action adverse to the United States. At Fort Warren in Boston Harbor, to which Morehead had been transferred, he took the oath prescribed and was paroled. Shortly afterwards, Secretary of War Stanton unconditionally discharged

[19] Simon Cameron to Oliver P. Morton, September 20, 1861, *ibid.*, 806.

[20] *Ibid.*, 808.

[21] Abraham Lincoln to William H. Seward, October 4, 1861, *ibid.*, 809.

[22] James Guthrie to Abraham Lincoln, October 25, 1861, *ibid.*, 814.

him from his parole. Durrett and Barr were released under similar conditions.

The other notable case of habeas corpus heard by Justice Catron in Kentucky early in the war was that of former Representative James B. Clay. Clay was among a group that was arrested by order of General Anderson on September 24, 1861. He was accused of promoting enlistment for the Southern cause. A writ of habeas corpus was sought in his behalf, and Justice Catron granted the writ on September 28. It was made returnable on September 30. General Anderson informed President Lincoln of the proceedings and stated: "I shall not resist it thinking that this course and his being placed under heavy bail for conspiracy if not treason will produce a good effect." [23]

Secretary Seward acknowledged the information that Anderson had sent the President and directed Anderson to "Consult James Guthrie . . . and unless he advises to the contrary, or in his absence James Speed, disregard the habeas corpus and send the prisoners . . . to Fort Lafayette." [24] But there had already been consultation with Guthrie, Speed, and Catron, and the plan to place Clay under heavy bail had been accepted.

Consequently, on September 30 Justice Catron took up the case of Clay. Catron admitted the accused "to bail in $5,000 for his appearance at the January term of the Court." [25] Most of the men arrested with Clay were released the next day upon taking an oath of allegiance, the oath being administered by General William T. Sherman.

In November, 1863, Justice Catron, presiding with Judge Connally F. Trigg in the Nashville, Tennessee, circuit court upheld the Confiscation Act in the case of *The United States v. The Nashville Republican Banner.* Trigg ruled, with Catron concurring, that "there being then a formidable rebellion in progress, the intention of Congress, in enacting this law, must have been to deter persons from so using and employing their property as to aid and promote the insurrection." [26]

Few of Catron's circuit decisions before the war were written. But when war came, he declared to District Judge Samuel Treat of St. Louis ". . . the necessity not only of announcing the law, but of explaining its wisdom. . . . Hence, the many written opinions since delivered from the Federal benches in his circuit; . . . . He had neither doubt, nor fear, nor hesitancy in that crisis." [27]

---

[23] Robert J. Anderson to Abraham Lincoln, September 28, 1861, *ibid.*, 885.

[24] William H. Seward to Robert J. Anderson, September 28, 1861, *ibid.*

[25] Louisville *Daily Journal,* October 1, 1861, p. 3.

[26] 27 Fed. Cas. 783; see also Washington *National Intelligencer,* November 13, 1863, p. 3.

[27] 70 U.S. x-xi.

CIRCUIT JUSTICE NOAH H. SWAYNE

Circuit Justice Swayne, like Catron, was inclined to deliver oral decisions. Consequently there is a dearth of Swayne circuit cases reported during the Civil War. Swayne's circuit first consisted of Ohio and Indiana but soon was changed to Ohio and Michigan.

In May, 1862, Justice Swayne arrived in Indianapolis to hold court with Federal Judge Samuel H. Treat of Springfield, Illinois, who was substituting for E. M. Huntington, the federal district judge in Indiana. During the term the most interesting case was that of *Hiram Wheeler v. Oliver Tousey*, a case which involved the Legal Tender Act of February 25, 1862. Disagreement between Swayne and Treat arose, and so the court certified its disagreement to the United States Supreme Court.[28]

Judge Huntington died the following October, and Justice Swayne presided alone over the circuit court in Indianapolis in November, 1862. He held court from November 17 to November 22 and then adjourned the court until January 5, 1863, at which time the newly appointed district judge for Indiana, Caleb B. Smith, took over and held court while Swayne was in Washington attending sessions of the Supreme Court.[29]

Swayne also held circuit court in Ohio, and a letter that he wrote to Secretary Chase indicates the extent to which he concerned himself with the court in Cleveland. "I understand [Swayne wrote] it has been suggested to take the Judges [sic] rooms on the Second Story of the court House . . . for the collector of taxes! & to require the Judges to occupy a room in the third story. . . . I must say I can see no good reason why our convenience should be sacrificed to that of other officers of the government." [30]

The two most notable cases that Swayne heard on circuit in Ohio in 1862 were the *United States v. James W. Chenowith* and the Rupert case.[31] Circuit Justice Swayne, presiding with District Judge Humphrey H. Leavitt, ruled in Cincinnati that James W. Chenowith, who was indicted on charges of treason, should be dismissed. George E. Pugh,

[28] Order Books of the United States circuit court in Indianapolis, vol. I, 428, Clerk's File, United States district court, Indianapolis, Indiana.

[29] *Ibid.*, 516.

[30] Noah H. Swayne to Salmon P. Chase, September 17, 1862, Chase MSS., Library of Congress.

[31] Two letters in the Thomas Ewing MSS. in the Library of Congress criticize rulings of "Judge Swayne" in Memphis, Tennessee in the year 1862. One letter is from William T. Sherman to J. H. Hammond, [?], 1862, and the other is from ————— to Swayne, November 12, 1862. The "Judge Swayne" referred to in these letters is not Justice Noah H. Swayne but Judge J. T. Swayne of the criminal court of Memphis. For information concerning the controversy between Sherman and Judge J. T. Swayne see the Memphis *Daily Bulletin*, November 15, 1862, p. 3 and the Memphis *Daily Appeal*, November 15, 1862, p. 2.

Chenowith's counsel, had made careful distinction between levying war against the United States and giving aid and comfort to the enemy. Swayne, who handed down the decision, said with obvious regret: "We sit here to administer the law, not to make it. With the excitement of the hour, we, as Judges, have nothing to do . . . Causeless and wicked as this Rebellion is, . . . it is not the less our duty to hold the scales of justice, in all cases, with a firm and steady hand." [32] The decision was not well received in certain quarters, and Secretary Chase wrote of it "Judge Swayne's opinion has take[n] many of his friends by surprise. It is a narrow and incorrect interpretation of the Constitution, in my judgment." [33]

The Rupert case came before Swayne and Leavitt in Cincinnati in the October Term, 1862. Swayne ruled, with Leavitt concurring that "this court would not grant the writ of habeas corpus, where it appeared that the detention or imprisonment was under military authority." [34]

In the fall of 1864 Swayne obligingly substituted for Circuit Justice Davis, to whom Indiana had been transferred, holding circuit court in Indianapolis during Davis's illness. It was urgent that a Supreme Court Justice be present in Indianapolis as District Judge Caleb B. Smith had died on January 7, 1864, and it was not until December 13, 1864, that Lincoln named David McDonald to fill the post. Justice Davis wrote to Swayne on October 27, 1864, "I am prostrated by illness, and am unable to . . . hold the next term of Circuit Court of Indiana. . . . You are requested to hold said Term for me, or such parts of the term as your other engagements will permit you to hold. . . ." [35] Swayne held court only briefly and adjourned so that he could proceed to Washington to participate in the December Term of the Supreme Court.

LIVELY ACTIVITY

A number of the Justices—Davis, Miller, Field, and Grier—not only were very energetic in holding circuit court during the war but delivered a large number of important written opinions as well. It is these written opinions that give insight into their feelings on numerous war-related subjects, many of which did not come before the Supreme Court itself.

CIRCUIT JUSTICE DAVID DAVIS

Early in his career as a Supreme Court Justice, David Davis narrowly averted a serious clash with the administration over the suspension of the

---

[32] Washington *National Intelligencer*, May 13, 1862, p. 2 (reprinted from the Cincinnati *Enquirer*).

[33] Salmon P. Chase to E. D. Mansfield, May 31, 1862, Chase MSS., Hist. Soc. of Pa.

[34] 28 Fed. Cas. 920.

[35] David Davis to Noah H. Swayne, October 27, 1864, quoted in the Order Books of the United States circuit court at Indianapolis, vol. J, 496.

Chicago *Times* on orders of General Ambrose E. Burnside. On June 3, 1863, the day that military authorities suspended publication of the *Times*, Justice Davis dined with Senator Orville H. Browning, Judge Samuel H. Treat, Lawrence Weldon, who was federal district attorney for the southern district of Illinois, and Antrim Campbell. Conversation drifted to a discussion of the suspension, and Browning later wrote into his diary: "We all agreed that it was a despotic and unwarrantable thing. . . ." Browning recorded that it was the opinion of all who were present that Judge Thomas Drummond should grant an injunction against the military authorities. "Judge Davis said if the application had been made to him, [Browning continued] he would not hesitate to grant it. He had been telegraphed to and will go to Chicago to night to sit with Drummond." [36]

Justice Davis, along with Senator Lyman Trumbull, telegraphed President Lincoln to rescind Burnside's order,[37] and while Drummond and Davis were hearing the case, Lincoln did so. Consequently, the judicial proceeding ended. The Washington *National Intelligencer* praised Lincoln editorially for not tolerating this additional "arbitrary" act by General Burnside.[38]

Following this term of court in Chicago, Davis returned to his home in Bloomington, his first experience as a Supreme Court Justice and as a Circuit Justice having been concluded. To his friend William W. Orme he wrote, "I have just returned from Chicago, where I have been holding Court for three weeks—The papers noticed me favorably, especially the Journal—I got along pretty well & satisfied myself—" [39]

In the course of the next year, 1864, Justice Davis participated in several terms of circuit court in the northern district of Illinois. One case in which he served along with Judge Samuel H. Treat in June, 1864, in Springfield, was of political consequence. In this case involving John Graham and others who resisted enrollment, the two jurists upheld the constitutionality of the enrollment act. Lawrence Weldon and William H. Herndon, both former close associates of the President, appeared for the government.[40]

Examination of the order books of the circuit court held at Indianapolis reveals that Circuit Justice Davis was present and served in that court during the May Term, 1863, the November Term, 1863, and the May Term, 1864. The following is typical of entries in the order books when Davis was present: "Tuesday morning 11. o'clock May 5th 1863, being

[36] Browning, *Diary*, I, 632 (June 3, 1863).

[37] Pratt, "David Davis," p. 107; Robert S. Harper, *Lincoln and the Press* (New York, 1951), p. 261.

[38] Editorial, Washington *National Intelligencer*, June 6, 1863, p. 3.

[39] David Davis to William W. Orme, July 29, 1863, Orme MSS.

[40] Washington *National Intelligencer*, June 22, 1864, p. 3.

the day fixed by law for holding circuit court of the United States for the district of Indiana, Present Honorable David Davis, one of the Justices of the Supreme Court of the United States, and the Honorable Caleb B. Smith District Judge of the United States for the District of Indiana." [41]

By 1864 Justice Davis had held two terms of Supreme Court and several terms of circuit court. Of his circuit duties he wrote, "I have just finished my summer term in Chicago. It lasted a month and was laborious. I disposed of the business to my own satisfaction, and I am led to believe, to the satisfaction of the bar." [42] Illness prevented him from serving either on circuit or in Washington during the fall of 1864 and the spring of 1865.

CIRCUIT JUSTICE SAMUEL F. MILLER

Samuel F. Miller, who held circuit court in Iowa, Kansas, Wisconsin, Missouri, and Minnesota during the war heard few cases that had political implications. The most significant case that Circuit Justice Miller heard was that of the *United States v. Michael Gleason*.[43] This case involved indictment on the charge of killing an enrolling officer and was heard in the circuit court for Iowa during the May Term, 1864. The indictment alleged that Gleason assaulted and wounded an enrollment officer, and that the wounds resulted in death.

Gleason's counsel maintained that the indictment was faulty in that "it contains no allegation that the assault was made with the intent to hinder, delay, obstruct, or oppose in any manner, the execution of the duties in which the officers were engaged."

Miller ruled that although offenses against such persons as enrolling officers must be punished, if the offenses are "committed against them, not as officers, but in personal difficulties totally disconnected with their official duties," the persons who committed the offenses were not answerable under the act in question before the court.

He agreed that the indictment in this case was faulty. "The true principle seems to be, [stated Miller] that it must appear that the animus of the assault grew out of, or had some relation to, the discharge by the officer of his official duties. And if this is necessary to appear in proof, it is equally necessary that some averment of it should be made in the indictment. Nothing of this kind is found here." Consequently, Miller sustained the contentions of Gleason's counsel. Gleason was retained in custody, however, and the grand jury agreed upon a new indictment which resulted in his conviction in 1867.

---

[41] Order Books of the United States circuit court at Indianapolis, vol. J, 121.

[42] Pratt, "David Davis" p. 104.

[43] 25 Fed. Cas. 1335.

CIRCUIT JUSTICE STEPHEN J. FIELD

It was Justice Stephen J. Field who had the longest and most difficult trip of all the Civil War Justices when he set out to go to his Far Western circuit. "He was . . . compelled, until the overland railroad was completed, [wrote one of his early biographers] to travel, going by the way of the Isthmus, over twelve thousand miles a year. . . ." [44] When his office was established, he was allowed one thousand dollars for traveling expenses.

During the war Circuit Justice Field heard a large number of the usual cases and a number of novel cases, as well. A case involving treason, the *United States v. Greathouse*, which was heard on October 17, 1863, at San Francisco, proved to be the most significant case that Field heard on circuit during the war. Serving with Field was District Judge Ogden Hoffman.

Revenue officers seized *The Schooner J. M. Chapman* in the harbor of San Francisco on March 15, 1863. The vessel was making ready to sail in the service of the Confederacy. Leaders of the expedition were Ridgeley Greathouse, Asbury Harpending, Alfred Rubery, William C. Law, and Lorenzo L. Libby. They were arrested on the charge of aiding the Confederacy.

Harpending, a native of Kentucky, and Rubery, a native of England, had received from Jefferson Davis a letter of marque giving authorization to prey upon the merchant shipping of the United States. Needing financial assistance, they contacted Greathouse, who supplied the necessary funds. In addition to privateering, their plan included an attempt to bring about an uprising in the state of California.[45]

Delos Lake and Alexander Campbell, attorneys for the defendants, argued that the schooner had not started on its voyage and that therefore no offense was committed. After arguments were completed, both Judge Hoffman and Justice Field charged the jury. Hoffman declared that it was inconsequential whether the voyage had begun or not. The intention of the defendants was clearly established, he explained, and as a consequence punishment was justified.

Justice Field not only charged the jury at length but took careful pains to instruct it as to its role. He discussed what constituted treason and stated: "War has been levied against the United States. . . . all who aid . . . are equally guilty of treason within the constitutional provision." [46] Justice Field did not hesitate to lead the jury to its decision. He

---

[44] Chauncey F. Black and Samuel B. Smith, eds., *Some Account of the Work of Stephen J. Field as a Legislator, State Judge, and Judge of the Supreme Court of the United States* (New York, 1881), second pagination, pp. 39-40.

[45] 26 Fed. Cas. 20.

[46] *Ibid.*, 22.

pointed out that when the defendants received the letter of marque they became "leagued with the insurgents." [47]

Field's charge to the jury was impressive. Furthermore, as Swisher, Field's most distinguished biographer has pointed out, "It is hard to read the charge without a conviction that Field . . . [was determined] that the jury, unless corrupt or a marvel of obtuseness would declare the prisoners guilty." [48]

When the case was presented to the jury, the defendants were found guilty. Alfred Rubery, the Englishman, soon gained his freedom, however, through special pardon by President Lincoln, who complied with the wishes of John Bright. And the other prisoners gained their freedom, too, as the result of proceedings that were heard by Judge Hoffman at San Francisco on February 15, 1864. Hoffman was presiding alone because Field was in Washington.

The prisoners claimed that under the President's proclamation of December 8, 1863, providing for pardon of those who would subscribe to an oath of allegiance, they were entitled to freedom if they took the oath. With great reluctance Judge Hoffman ruled that the prisoners were covered by the President's pardon. He emphasized that the legality of the earlier sentence was neither questioned nor denied. And he expressed the view that if this case had been brought to the attention of President Lincoln, he would have made a special exception of these petitioners. [49]

CIRCUIT JUSTICE ROBERT C. GRIER

Justice Robert C. Grier had occasion to demonstrate his loyalty and devotion to the Union early in the war. It was in circuit cases in Pennsylvania that he stated the views that later were enunciated by the Supreme Court in the *Prize Cases.*

In October, 1861, there came before District Judge John Cadwalader and Circuit Justice Grier at Philadelphia the case of the *United States v. William Smith.* Smith was charged with piracy. This case gave Grier an opportunity to state his views in relation to the events that were interfering with federal authority. And Grier helped point the way, too, for the reasoning that was to sustain Lincoln's policy of blockade.

In charging the jury Grier expressed disagreement with Smith's counsel who contended that Smith was not guilty because he acted under authority granted by the Confederacy. Grier recognized in this an implication that the Confederacy was an independent and sovereign state. In refuting this position Justice Grier declared: "A successful rebellion

---

[47] *Ibid.,* 25.

[48] Swisher, *Stephen J. Field,* p. 132.

[49] 10 Fed. Cas. 1062.

may be termed a revolution; but until it becomes such it has no claim
to be recognized as a member of the family, or exercise the rights or
enjoy the privileges consequent on sovereignty." [50]

Grier demonstrated a sound grasp of the problems that the administration faced. He explained to the jury the role of the government and
of the courts in time of rebellion. He pointed out that when rebellion
occurs, the courts must "view such contested government as it is viewed
by the legislative and executive departments of the government. . . ."
"Consequently," he concluded, "this court . . . can view those in rebellion
. . . in no other light than as traitors to their country and those who
assume by their authority a right to plunder the property of our citizens
on the high seas as pirates and robbers." [51]

In two instances in 1863 special emphasis was made by federal judges
in Pennsylvania of the fact that Justice Grier endorsed decisions handed
down in federal district courts of the state. One was a case in which
Judge Cadwalader, in the United States district court in Philadelphia,
upheld the constitutionality of the conscription act.[52] The other was a
case involving Joseph Will, who was found guilty of violating the enrollment act by assaulting an enrollment officer. Federal District Judge
Wilson McCandless announced that this case, heard in Pittsburgh, was of
such importance that he had conferred with Justice Grier.[53]

In 1864 Justice Grier in two notable circuit cases upheld property
rights and contractual obligations. In charging the jury in one of the
cases, that of the West Chester *Jeffersonian*, a Democratic newspaper
which had been seized in August, 1861, Justice Grier declared that
"There was no justification for the seizure, that the District Attorney had
no right to issue such an order and the Marshal none to execute it." [54]
In the other case Grier ruled that legal tender notes could not be offered
to satisfy Pennsylvania ground rents because ground rents could not be
considered debts. Although the ruling had no relation to the constitutionality of the Legal Tender Act, Grier declared, "The treasury notes are
made lawful or current money, and a legal tender for debt, etc., as
between individuals. As this is the first act in which this high prerogative
of sovereignty has been exercised, it should be construed strictly. It is
doubtful in policy and dangerous as a precedent." [55]

---

[50] 27 Fed. Cas. 1135.

[51] *Ibid.*, 1136.

[52] Washington *National Intelligencer*, September 11, 1863, p. 3.

[53] 28 Fed. Cas. 608.

[54] Washington *National Intelligencer*, October 29, 1864, p. 3 (reprinted from the
Philadelphia *Ledger*).

[55] 19 Fed. Cas. 492.

THE ADMINISTRATION DEFIED

CIRCUIT JUSTICE SAMUEL NELSON

Justice Samuel Nelson fulfilled his circuit duties devotedly during the Civil War. Although he heard cases throughout his circuit, the circuit court for the southern district of New York demanded much of his attention because of the vast quantity of litigation that came before it.

Cases which related to condemnation of vessels as prize came before Circuit Justice Nelson in the fall of 1861 while he was presiding in New York City. And in charging the jury on November 4, he commented generally on the crisis that faced the nation and upon the crime of treason.[56]

Early in the war Circuit Justice Nelson heard piracy cases. On October 30, 1861, he heard the case of the *United States v. Thomas H. Baker*, involving the private armed schooner, *The Savannah*, of which Baker was master. Baker acted under a commission from Jefferson Davis and was charged with piracy. In charging the jury Nelson declared: "Until . . . the recognition of the new government, the courts are obliged to regard the ancient state of things as remaining unchanged. This has been the uniform course of decisions and practice of the courts of the United States." [57] But no verdict could be arrived at because Nelson left the jury to decide whether the federal government had or had not granted recognition to the Confederacy.

Emphasizing the need for the Supreme Court to clarify the subject of prize law, two cases in which District Judge Samuel R. Betts of the southern district court of New York had condemned vessels as prize— *The Hiawatha* and *The Crenshaw*—were appealed in November, 1861, to the circuit court over which Nelson presided. In order to facilitate the obtaining of a decision of the Supreme Court, Nelson affirmed the decrees of Judge Betts "without delivering any opinion, or expressing any." [58] Nelson delayed the hearing of other prize cases, such as *The Sarah Starr* and *The Sunbeam*, until the Supreme Court had spoken.

Following the decision of the Supreme Court on March 10, 1863, regarding the *Prize Cases*, Justice Nelson took up the cases pending in his circuit. On July 17, 1863, he handed down a large number of decisions involving prize. In most instances, of course, in harmony with the ruling of the Supreme Court, vessels and cargoes were condemned. Nonetheless, Nelson made a careful examination of each case, and whenever special circumstances existed, his tendency was to make some exception.[59]

[56] 30 Fed. Cas. 1035.
[57] 24 Fed. Cas. 966.
[58] 12 Fed. Cas. 94.
[59] 8 Fed. Cas. 695-96; 10 Fed. Cas. 574-75.

CIRCUIT JUSTICE NATHAN CLIFFORD

One case alone, the Winder case, stands out among the numerous cases that Circuit Justice Nathan Clifford heard in Maine, Massachusetts, Rhode Island, and New Hampshire during the Civil War. William H. Winder of Philadelphia and his brother Charles H. Winder of Washington carried on treasonable correspondence with rebels and rebel sympathizers. Both were arrested, and Charles Winder was soon paroled, but the case of his brother, William, took on many complexities and became widely known.

William Winder was arrested in Philadelphia on September 10, 1861, on the order of Brigadier General Andrew Porter, Provost-Marshal of the Army. The charge against him was that he conspired to overthrow the government of the United States, and a hearing was conducted on September 13.

At the hearing the United States district attorney, George A. Coffey, produced a telegram from Secretary of War Cameron which stated, "Have telegraphed Marshal [William] Millward to arrest Wm. H. Winder and transfer him to Fort Lafayette." [60] Millward actually had received such orders both from Secretary Cameron and Secretary Seward. Consequently Winder was transferred that night to Fort Lafayette, New York. Before his removal from Fort Lafayette to Fort Warren in Boston Harbor early in November, 1861, he was permitted to consult with Richard M. Blatchford, a New York lawyer.

While Winder was at Fort Warren, a letter from Secretary of State Seward was read to all prisoners of state which invited them to present the facts of their case to the Secretary. "I have been confined now," wrote Winder, taking advantage of Seward's invitation, "nearly thirteen weeks, and during all that time I have been unable to learn of my charge whatever; consequently, I can only state that I am unconscious of word or act inconsistent with the character of a true American citizen. . . ." [61]

The result of his letter was that Assistant Secretary of State Frederick W. Seward wrote Colonel Justin Dimick, commandant of Fort Warren, to release Winder if he would take an oath of allegiance to the United States and if he would agree not to enter the insurrectionary states.[62] Winder promptly refused.

Following these events, Winder addressed himself to the new Secretary of War, Edwin M. Stanton, complaining that he had been held for five months without "process or form of law." "If there be any charge of crime against me, [Winder concluded] I am ready to meet it. If there be none, I trust the secretary will see that to impose conditions on me as

[60] 30 Fed. Cas. 288.

[61] Ibid.

[62] Frederick W. Seward to Justin Dimick, January 10, 1862, Offic. Rec., ser. II, vol. 2, 736-37.

the price of my liberation, is to aggravate the wrong which will then stand confessed." [63]

Three weeks later, March 15, 1862, Winder wrote to former Secretary of War Cameron to learn why he had ordered his arrest. Cameron denied that he was responsible and said that he assumed that Secretary Seward had ordered it. Nonetheless, Cameron's request for the arrest does exist in the records of the War Department.[64]

United States commissioners visited Fort Warren in May, 1862, to question prisoners of state, and they talked to Winder on May 7 and informed him that his offense was his correspondence with rebels as well as his newspaper articles. They concluded that his case should be taken under advisement, but he never heard from them.

Winder's counsel entered the October Term, 1862, of circuit court for the district of Massachusetts, over which Circuit Justice Clifford presided, to obtain a writ of habeas corpus. The facts of the case were presented on October 25. Without hesitation Justice Clifford issued the writ. "Nothing need be added to the narrative of the facts as set forth in the petition, [Clifford announced] to demonstrate that the petition shows probable ground to conclude that he is imprisoned and restrained of his liberty without just cause." [65]

Since the United States marshal refused to serve the writ, Justice Clifford assigned the task to B. F. Bayley, a deputy sheriff, who proceeded to the commercial wharf on October 28. But the captain of the steamboat which went out to Fort Warren refused passage to Bayley, saying that no one could come aboard without a pass from Colonel Dimick.

The next day at three P.M. Bayley arrived at the landing place for the fort aboard a sailboat that he had hired to provide passage. He faced a body of some fifty armed men who warned him to leave, although he announced that he brought a writ from the circuit court at Boston to serve upon Colonel Dimick and he withdrew.

Bayley recounted his experience to Clifford when court reconvened on the thirteenth. Bayley declared that if he had attempted to land he "should have been prevented from so doing by the force of armed men drawn up at the landing. . . ." [66] Clifford stated that he did not see any possibility of making the writ effective. He said that "The court deeply regrets that officers of the United States should obstruct process out of a court of the United States, especially this process." He directed that the writ be placed on file and served when it became "practicable" to do so.

William B. Reed, a member of Winder's counsel, thanked the court

---

[63] 30 Fed. Cas. 290.

[64] Ibid.

[65] Ibid., 293.

[66] Ibid., 294.

for its sympathetic treatment and pointed out that the case was similar to that of John Merryman of Maryland. He lamented that ". . . here in Massachusetts, many hundreds of miles away from any scene of war, where perfect peace reigns, and every peaceful relation of life is maintained . . . the writ which your honor granted is both evaded and resisted, and an imprisoned American citizen is denied the common right of knowing who are his accusers and of what he is accused." [67]

The New York *World* and the Washington *Morning Chronicle* reacted to the Winder case as could be expected. "What true American citizen does not hang his head in shame [editorialized the *World*] as he reads the record of the closing scenes in the Winder case—a long course of outrageous tyranny fitly consummated with insult and mockery to the very forms of decency and law! . . . And this happened in Massachusetts—in Boston harbor, near by where Liberty was cradled, where patriots gave their lives in her behalf. . . ." [68] But the *Chronicle* could find only praise for the detention of Winder. "Has Mr. Justice Clifford, [asked the *Chronicle*] who recently issued the writ of *habeas corpus* to deliver a prisoner from Fort Warren, done any act or said a word during the war to suppress treason or aid the Government? . . . Where has judicial power and influence been executed but *against* the Government, and where has it not been the favorite shelter of public enemies?" [69]

Despite the refusal of the military authorities to bow to the demands of Clifford, within a month orders were issued by the adjutant-general's office in Washington, and Colonel Dimick released William H. Winder on November 26, 1862. So the judicial process of the United States, issued by Circuit Justice Clifford, finally won out. But the refusal of Colonel Dimick to accept the writ provided evidence again that Lincoln's policy was to allow federal judicial process to go unheeded if it seemed best to ignore it. That the writ granted by Clifford did influence the administration cannot be denied however. Here again, the federal judiciary was flouted by the administration of Abraham Lincoln.

The circuit duties of the members of the Taney Court, as this discussion reveals, brought the Justices intimately into contact with the people and their legal controversies. In fact it is correct to say that circuit activities of the Justices were almost as important as their duties in Washington. Although the oppressive nature of circuit duties inevitably was to dictate modification, one cannot but express some regret that the intimate circuit relations between the Justices and the people came to an end in the years after the war.

---

[67] *Ibid.*

[68] Editorial, New York *World*, November 3, 1862, p. 4.

[69] Editorial, Washington *Morning Chronicle*, November 24, 1862, p. 2.

CHAPTER FIFTEEN

Avalanche of Ambition

TANEY DEAD

As time went on Attorney General Bates became more and more convinced that death would intervene in the Court to enable the Republicans to make additional appointments. In 1864 he repeatedly predicted the death of Taney, or Wayne, or Catron, or Grier. All evidence seemed to fortify the Attorney General's feeling, but the fulfillment of his anticipations was delayed.[1]

At 7:13 A.M. on October 13, 1864, Edwin M. Stanton filed a telegram bearing these tidings to his friend Salmon P. Chase: "Chief Justice Taney died last night." [2] Taney had been able to serve on the bench only a few days during the previous term. Announcement of his death, an impatiently anticipated event in Republican circles, set in motion the machinery that would produce the first Republican Chief Justice of the United States.

Taney's death was a signal for rejoicing among most of Washington officialdom as well as most of the press. But one adviser of the President, the Attorney General, the member of the administration whose duties brought him most closely in contact with the Supreme Court, had gained a deep respect for the aged Chief Justice although their views were in conflict. Bates recorded in his diary that he had called at the residence shortly before Taney's death and "was told that he was *no better*, and I was prepared at any moment to hear of his death."

It is interesting to note Bates's final judgment of this man who had been in such bitter dispute with the Lincoln administration. "He was [recorded Bates] a man of great and varied talents; a model of a presiding officer; and the last specimen within my knowledge of a graceful and polished old gentleman." Bates concluded that although Taney's reputation was "dimmed by the bitterness of party feeling arising out of his unfortunate judgment in the Dred Scott case," in time his fame would be properly restored.[3]

The Washington *Morning Chronicle*, which had abused Taney in its

---

[1] Bates, *Diary*, pp. 341-42 (March 2, 1864). See also *ibid.*, pp. 354-55 (April 6, 1864); *ibid.*, 355 (April 6, 1864); *ibid.*, 358 (April 11, 1864).

[2] Edwin M. Stanton to Salmon P. Chase, October 13, 1864, Chase MSS., Hist. Soc. of Pa.

[3] Bates, *Diary*, p. 418 (October 13, 1864).

columns, informed its readers, "Scarce any knew that the beloved and honored jurist had been for days at the point of death. . . . To the last, he exhibited to his relatives, and even to servants, that thoughtful gracious-ness of manner, that effort to lighten their attentive labors, which has marked his entire life." [4]

One of Taney's daughters, in a letter she wrote shortly after his death, said that he had survived so many earlier attacks that his death, though long expected, came upon the family quite suddenly. "His mind was always so clear & strong," she continued, "that I think it made us lose sight of his great age." On the day of his death he said to her, " 'My dear child my race is run—'. . . . He asked . . . to receive the last rites of his Church, calmly & distinctly gave directions for such preparations as he wished to make for them. . . ." [5]

The death of Chief Justice Taney was discussed in a meeting of Lin-coln's cabinet on October 14. Plans for the funeral were considered, and the President and his advisers debated the propriety of attending the services. Burial was to be in Frederick, Maryland, the boyhood home of Taney.

Secretary of State Seward felt that it was his duty "to attend the funeral in this city but not farther, and advised that the President should also," Secretary of the Navy Welles recorded in his diary. Bates indicated that he felt it was his duty to proceed to Frederick. President Lincoln inquired of Welles what he thought was proper, and Welles answered that perhaps the President, the Secretary of State, and the Attorney General should attend the funeral, but he believed that "it would be best not to take official action but to let each member of the Cabinet act his pleasure." [6]

Taney had directed that there be no public display at the funeral, so no effort was made to take his body to the Supreme Court chambers to lie in state. The Washington *Evening Star* reported that arrangements, in charge of Marshal Ward H. Lamon, provided for a special train departing at 7:00 A.M., October 15, to carry the remains of the Chief Justice to Frederick. Officers of the Court, members of the Supreme Court bar, friends, and relatives were to be aboard. [7]

Bates closed the Attorney General's office the day of the funeral and accompanied the funeral party to Frederick. President Lincoln, Secretary of State Seward, and Postmaster General Dennison "attended the body, from the [Taney] dwelling to the [railroad] cars." Bates wrote of the

[4] Washington *Morning Chronicle*, October 14, 1864, p. 2.

[5] Anne A. Campbell to Margaret Birnie, October 31, 1864, Delaplaine Collection.

[6] Welles, *Diary*, II, 176-77 (October 14, 1864).

[7] Washington *Evening Star*, October 14, 1864, p. 2.

funeral: "High Mass was sung in the Jesuits' church . . . and I saw his body placed in the grave (beside his mother, as he had ordered) in the old church yard. . . ." [8]

When the Supreme Court assembled for its December Term, 1864, a committee of the bar under the chairmanship of Thomas Ewing of Ohio presented a resolution of tribute to the deceased Chief Justice. Supreme Court Reporter Wallace recorded that "the Honorable Mr. Justice Wayne, Senior Associate of the Court, who had sat on the bench for a longer time than even the whole of the term in which the late Chief Justice was here," responded in behalf of the Court. In acknowledging the tribute, Wayne drew parallels between Roger B. Taney and John Marshall, affirming that these two men were responsible for building up the great prestige of the Court.[9]

The death of Taney ended an epoch in the history of the Supreme Court. It occurred almost six months before the end of the war, and some Republicans were quickly able to overcome their bitterness toward him. Greeley's New York *Tribune* declared, "He was the product of circumstances which (we trust) will mold the character of no future Chief Justice . . . but it is unjust to presume that he did not truly and earnestly seek the good of his country." [10] But Andrew Johnson, who was soon to be elected Vice President of the United States, declared: "Taney is dead! and let freedom and justice rejoice. He has gone into his tomb, remembered only to be despised." [11]

THE LESSER CONTENDERS

The vacancy in the Chief Justiceship was sought by a number of contenders—contenders who exerted almost every conceivable pressure upon President Lincoln. The Chief Justiceship had been vacant only once before since the century began. The four appointees of Lincoln had already heralded the opening of a new constitutional era. Taney had been a link with the past; by 1850 all of the Associate Justices who were on the bench when he became Chief Justice were gone except two— Justice McLean and Justice Wayne. And by 1861 only Justice Wayne remained. With the appointment of a new Chief Justice, Lincoln's remolding of the Court would be complete.

Immediately after the death of Taney Lincoln was given advice as to the proper procedure in naming his successor and what qualifications a new Chief Justice should have. Election day was around the corner—

[8] Bates, *Diary*, p. 419 (October 15, 1864).

[9] 69 U.S. ix-xii.

[10] Editorial, New York *Tribune*, October 14, 1864, p. 4.

[11] Editorial, New York *World*, October 25, 1864, p. 4, quoting the Nashville *Times*.

November 8, 1864—and it appeared expedient to many of Lincoln's followers to delay making the appointment until after the presidential election. It would be sound strategy to keep all aspirants guessing.[12]

Alfred Conkling, a prominent jurist of New York, wrote Secretary Seward a letter covering the problems to be considered in naming a Chief Justice, and Seward turned the letter over to the President. Conkling doubted that any candidate possessed fully the qualities that he deemed essential. He declared that the new Chief Justice must be a man of "commanding talent" because the court "stands sadly in need of a strong balance wheel," that he must be a "*young* man" and a "sound & *learned* lawyer." Conkling feared that the appointment would go to Salmon P. Chase, who was mentioned as the leading candidate. Conkling found Chase too "far advanced in years (more than 60, is he not?)," and in addition he believed Chase too little learned in the law.[13]

One Ohioan, writing Lincoln on the subject of the new Chief Justice, said that the man chosen should be a lawyer who fully understood the genius of the American government, but his final remark was one of pessimism: "I do not pretend to know *who* that man is." [14] Many men not only pretended to know who should preside over the Supreme Court, they waged energetic battles and intrigued in behalf of their favorites. The consequence was that in addition to the leading contenders there were many other men recommended to the President.

Among those of lesser importance suggested were John Jay of New York, grandson of the first Chief Justice; Judge William Strong of the supreme court of Pennsylvania; Lewis B. Woodruff, who served for twelve years as New York superior and common pleas judge; Daniel S. Dickinson, formerly attorney general of New York; Senator Ira Harris of New York; William Curtiss Noyes, a leading New York lawyer; Frederick K. Fogg of Boston; and John K. Porter of the New York court of appeals.

Lincoln was overwhelmed not only by the outpouring of recommendations for the leading contenders but also by recommendations in behalf of these lesser public figures. Senator John P. Hale wrote Lincoln: "There is a John Jay of New York who would make a Chief Justice of the same Court now in no respect unequal to the first [Chief Justice]." [15] Proposing Judge William Strong of Pennsylvania, M. P. Boyer of Reading wrote the President: "I have no doubt you are very much perplexed whom to appoint," as he, himself, added to the President's perplexity.[16] Another

---

[12] James A. Briggs to William Dennison, October 13, 1864, Lincoln MSS.

[13] Alfred Conkling to William H. Seward, October 21, 1864, *ibid*.

[14] Milton Sutliff to Abraham Lincoln, October 16, 1864, *ibid*.

[15] John P. Hale to Abraham Lincoln, October 16, 1864, *ibid*.

[16] M. P. Boyer to Abraham Lincoln, October 18, 1864, *ibid*.

correspondent advised the appointment of Lewis B. Woodruff, telling Lincoln: "The recent dispensation of Providence, in removing . . . [Taney] has revived a wish, whose nature it may not be improper to whisper in the Ear of my president." [17] Pushing Daniel S. Dickinson for the post, Judge Ransom Balcom of Binghamton, New York, wrote: "He is sound and entirely reliable. . . ." [18]

Senator Ira Harris, who had had a notable career as a judge, was recommended to the President in these terms: "You will find him a true friend, a safe counsellor & an able Judge—" [19] Senator Edwin D. Morgan of New York recommended William C. Noyes of the New York bar, writing, "He would be safe and discreet upon the great and important questions which in the next few years will necessarily come before the Supreme Court—" [20] Another correspondent counseled Lincoln: "Frederick K. Fogg [of] Boston should be made Chief Judge, ask Sumner." [21] And John T. Hall of Albany urged Lincoln to appoint Judge John K. Porter of the New York court of appeals.[22]

Although Lincoln was approached by the followers of these men of lesser importance, greater pressures were built up in behalf of the men who were deemed to be first-rate contenders for the office.

ASPIRANTS OF THE COURT AND BAR

Lincoln might have chosen to elevate a member of the Supreme Court. Custom dictated selection of a person who was not serving on the Court however. Several members either had an interest in obtaining the headship of the Court or were seriously mentioned in relation to it, including Justices Wayne, Davis, and Swayne. And William M. Evarts, a member of the Supreme Court bar, was prominently mentioned as a candidate.

Justice Wayne was discussed favorably by the Washington *National Intelligencer* which noted that "The Kentucky *Commonwealth*, speaks of Judge Wayne . . . as an eminently proper appointment for the vacant Chief Justiceship, and as a suitable acknowledgment of his pure patriotism. . . ." [23] As to the possibility of Justice Davis becoming Chief Justice, the New York *Times* declared: "Justice Davis . . . will all but certainly, be Chief Justice. . . ." [24] But Davis was well aware that he was not in the running.[25]

---

[17] Las Casos L. Dean to Abraham Lincoln, October 14, 1864, *ibid.*

[18] Ransom Balcom to Abraham Lincoln, November 18, 1864, *ibid.*

[19] Thomas W. Olcott to Abraham Lincoln, November 1, 1864, *ibid.*

[20] Edwin D. Morgan to Abraham Lincoln, November 9, 1864, *ibid.*

[21] Richard W. Henshaw to Abraham Lincoln, November 14, 1864, *ibid.*

[22] John T. Hall to Abraham Lincoln, October 17, 1864, *ibid.*

[23] Washington *National Intelligencer*, December 6, 1864, p. 3.

[24] New York *Times*, November 28, 1864, p. 4.

[25] David Davis to William W. Orme, December 19, 1864, Orme MSS.

Justice Swayne was widely supported. Rumors that he would become Chief Justice were reported to Senator Charles Sumner by John Jay the day after Taney died. These reports were based upon the fact that early in 1864 a strong movement developed within the Court to have one of its members succeed Taney. Justice Swayne had written to his friend Samuel J. Tilden on February 19, 1864, telling him of the movement: "while he [Taney] was so ill the Court expressed a wish, that in the event of a vacancy—the most worthy of its members should succeed him. The intimation was most kindly received at the Whitehouse [sic]." [26]

Chase, writing to Sumner while the appointment pended, reported that he had heard that the Justices had drawn up a statement asking for the appointment of Swayne if a vacancy occurred. It was his conclusion, however, that such a petition would carry no more weight than other petitions sent to the President. [27] Whether or not the request of the Justices was in written form, no such petition is found today in the Robert Todd Lincoln collection.

Henry S. Foote, a former governor of Mississippi, sheds light upon this recommendation by the Court. Foote explained in his *Casket of Reminiscences* that after the request of the Justices, Lincoln promised to appoint Swayne when the occasion presented itself. When the vacancy occurred in October, 1864, the presidential campaign was in progress, and Lincoln feared greatly for his re-election. According to Foote, prominent men in the Republican party visited him, urging that Chase be given the post, and these complications forced the President to seek release from the pledge he had given Swayne. "When President Lincoln approached . . . [Swayne] and informed him of the perplexing dilemna [Foote related] he cheerfully consented to sacrifice his own claims to official promotion upon the altar of his country's happiness." [28]

The Robert Todd Lincoln collection includes numerous recommendations sent to the President supporting Justice Swayne. Prominent among those who wrote in his behalf were members of the bench and bar within the circuit over which he presided. Alfred Russell, the United States district attorney for the eastern district of Michigan, wrote Lincoln that "a large and respectable portion of the Republican party in Michigan" felt that Swayne "would honor the place and the administration." [29] Federal District Judge Hiram V. Willson of the northern district of Ohio told Lincoln that the chief judicial officer of the nation should be chosen from the *"Great West."* [30]

[26] Noah H. Swayne to Samuel J. Tilden, February 19, 1864, Tilden MSS., N.Y. Pub. Lib.

[27] Salmon P. Chase to Charles Sumner, November 12, 1864, Chase MSS., Library of Congress.

[28] Henry S. Foote, *Casket of Reminiscences* (Washington, 1874), pp. 413-15.

[29] Alfred Russell to Abraham Lincoln, November 7, 1864, Lincoln MSS.

[30] H. V. Willson to Abraham Lincoln, November 10, 1864, *ibid.*

Another correspondent who wrote to Lincoln in Swayne's behalf declared that the new Chief Justice should be "one, who *is* and always *has* been a lawyer, and never an office-seeking politician; one, who desires to be only a Chief Justice, and will never seek to be President." [31] Samuel Galloway, a leading Ohio Republican said that he preferred Swayne because Chase "would accept the place if chosen, as a mere stepping stone to the Presidency—" [32]

With a considerable lack of discretion even the newly appointed reporter of the Court, John W. Wallace, entered into the struggle. Wallace expressed his views to William Dennison. He said that many people were speaking to him about the vacancy and that he "generally replied that the President was a lawyer, and his appointments to the bench . . . had been good, & that I thought the matter safe in his hands." As to the general attitude toward Swayne, Wallace said that the bar felt it knew him, and that he was a "good judge" and a "good man." Wallace explained that he was writing because of Dennison's friendly relations with Swayne, adding: "I am not intimate with him at all, but I have respect for him." [33] Dennison passed the Wallace letter on to the President, and today it is in the Robert Todd Lincoln collection.

Two other interesting letters directed to Lincoln in Swayne's behalf should be mentioned. Both were written by Justice David Davis. In the first letter Davis informed Lincoln that his views were unchanged since the last winter; he believed Swayne should be made head of the Court. Speaking boldly, Davis said: "No regular partisan ought to be elevated to such a place[.] Judicial life should be kept as free as possible from party politics." [34] In the second letter Davis wrote more earnestly yet. He admitted that Marshall and Taney were taken from the bar rather than the bench but argued, "when a gentleman is on the bench, who is equal to the place, and the equal of any who are talked of, it Seems to me, that he is entitled to the position." [35]

And here rested the case of Justice Swayne. It had been presented to Lincoln with great care. Whether Swayne could overcome the competition of others remained to be seen.

One other person associated with the Supreme Court remains to be discussed, William M. Evarts, grandson of Roger Sherman. Secretary Welles, who spoke with Lincoln on November 23 about the Chief Justiceship, reveals in his diary that they discussed the candidacy of Evarts. Welles recorded that Lincoln remarked that " 'There is a tremendous pressure just now for Evarts of New York, who, I suppose, is a

[31] B. White to Abraham Lincoln, November 7, 1864, *ibid.*
[32] Samuel Galloway to Abraham Lincoln, November 15, 1864, *ibid.*
[33] John W. Wallace to William Dennison, November 28, 1864, *ibid.*
[34] David Davis to Abraham Lincoln, October 22, 1864, *ibid.*
[35] David Davis to Abraham Lincoln, November 29, 1864, *ibid.*

good lawyer?' This he put inquiringly. I stated that . . . perhaps no one
was more prominent as a lawyer." Welles wished to promote the candidacy of Montgomery Blair, so he went on to tell Lincoln that the new
Chief Justice must be more than a prominent lawyer.[36]

Support for Evarts came especially from Rhode Island, Maryland,
Massachusetts, and, of course, New York. Congressman Thomas A.
Jenckes of Rhode Island wrote Secretary Seward that he could obtain
the "almost unanimous recommendation" of the entire eastern bar in
behalf of Evarts.[37] Massachusetts gave Evarts considerable support.
Judge Ebenezer R. Hoar and Richard H. Dana, Jr., mobilized the sentiment of the state in Evart's behalf.[38]

The strongest support for Evarts, however, came from his home state
of New York. Several members of the New York court of appeals
petitioned Lincoln, stating that they could "speak with entire confidence
of his eminent qualifications for that high position. . . ."[39] And a former
judge of that court, Alexander S. Johnson, who had served on the New
York appeal court "at different times with thirty-seven associates," declared that Evarts had displayed unusual mastery of judicial problems in
New York.[40] Edwards Pierrepont, a war Democrat and formerly a judge
in New York City, wrote Lincoln an elaborate letter in support of Evarts.
Pierrepont suggested to Lincoln that the man he named would probably
"remain before your eyes, and the eyes of your countrymen for the next
twenty years—" He declared that Evarts was ideal for the post, adding,
"There is as sure to be a leader in a bench of ten judges, as there is to be
a stronger ox in a lot of ten. . . ."[41]

But before Lincoln could make his choice he had to examine the
claims and qualifications of another group of aspirants that presented him
with insistent demands.

ADVISERS AND FORMER ADVISERS

Three advisers of the President, none of whom was seriously con-
sidered for appointment as Chief Justice, were Secretary of State William
H. Seward, Secretary of the Treasury William P. Fessenden, and Judge
Advocate General Joseph Holt.

One correspondent told Lincoln that in considering a suitable successor to Taney "the name of Mr. Seward should not be omitted."[42]

[36] Welles, Diary, II, 181-82 (November 26, 1864).
[37] Thomas A. Jenckes to William H. Seward, October 17, 1864, Lincoln MSS.
[38] E. L. Pierce to Salmon P. Chase, November 14, 1864, Chase MSS., Hist. Soc. of Pa.
[39] H. Denio and others to Abraham Lincoln, November 4, 1864, Lincoln MSS.
[40] Alexander S. Johnson to Abraham Lincoln, November 7, 1864, ibid.
[41] Edwards Pierrepont to Abraham Lincoln, November 24, 1864, ibid.
[42] Benjamin H. Brewster to Abraham Lincoln, October 14, 1864, ibid.

Vice President Hannibal Hamlin interceded in behalf of Secretary Fessenden. Hamlin informed Lincoln that he was going to New York and Pennsylvania "to engage in the Pres[iden]t[ial] canvass" but that he would come to Washington if it "would be of any avail." Hamlin declared: "if you can . . . give him the place it will confer a lasting obligation upon me—" [43] The New York *Times* reported that Joseph Holt was being given careful consideration.[44] But Lincoln revealed to John Hay that although he would appoint Holt to the Supreme Court "if a vacancy should occur . . . in any Southern district," he was not seriously considered for the Chief Justiceship.[45]

Three others who associated closely with Lincoln or who had associated closely with him—Secretary of War Stanton, former Postmaster General Blair, and Attorney General Bates—were given wide support for the appointment or energetically solicited the post.

Stanton had vast support in this race for the Chief Justiceship. Shortly after Taney died, a friend in Pennsylvania inquired of Stanton whether he had any interest in the post. "I do not want to move in this matter [he informed Stanton] except to further *you* or your candidate if you are going to *be* or have one—" [46] Justice Grier wrote Stanton: "It would give me the greatest pleasure and satisfaction to have you preside on our bench—I am sure you would be the *right man* in the *right* place." [47] Another correspondent urged Stanton to seek the post "and build up the court as you have" the War Department.[48]

Several persons urged the President to appoint Stanton. One cited Stanton's Herculean capacity for work, concluding, "we want a Chief Justice who will not hesitate to hang traitors—" [49] And Governor Tod of Ohio counseled Lincoln to leave the post vacant "until after the fall of Richmond" and then appoint Stanton. "I know whereof I speak," he concluded.[50] But the New York *World*, which viewed with alarm any move to elevate Stanton to the Supreme Court, attacked him as unfit for the post. It informed its readers that "His quick, hot, impetuous temper is inconsistent" with those qualities required of a Chief Justice.[51]

Orville H. Browning sheds interesting light upon his attitude toward Stanton's candidacy. Following a call he made upon Mrs. Stanton—

---

[43] Hannibal Hamlin to Abraham Lincoln, October 15, 1864, *ibid.*
[44] New York *Times*, October 15, 1864, p. 4.
[45] Nicolay and Hay, *Abraham Lincoln*, IX, 345.
[46] George Harding to Edwin M. Stanton, October 15, 1864, Stanton MSS.
[47] Robert C. Grier to Edwin M. Stanton, October 13, 1864, *ibid.*
[48] James Bates to Edwin M. Stanton, October 16, 1864, *ibid.*
[49] Cortlandt Parker to Abraham Lincoln, October 25, 1864, Lincoln MSS.
[50] David Tod to Abraham Lincoln, October 17, 1864, *ibid.*
[51] Editorial, New York *World*, November 18, 1864, p. 4.

Stanton had gone to City Point—he wrote in his diary that Mrs. Stanton had "great desire to have her husband appointed Chief Justice" and requested him to talk to the President. Consequently, on October 17, Browning had an interview with Lincoln, during which the President kept his own counsel. "He said nothing in reply to what I urged [Browning wrote] except to admit Mr. Stantons [sic] ability, and fine qualifications." [52]

Strenuous efforts were made by Montgomery Blair, who represented a moderate point of view in the cabinet until his resignation on September 23, 1864, to convince Lincoln to appoint him to the office. Blair's father, Francis P. Blair, Sr., a leading politician and one of the organizers of the Republican party, fought a tireless battle for his son. The vacant Chief Justiceship was looked upon by the Blairs as their supreme opportunity, and they exerted every pressure upon Lincoln. But as Nicolay and Hay point out, although Blair was "eminently fitted" for the post, "the competition of Mr. Chase was too strong for any rival, however worthy." [53]

There exists in the Blair manuscripts in the Library of Congress a corrected draft of a letter from the senior Blair to the President in which he poured out his heart. Whether it was re-written and sent to Lincoln cannot be determined with certainty, but it is not to be found in the Robert Todd Lincoln collection.

Blair sketched a brief history of the Blairs in politics and asked Lincoln to "indulge me with a little conference with you on paper about a thing which is involving a good deal of egotism, [that] I am ashamed to talk about face to face—" He asked Lincoln to appoint Montgomery so that he could be "your representative man," heading the Court in a day when it would face problems of the freedmen and reconstruction. "If you cannot give him a seat on the bench, [Blair wrote] I do not know that you can do anything to remove the cloud which his ostracism from your Cabinet [resulted in]. . . ." In conclusion, Blair built up an emotional appeal that was designed to make refusal impossible. "See what castles an old man can build [wrote Blair]—Montgomery to be a Judge of the Supreme Court. . . . I wish you would make this dream a reality. . . . I have opened [my] heart to you . . . like a book—pray pardon the trespass & I will sin no more." [54] But if Lincoln received this appeal, he was unmoved by it.

Gustavus V. Fox, the Assistant Secretary of the Navy, who supported the appointment of Montgomery Blair, wrote General Benjamin F.

---

[52] Browning, *Diary*, I, 687-88 (October 16 and October 17, 1864).

[53] Nicolay and Hay, *Abraham Lincoln*, IX, 342.

[54] Francis P. Blair, Sr. to Abraham Lincoln, corrected draft of a letter, October 20, 1864, Blair Family MSS., Library of Congress.

Butler on November 17 seeking his aid. "The President [Fox wrote] has not yet determined who shall be the Chief Justice; on the contrary, he invited that pressure upon himself, which now seems necessary to obtain the great office." "I beg of you, [Fox implored] . . . that you write a letter in the Judge's behalf." [55]

Blair's father was unwilling to leave any stone unturned. He spoke with Mrs. Lincoln about the Chief Justiceship and finally even had a personal interview with the President. In a letter to Governor John A. Andrew of Massachusetts, Blair related the details of these conversations. He informed Andrew that on an occasion when he was chatting with Mrs. Lincoln about "Town topics," she suddenly changed the course of conversation and said, "Mr. Blair, Chase and his friends are beseiging [sic] my husband for the Cheif [sic] Justiceship. I wish you could prevent them." Blair took this as a hint and proceeded to Lincoln's office.

The main point that Blair made to Lincoln was that in the past Montgomery had supported the administration fully. Lincoln was noncommital, Blair informed the Governor; all that he would say was that he must consult with others whose desires could not be denied. Blair quoted him as declaring, "although I may be stronger as an authority yet if all the rest oppose, I must give way. Old Hickory who had as much iron in his neck as any body, did so some times. If the strongest horse in the team *would* go ahead, he *cannot*, if all the *rest hold back*" Blair took Lincoln's remarks to be "delphic hints" and inferred that Lincoln was not ill-disposed toward Montgomery. He suggested to Andrew that if he were inclined to, he should write a letter so that it could be presented to the President.[56]

The fullness of the pressure that Lincoln faced in naming a Chief Justice is even more apparent when it is pointed out that there was another aspirant yet, Attorney General Bates. Bates looked upon the office as suitable reward for his devotion and service. In the letter in which he informed Lincoln officially of the death of Taney, Bates stated his claims. He said to Lincoln that he wished to "recall to your memory . . . our former conversations in regard to a vacancy on the Supreme bench. . . . I could not desire to close my public life more honorably, than by a brief term of service in that eminent position."

Bates's request is remarkable because of a proviso which he included: he suggested to Lincoln that he had no desire to occupy the Chief Justiceship more than two or three years "and so it would still be within

[55] Gustavus V. Fox to Benjamin F. Butler, November 17, 1864, Jessie A. Marshall, ed., *Private and Official Correspondence of Gen. Benjamin F. Butler during the Period of the Civil War* (Norwood, Massachusetts, 1917), V, 353-54.

[56] Francis P. Blair, Sr. to John A. Andrew, November 19, 1864, quoted in Massachusetts Historical Society, *Proceedings*, LXIII, 88-89.

your disposal during your second term. In fact I desire it chiefly—almost wholly—as the crowning, retiring honor of my life." [57]

Lincoln discussed Bates's desires with Orville H. Browning as well as Commissioner of Agriculture Isaac Newton. Apparently Lincoln merely informed Browning that Bates "had personally solicited the Chief Justiceship of him." [58] But Lincoln discussed the matter at length with Newton, who later reported the conversation to Bates. Lincoln told Newton, Bates recorded in his diary, that he, "if not overborne by others, would gladly make me Ch.[ief] J[ustice]—That Chase was turning every stone, to get it, and several others were urged, from different quarters—" [59]

While Lincoln was continuing consideration of the vacancy Bates resigned his post on November 24, 1864. He explained that he had considered it his duty to continue in office until the success of the Union was assured and until Lincoln's re-election was attained. In resigning Bates expressed deep gratitude "not only for your good opinion which led to my appointment, but also for your . . . courtesy and kindness. . . ." [60]

Thus Edward Bates had added additional pressure in seeking from Lincoln appointment as Chief Justice. But Lincoln did not permit Bates's resignation to influence the decision that had to be made. Despite all the pressure Lincoln did not permit himself to swerve from his intention of placing at the head of the Supreme Court his onetime cabinet member and competitor, Salmon P. Chase.

[57] Edward Bates to Abraham Lincoln, October 13, 1864, Lincoln MSS.

[58] Browning, *Diary*, I, 688 (October 18, 1864).

[59] Bates, *Diary*, 428 (November 22, 1864).

[60] Edward Bates to Abraham Lincoln, November 24, 1864, Lincoln MSS.

CHAPTER SIXTEEN

Reward for Rivalry

CHASE SPECULATES

None awaited Taney's departure more eagerly than did Salmon P. Chase and his friends. Even before the first year of the Lincoln administration ended, Chase had evidenced a keen interest in the office of Chief Justice. Hiram Barney, Chase's intimate friend whom Lincoln appointed collector of the Port of New York, discussed Supreme Court vacancies with the President on December 16, 1861. At that time there were three vacancies on the Court. Barney returned to his room in Willard's Hotel following the interview, and fearing that there might be misunderstanding, wrote Lincoln: "I am not satisfied that I stated my request very clearly. . . . it is the *chief* office only that our friend desires. That is not vacant and it is uncertain when it will be."

The two had discussed the vacancy created in the Ohio circuit by the death of Justice McLean. Barney feared that if Lincoln filled it with an Ohioan, Chase's chances of someday replacing Taney might be jeopardized. Therefore, he suggested that Lincoln fill that vacancy with a non-Ohioan since "it might be embarassing [*sic*] to take a *chief* from the same state which already has a judge on the same bench." [1]

In his letter Barney never mentioned the name "Chase" but referred to Chase as "our friend." When Lincoln received it he continued the game of evasion and endorsed the letter: "Hiram Barney, Dec. 16, 61 wants office for 'our friend.' " But "our friend" was Salmon P. Chase. And when Taney died three years later, Barney was at once energetic in seeking support for "our friend." [2]

Friends had frequently attempted to convince Chase that the Chief Justiceship was more to be coveted than the presidency. Joshua Leavitt, a Chase supporter, suggested that "a Four years' Presidency is soon over" and maintained that it would be better "to have the Supreme Court in your hands for the coming twenty years." [3] Chase probably was impressed by these arguments because in 1863 he told Hugh McCulloch, United States comptroller of the currency, that "there was only one

[1] Hiram Barney to Abraham Lincoln, December 16, 1861, Lincoln MSS.

[2] Hiram Barney to Salmon P. Chase, October 14, 1864, Chase MSS., Hist. Soc. of Pa.

[3] Joshua Leavitt to Salmon P. Chase, September 30, 1863, Chase MSS., Library of Congress.

office which he had heartily desired—the office of Chief Justice. . . ." [4]

Shortly before Chase's resignation from the cabinet on June 29, 1864, the New York *World* pointed out that Chase had his eye on the Chief Justiceship. It said that Lincoln could afford to promise Chase the Chief Justiceship (when it became vacant) in order to induce him not to seek the presidency. "We shall, accordingly, [predicted the *World*] see Mr. Chase supporting for reelection a man whom in his heart he despises and derides." [5]

The day after his resignation Chase recorded in his diary information that was brought to him by Representative Samuel Hooper of Massachusetts. Hooper told him that in an interview several days earlier, Lincoln had regretted that his relations with Chase were embarrassing. Lincoln expressed esteem for Chase and revealed that "he had intended in case of vacancy in the Chief Justiceship to tender it to me and would now did a vacancy exist." [6] Representative Hooper said that he believed that Lincoln had stated these facts so that they would be repeated to Chase. Chase's reaction was that if he had known Lincoln's feelings misunderstandings could have been averted.

It was with the election impending and this background of strained relations that Chase received Stanton's telegram stating that "Chief Justice Taney died last night." Chase replied at once, "Within the last three or four months I have been afraid[!] that it was the President's intention to offer the place to me in case of a vacancy. I think I should accept it . . . I am weary of political life & work. What do you think?" [7]

Rumor had circulated about the Chief Justiceship even before Taney's death. J. K. Herbert wrote General Butler that Lincoln had sent for Chase "and took him out to the Soldiers' Home, where a long, private interview took place of which nobody knows anything. But Chase is going to Ohio to make speeches. Gurowski says that the Ch[ie]f Justiceship is still his contract. I should say that [David] Davis told me Lincoln had begged Chase's pardon most humbly for his treatment, &." [8]

"THE POT BOILS"

Chase quickly acquired support for the Chief Justiceship, his friends

---

[4] Hugh McCulloch, *Men and Measures of Half a Century: Sketches and Comments* (New York, 1900), p. 186.

[5] Editorial, New York *World*, May 26, 1864, p. 4.

[6] David Donald, ed., *Inside Lincoln's Cabinet: The Civil War Diaries of Salmon P. Chase* (New York, 1954), p. 221 (June 30, 1864). Also quoted in Robert B. Warden, *An Account of the Private Life and Public Services of Salmon Portland Chase* (Cincinnati, 1874), p. 618.

[7] Salmon P. Chase to Edwin M. Stanton, October 13, 1864, Stanton MSS., Library of Congress.

[8] J. K. Herbert to Benjamin F. Butler, September 26, 1864, Marshall, ed., *Correspondence of Gen. Butler*, V, 167-68.

springing to action with determination. Typical was the statement of Judge Jacob Brinkerhoff of the supreme court of Ohio who informed Lincoln that ninety-nine out of every hundred loyal men supported Chase. And Brinkerhoff advised Lincoln that past differences should not prevent the appointment.[9] One friend wrote Chase that "I shall regard your appointment as Chief Justice of more importance to the cause of Emancipation than the election of Abraham Lincoln." [10]

Not only did the friends of Chase spring into action; his enemies moved swiftly, too. The morning after the death of Taney, Orville H. Browning transacted business with Secretary of the Treasury Fessenden and proposed that Fessenden compete for the appointment. But the Secretary replied that the place "was designed for Mr. Chase, and that the appointment would be tendered to him and accepted by him —" Fessenden pointed out, too, that at the time of Chase's resignation from the cabinet Lincoln had declared that "he had great respect for Mr. Chase," [11] and that he intended to appoint Chase to the Chief Justiceship.

Thomas Ewing entered the struggle against Chase. Warning Lincoln that Chase would not be acceptable, the former senator declared: "He is a politician rather than a lawyer & . . . I am unwilling to see a Chief Justice . . . intriguing & trading for the Presidency." [12]

But a week after Taney's death Fessenden informed Chase that Lincoln was going to keep his promise. "The Pres[iden]t said to me [Fessenden wrote] that he 'had not forgotten' our conversations, but as things were going on well he thought it best not to make any appointment or say anything about it, until the election was over. Do not give yourself any anxiety, whatever you may see in the papers—" [13]

When news of Taney's death first reached Senator Sumner, he demanded that Lincoln name Chase at once. He wrote the President: "Providence has given us a victory in the death of Chief Justice Taney. It is a victory for Liberty and for the Constitution." [14] And the same day Sumner wrote to Dr. Francis Lieber that "Last spring, after a long conversation, Mr. Lincoln promised me to tender the chief justiceship to Chase. He has referred to that promise since his break with Chase, and declared his willingness to nominate him." [15]

---

[9] Jacob Brinkerhoff to Abraham Lincoln, October 14, 1864, Lincoln MSS.

[10] George Wood to Salmon P. Chase, October 15, 1864, Chase MSS., Library of Congress.

[11] Browning, *Diary*, I, 686-87 (October 13, 1864).

[12] Thomas Ewing to Abraham Lincoln, December 3, 1864, Lincoln MSS.

[13] William P. Fessenden to Salmon P. Chase, October 20, 1864, Chase MSS., Hist. Soc. of Pa.

[14] Charles Sumner to Abraham Lincoln, October 12, 1864, Lincoln MSS.

[15] Charles Sumner to Francis Lieber, October 12, 1864, quoted in Edward L. Pierce, *Memoir and Letters of Charles Sumner*, (London, 1893), IV, 207-08.

Chase wrote Sumner a letter on October 19 in which he stated that he would accept the appointment if Lincoln tendered it.[16] Sumner at once wrote Lincoln again and quoted from Chase's letter this statement: "It is perhaps not exactly *en règle* to say what one will do in regard to an appointment not tendered to him; but it is certainly not awry to say to you that I should accept." Sumner even quoted to Lincoln, Chase's lavish praise: "Happily . . . the next Administration will be in the hands of Mr. Lincoln from whom the world will expect great things. God grant that his name may go down to posterity with the two noblest additions historians ever recorded—Restorer & Liberator." [17] The friends of Chase were losing no opportunity to impress upon Lincoln the newly found loyalty of Chase.

In his reply to Chase's letter of the nineteenth, Sumner related that in the spring he and Lincoln had canvassed the potential candidates for the Chief Justiceship, and Lincoln declared that he considered Swayne the most capable of the new Justices and "a candidate for Chief Justice." Sumner spoke out against Swayne and it was then that Lincoln said that "he would tender the place to you." Furthermore, Sumner stated, Lincoln has "repeated this determination since, expressly to the Senate Com[mi]ttee when it visited him to know the occasion of your resignation." [18]

Whitelaw Reid, serving as a war correspondent of the Cincinnati *Gazette*, suggested to Chase that he make a speech at Cooper Institute in behalf of Lincoln's re-election. "One of two things [Reid concluded] is certain. Either Mr. Lincoln has determined to make you Chief Justice; or he has determined to make your friends believe so till after the election. I prefer to believe the former." [19]

Two Justices of the Supreme Court let President Lincoln know of their desire that Chase be appointed. Justice Field joined Governor Frederick F. Low of California in sending this telegram to Lincoln: "The appointment of Hon[orable] S. P. Chase as Chief Justice . . . vice Taney deceased would in our opinion be eminently Judicious & highly satisfactory to the loyal people of the Pacific coast." [20] And Justice Miller, who along with Justice Field had once urged the appointment of Swayne, now favored Chase. Miller authorized Senator John Sherman to make his new

---

[16] Salmon P. Chase to Charles Sumner, October 19, 1864, Chase MSS., Library of Congress.

[17] Charles Sumner to Abraham Lincoln, October 24, 1864, Lincoln MSS.

[18] Charles Sumner to Salmon P. Chase, October 24, 1864, Chase MSS., Library of Congress.

[19] Whitelaw Reid to Salmon P. Chase, October 19, 1864, Chase MSS., Hist. Soc. of Pa.

[20] Frederick F. Low and Stephen J. Field to Abraham Lincoln, October 16, 1864, Lincoln MSS.

feelings known to Lincoln.[21] Miller's change of mind may have resulted from the bitterness that he and Swayne engaged in during the previous term of Court.

Schuyler Colfax, the Speaker of the House, who was on a campaign trip in the Middle West, informed Lincoln a few days before the election that "I have spoken in five States since the Oct. election, & have never known public opinion to be as unanimous as it is in favor of Gov. Chase. . . ." [22]

Following the presidential election on November 8, 1864, Chase's friends grew increasingly impatient. Finally, they became exasperated that Lincoln withheld the appointment. Despite a letter of congratulations from Chase the President took no action. Senator Sumner decided, therefore, to throw all caution to the winds. On November 20, he wrote Lincoln that delay in making the nomination provoked anxiety in the nation. He declared that although Lincoln had been counseled to make no appointment until after the election, "I thought it ought to have been made on the evening of Taney's funeral. The promptitude . . . would have had an inspiring effect. But I can see no ground of delay now. . . ." [23] Was it that Lincoln was enjoying the uneasiness that was being evinced by Chase and his friends? Was it that Lincoln was having fun at the expense of those waiting for the deed to be done?

The champions of Chase continued to await the event nervously. Every bit of gossip that fell from the mouths of the politicians, every newspaper report that hazarded a guess as to who would be the new Chief Justice, contributed to their apprehension and discomfort. Lincoln had appointed David Davis during a recess of Congress. Delay in making the appointment of Chase until Congress reassembled cannot be interpreted in any other way than willful procrastination.

After the election, Chase, himself, began to question Lincoln's intentions. He made his fears known to his friends, writing Senator Sherman, "Please write me, if you can, when the President will act." [24] Secretary of War Stanton counseled Chase not to become too apprehensive, declaring, "Your experience has taught you that the newspaper reports are all lies, invented by knaves for fools to feed on." [25]

Chase's friend, E. T. Carson, with whom he was staying in Cincinnati, asked Sherman what the prospects were, assuring him that even bad news

[21] John Sherman to Abraham Lincoln, October 22, 1864, *ibid*.

[22] Schuyler Colfax to Abraham Lincoln, November 3, 1864, *ibid*.

[23] Charles Sumner to Abraham Lincoln, November 14, 1864, *ibid*.

[24] Salmon P. Chase to John Sherman, November 12, 1864, Sherman MSS.

[25] Edwin M. Stanton to Salmon P. Chase, November 19, 1864, cited in Jacob W. Schuckers, *The Life and Public Services of Salmon Portland Chase, United States Senator and Governor of Ohio; Secretary of the Treasury, and Chief-Justice of the United States* (New York, 1874), p. 513.

would be preferable to the terrible suspense. "Cant 'Abraham' settle this matter now [asked Carson] as well as two or three weeks hence—?" [26] And it was Senator Sherman who came up with the forecast that ultimately proved correct. He believed that no appointment would be made until Congress convened. He told Chase that he was to see the President shortly and would transmit any late news.[27]

Chase was encouraged by this report and wrote R. C. Parsons: "All I learn from Washington is that the pot boils. If Blairs [sic] wishes prevail, yours will not. I have made up my mind to take things as they come." [28] As Chase became a little more certain in his own mind that Lincoln would proffer the post, he began to feel a reluctance to have it appear that he was soliciting it. As the assembling of Congress drew near, he became more independent and wrote to Hugh McCulloch: "I supported him [Lincoln] for reelection wholly without reference to any personal advantage for myself, because I thought it my duty to the country, our cause, & my political friends required it of me. . . . If he offers the appointment . . . I desire that he may do so because his own judgment is satisfied that it is one fit to be made. . . ." [29]

THE SPHINX ACTS

The tension upon the interested parties was almost intolerable as the members of Congress returned to Washington in December, 1864. Chase, who had personal business in the national capital, had delayed the trip, anticipating that Lincoln could not avoid taking action soon. By the first of December, however, his business could be delayed no longer, and he wrote both to Sumner and to Sherman telling them of his impending trip. His feelings were that "though I hate to come before I know that there remains nothing to hope or fear . . . I must." [30] The withholding of the appointment, however, was making him belligerent and the next day he wrote Sumner: "I would not have the office on the terms of being obliged to ask for it. . . ." [31]

Information finally trickled down to Chase, as to the actual thinking of Lincoln on the subject. Schuyler Colfax had an interview in which Lincoln spoke his mind freely, and he immediately related to Chase the course that the interview took. Lincoln had told Colfax of the objections

[26] E. T. Carson to John Sherman, November 18, 1864, Sherman MSS.

[27] John Sherman to Salmon P. Chase, November 27, 1864, Chase MSS., Hist. Soc. of Pa.

[28] Salmon P. Chase to R. C. Parsons, November 27, 1864, ibid.

[29] Salmon P. Chase to Hugh McCulloch, November 27, 1864, McCulloch MSS., Library of Congress.

[30] Salmon P. Chase to John Sherman, December 2, 1864, Sherman MSS.

[31] Salmon P. Chase to Charles Sumner, December 3, 1864, Chase MSS., Library of Congress.

that were being presented against Chase, and the President especially emphasized that the Chief Justiceship should not be a stepping-stone to the presidency: "I asked Mr. Lincoln [Colfax continued] if you had not yourself told him you preferred to be C[hief] J[ustice] rather than President. He replied yes; & I added that, if appointed, I felt certain you would dedicate the remainder of your life to the Bench. . . ."

Colfax did not think the interview went well, and wrote Chase that he neglected to make a point that only occurred to him after he left the President. Colfax said that he failed to ask "if . . . he app[ointe]d some one else, History might not say that he did so because you had dared to be a candidate for the Pres[iden]t[ial] nomination ag[ain]st him. It would have touched him on a point of honor & magnanimity. I asked Garfield yesterday [December 4] to hint it to him to day." [32]

The Supreme Court met on December 5 for its first session of the December Term, 1864. Still there had been no announcement from the Executive Mansion. Justice James M. Wayne presided over the Court. Only Justices Wayne, Grier, Clifford, Swayne, and Miller were present, and the Court lacking a quorum, adjourned until the next day.

It was on December 6 that Lincoln took action. He surprised many of his closest advisers, some of them revealing that they had no knowledge of his intentions as late as ten minutes before the nomination was sent to the Senate. The nomination, written in full in Lincoln's hand read, "I nominate Salmon P. Chase of Ohio, to be Chief Justice of the Supreme Court of the United States, vice Roger B. Taney, deceased." [33] Lincoln had broken the supense, but no man could say that the appointment of Chase was marked by graciousness and good will.

Senator Samuel C. Pomeroy of Kansas at once informed Chase, "I am gratified, beyond measure, to be able, at this moment to vote—'Aye'—with a *unanimous Senate:* confirming you: Chief Justice of the United States." [34] The nomination had been made and confirmed—it was not referred to committee—on the same day. This was a compliment to Chase and perhaps a rebuke to the President for his prolonged delay.

Even Chase was not forewarned when Lincoln was ready to act. The night of his appointment Chase wrote the President: "On reaching home tonight I was saluted with the intelligence that you this day nominated me to the Senate for the office of Chief Justice." The new Chief Justice wrote further: "I cannot sleep before I thank you for this mark of your confidence, & especially for the manner in which the nomination was

[32] Schuyler Colfax to Salmon P. Chase, December 5, 1864, Chase MSS., Hist. Soc. of Pa.

[33] Nomination of Salmon P. Chase to the Supreme Court, December 6, 1864, photostat, Papers of the Attorneys General.

[34] S. C. Pomeroy to Salmon P. Chase, December 6, 1864, Chase MSS., Library of Congress.

made. I shall never forget either and trust that you will never regret either. Be assured that I prize your confidence & goodwill more than nomination or office." [35] In view of the delay and taciturnity that Lincoln invoked, the latter part of Chase's remarks could easily have a double meaning.

Secretary Welles testifies in his diary as to how well Lincoln guarded his secret. He recorded that not a word concerning the nomination was mentioned during the cabinet meeting on December 6 despite the fact that Lincoln announced that he had nominated William Dennison to be Postmaster General and James Speed to be Attorney General. Welles was piqued that Lincoln should have withheld the news "which we all knew in less than one hour." He added that Dennison later informed him that the night prior to the nomination he accompanied Lincoln to the theater "and parted with him after 11 o'clock, and not a word was said to him on the subject." [36]

The new Chief Justice had had a notable political career. He was born in New Hampshire in 1808, but was brought up in Ohio by an uncle, Bishop Philander Chase of the Protestant Episcopal Church. He was graduated from Dartmouth, conducted a school for boys, read law, and was admitted to the bar in 1829. Chase began practice in Cincinnati and soon became active in the antislavery movement. His political experience included service as United States Senator from Ohio and as Governor of the state. He sought the Republican nomination for the presidency in 1856 as well as 1860. With the beginning of the Lincoln administration, Chase accepted appointment as Secretary of the Treasury, a post he retained until after his effort to replace Lincoln as the Republican nominee in 1864 failed.

The press heralded Chase's appointment as Chief Justice as the ushering in of a new era in American jurisprudence. That the break with the past was complete was emphasized by many of the leading newspapers. The New York *Tribune* commented that if any one in 1860 had suggested that Chase would be the successor of Taney, the individual "would have been regarded as in need of a straight jacket." [37] Maintaining that even the Union Democrats were pleased, the New York *Times* declared: "There is no public man in the country whose anti-slavery record has been longer, or more consistent, or more decided than that of Salmon P. Chase." [38] The Washington *National Intelligencer* lavishly praised Chase and declared: "The fifth in line of the Chief Justices, he will, we may be sure, worthily sustain the high traditions handed down by his illustrious

[35] Salmon P. Chase to Abraham Lincoln, December 6, 1864, Lincoln MSS.

[36] Welles, *Diary*, II, 192-93 (December 6, 1864).

[37] Editorial, New York *Tribune*, December 9, 1864, p. 4.

[38] Editorial, New York *Times*, December 8, 1864, p. 4.

predecessors on the bench of the American Themis." [39] The Washington *Morning Chronicle* interpreted Chase's appointment as a "pledge that the Constitution and laws will in the future be expounded from the standpoint of freedom." [40]

The New York *World*, however, unleashed a bitter attack against him. It charged that even Lincoln's preference for Chase was questionable since he delayed so long in appointing him. "The controlling and decisive consideration in making the appointment, [said the *World*] was probably an unequivocal intimation that if he [Lincoln] sent in any other name than that of Mr. Chase the Senate would reject it." Speaking with a remarkable degree of accuracy, the *World* added, "The tendency of the bench is conservative; and Mr. Chase is strong enough to obey his convictions without subjecting himself to the suspicions or censures of his party should he refuse to go to immoderate lengths." [41] The *World* had spoken well. Chief Justice Chase would break with his Radical friends before he would bow to their dictates.

Salmon P. Chase was installed as Chief Justice on December 15, 1864. The installation was a scene, said the Washington *Morning Chronicle*, "whose simple grandeur is a noble testimonial to republican institutions." Emphasizing that almost a generation had passed since a Chief Justice had been installed, the *Chronicle* reported that the oath was administered to the new Chief Justice "in the presence of his associates and a few friends" in the consultation room. The courtroom itself was crowded with "ladies and gentlemen, comprising the *elite* of fashion and of talent, of beauty and of worth." Into it, at eleven o'clock, with the audience and bar standing, filed the procession of Justices "in their robes of office, preceded by the senior associate the venerable Justice Wayne. The Chief Justice-elect followed, moving towards his appointed seat when Justice Wayne handed him the written oath of office, which he proceeded to read in a firm, audible voice, amid profound silence." [42] With that the ceremony was at an end. The Crier announced the opening of the Court, and Salmon P. Chase entered upon his new duties.

Congratulatory messages poured in upon the new Chief Justice. Several of Chase's friends took pains to emphasize that in many ways it was better to be Chief Justice than to be President. Alphonso Taft, Ohio politician and lawyer, rejoicing that liberty would be protected "in that High Court," said that he would "forgive Mr. Lincoln much for this." He added that "To be Chief Justice . . . is more than to be President." [43]

[39] Washington *National Intelligencer*, December 7, 1864, p. 3.

[40] Editorial, Washington *Morning Chronicle*, December 7, 1864, p. 2.

[41] Editorial, New York *World*, December 7, 1864, p. 6.

[42] Editorial, Washington *Morning Chronicle*, December 16, 1864, p. 2.

[43] Alphonso Taft to Salmon P. Chase, December 7, 1864, Chase MSS., Library of Congress.

William Cullen Bryant declared to Chase that problems arising out of the war would make the Chief Justiceship "more important to the country, for many years after the war shall have ended, than the Presidency itself." [44]

Many friends told Chase that his appointment was providential and guaranteed the doom of the institution of human bondage. Whitelaw Reid, writing from the Cincinnati *Gazette* offices, sent Chase newspaper clippings concerning the appointment and declared: "Since Judges are mortal, and their sympathies tinge their decisions, slavery has all too long possessed this advantage at the feet of the Chief Justice of the United States." [45] "May you long live [wrote John Jay] to impress upon the Supreme Court of the Nation, that regard for the constitutional Right & eternal justice, which has marked your political career, & secured for you the admiration & confidence of your country." [46]

FIRES AROUND LINCOLN

There remains to be examined why Lincoln, although he delayed the appointment of Chase until it smacked of ungraciousness, finally named this rival who had caused so much pain to the administration. A forceful argument that was used was that Chase should be appointed out of gratitude for the assistance he gave Lincoln in his bid for re-election. This sentiment was best stated by Thomas L. Kane of Pennsylvania who wrote Lincoln that there could "be no impropriety in my reminding you how earnest was the support which you received in this portion of Pennsylvania from the friends of *Mr. Chase* of whom I was one." Both with frankness and conviction Kane added, "You did not know us to be his friends because we were so cordially yours. We would be very grateful for your recognition at this time of Mr. Chase's service." [47]

Another argument was that elevation of Chase would go far to heal the breach in the Republican party. The day after Taney died George B. Senter of Cincinnati wrote Lincoln: "It is believed by our friends that to tender the place of Gov. Chase would do much to harmonize our difficulties & believe all our best interests requires [*sic*] this." [48] And William Sheffield of Ohio stated that although in "ordinary times" no man could be asked to ignore the provocation that Chase had given him, Lincoln should appoint Chase "in the interest of the country" and should forget the way in which Chase "& his friends in the interest of

---

[44] William Cullen Bryant to Salmon P. Chase, December 10, 1864, Chase MSS., Hist. Soc. of Pa.

[45] Whitelaw Reid to Salmon P. Chase, December 9, 1864, *ibid.*

[46] John Jay to Salmon P. Chase, December 7, 1864, Chase MSS., Library of Congress.

[47] Thomas L. Kane to Abraham Lincoln, November 19, 1864, Lincoln MSS.

[48] George B. Senter to Abraham Lincoln, October 13, 1864, *ibid.*

the succession, have reviled you with a bitterness, unsurpassed by our open opponents." [49]

The argument most frequently used was that the appointment of Chase would place at the head of the Court a man with sound views concerning issues growing out of the war. Timothy Danielson of Cincinnati expressed this view very well when he wrote Lincoln: "The national welfare, the national dignity, the peace and the honor, and the honesty of the republic demand an anti-slavery Chief Justice to meet the great and complicated questions that already cast the lurid gloom of their approach over the future of our jurisprudence. Mr. Chase is the man of men to meet them." [50]

These were the main arguments presented to President Lincoln in behalf of Salmon P. Chase. Their appeal was broad. Their logic was overwhelming. And with obvious misgivings, Lincoln finally complied. Less than a week after the appointment was made Secretary of the Navy Welles recorded in his diary that "The President told Chandler of New Hampshire, who remonstrated against such selection, that he would rather have swallowed his buckhorn chair than to have nominated Chase." [51]

Hugh McCulloch also gained information concerning Lincoln's reluctance in naming Chase. McCulloch declared that Lincoln had fears that Chase "might be somewhat rigorous in his judgment of some of the executive acts, and especially those of the Secretary of War, if suit should be brought involving questions that could only be settled by the Supreme Court." Consequently, while Lincoln was delaying the appointment, he sent for McCulloch, knowing of the close relations between McCulloch and Chase. Lincoln stated his fears and asked "what I thought about them," McCulloch later related. McCulloch replied, "you have no reason for fears on that score. Mr. Chase is in the same box with yourself and Mr. Stanton. He favored and advised, as he has himself informed me, the dispersion by force of the Maryland legislature, and if anything more illegal than that would have been done I have not heard of it." [52]

After the appointment was made Lincoln still entertained fears that Chase would not be satisfied. Representative George S. Boutwell of Massachusetts told Lincoln that he was glad that Chase had been selected. And according to Boutwell, he replied:

There are three reasons in favor of his appointment, and one very strong reason against it. First, he occupies the largest place in the public mind in

[49] William Sheffield to Abraham Lincoln, November 12, 1864, *ibid*.

[50] Timothy Danielson to Abraham Lincoln, November 28, 1864, *ibid*. See also Timothy Danielson to Abraham Lincoln, October 17, 1864, *ibid*.

[51] Welles, *Diary*, II, 196 (December 10, 1864).

[52] McCulloch, *Men and Measures*, p. 187.

connection with the office, then we wish for a Chief Justice who will sustain what has been done in regard to emancipation and the legal tenders. We cannot ask a man what he will do, and if we should, and he should answer us, we should despise him for it. Therefore we must take a man whose opinions are known. But there is one very strong reason against his appointment. He is a candidate for the Presidency, and if he does not give up that idea it will be very bad for him and very bad for me.[53]

Before the appointment was made certain political associates brought to Chase's attention the charge that he would never be satisfied in the office of Chief Justice. A. P. Stone wrote him that he had been told by Judge Pierrepont and others that Chase would "not be satisfied with it six months." Stone's reply was: "I told them you had said you would sooner reverse the Dred Scott decision than be President, and that I thought the Lord had been educating you for twenty years for that place, and that he would put you there." [54]

A few friends opposed Chase's acceptance of the Chief Justiceship. Edward L. Pierce, Charles Sumner's secretary, told Chase that "for one who had been so active in directing public opinion, it seems very much like going into a monastery. There is something in the seclusion of judicial office that I do not like." [55] Another lamented that "I and others whom you used to encourage will hardly be able to see much of you, or to approach you with the friendly freedom of old times." [56]

A few weeks after Chase assumed his new duties he dined with Hugh McCulloch and revealed that he began to see the political limitations imposed by a seat upon the highest court of the land. McCulloch said that he "was pained by discovering that . . . Chase was far from being satisfied. As Chief Justice of the Court, he had no favors to grant, no patronage to wield. High as the position was, it was not the one to which he had really aspired." Chase found that the duties of the Court would be laborious, particularly since he had neglected his legal knowledge during the years when he was Governor, Senator, and cabinet member. "It was undoubtedly this hard work," McCulloch stated, "and the disappointment of his political ambition that shortened his life." [57]

As Chief Justice, Salmon P. Chase was quite different from what had been anticipated by those who favored his appointment. Although he kept his promise to inform Stanton of the occasion upon which he

[53] George S. Boutwell, *Reminiscences of Sixty Years in Public Affairs* (New York, 1902), II, 29.

[54] A. P. Stone to Salmon P. Chase, December 9, 1864, Chase MSS., Library of Congress.

[55] Edward L. Pierce to Salmon P. Chase, November 14, 1864, Chase MSS., Hist. Soc. of Pa.

[56] W. Prescott Smith to Salmon P. Chase, December 17, 1864, Chase MSS., Library of Congress. See also R. B. Warden to Salmon P. Chase, December 19, 1864, *ibid.*

[57] McCulloch, *Men and Measures*, pp. 186-87.

would deliver his first opinion,[58] the administration soon began to question his cooperation and his friendliness.

As early as February, 1865, there was indication that Chase, whether from personal inclination or personal ambition, might choose to oppose certain administration policies if they were tested before the Court. These prospects aroused Lincoln. Welles wrote in his diary that on February 21, when he went in to see Lincoln, "I found the President . . . in consultation over an apprehended decision of Chief Justice Chase, whenever he could reach the question of suspension of the writ of *habeas corpus*. Some intimation comes through Stanton, that his Honor the Chief Justice intends to make himself felt by the Administration. . . . I shall not be surprised, for he is ambitious and able. Yet on that subject he is as much implicated as others." [59] Welles recorded that Lincoln "expresses and feels astonishment" that Chase would adopt a position out of harmony with the view of the administration. Welles's conclusion was that Chase's political ambitions were "fierce" and might lead him to assume a position of opposition to Lincoln.[60] Once the judicial ermine enveloped him Chase did change. Perhaps politics did dictate his change of viewpoint. At any rate, he continued to have aspirations for the presidency.

Shortly after Chase's elevation to the Supreme Court an event took place that was symbolic of the new day that was dawning. On February 1, 1865, Senator Charles Sumner stood before his friend, who had presided over the Supreme Court scarcely two months, and moved the admission of John S. Rock of Massachusetts to the Supreme Court bar. With that act the first Negro was admitted to practice before the Supreme Court. The principles of the Dred Scott decision were dead indeed.

---

[58] Salmon P. Chase to Edwin M. Stanton, January 28, 1865, Stanton MSS.

[59] Welles, *Diary*, II, 242-43 (February 21, 1865).

[60] *Ibid.*, II, 245-46 (February 22, 1865).

CHAPTER SEVENTEEN

The Court Under Chase

HINTS OF THE FUTURE

The December Term, 1864, was to prove eventful for the Supreme Court. Not only was it under the leadership of Chief Justice Salmon P. Chase, it was served by a new Attorney General, and it heard a considerable number of vital war-related cases. Before the Court assembled, Lincoln had to turn to the task of appointing an Attorney General to fill the vacancy created by the resignation of Edward Bates. With re-election to office recently attained, the appointment involved fewer political considerations than would have been involved earlier. It was anticipated that Lincoln would turn to a border state to fill the post because Postmaster General Montgomery Blair had resigned also, and the border states were no longer represented in the cabinet.

It was generally forecast that Lincoln would select Judge Advocate General Joseph Holt.[1] But Holt declined because he did not wish the responsibility of managing cases before the Supreme Court.[2] In refusing the appointment, he wrote Lincoln, "In view of all the circumstances, I am Satisfied that I can serve you better in the position which I now hold at your hands, than in the more elevated one to which I have been invited."[3] So Lincoln sought further in Kentucky and James Speed, brother of Joshua F. Speed, accepted the cabinet seat. The new Attorney General had been a leading adviser of Lincoln on affairs in Kentucky early in the war.

The Supreme Court met on December 5, 1864, and the new Attorney General appeared before it on December 14, the day before Chase took over as Chief Justice. The term lasted until March 10, 1865. During the session the Court decided some sixty cases. Although most of them were commonplace, the Court, in which five of the ten members were appointees of Lincoln, dealt with many controversies that grew out of the war.

Land title cases in California and elsewhere again comprised a considerable part of the litigation, forming almost twenty per cent of the cases heard. Other cases involved mortgage, patent rights, the slave trade, contract, collision at sea, jurisdiction of the Court, land formed

---

[1] New York *Times*, December 1, 1864, p. 1.

[2] Nicolay and Hay, *Abraham Lincoln*, IX, 347.

[3] Joseph Holt to Abraham Lincoln, November 30, 1864, Lincoln MSS.

by accretion, property rights, bridges, estates, bank collections, and prize.

In one instance during the term the hand of Roger B. Taney was felt even though the Court was under new leadership. A case pending at the end of the previous session involved appeal from the court of claims in a case concerning damages by United States troops during the War of 1812. The case, *Gordon v. the United States,* had been submitted to the Court on December 18, 1863. On April 4, 1864, four days before the 1863 Term ended, the Court ordered that argument of the case take place on the second day of the December Term, 1864.

Chief Justice Taney prepared a statement giving his views and although he did not live to hear the case argued, his opinion guided the decision that finally was made. During the summer of 1864 Taney had sent his statement to the Clerk, Daniel W. Middleton, and instructed him to deliver it to the Justices when the new term began. Taney's statement was not included in the *United States Reports* until the October Term, 1885, but when it was printed, J. C. Bancroft Davis, the Clerk at that time, declared that "It is the recollection of the surviving members of the court, that this paper was carefully considered by the members . . . in reaching the conclusion . . . in [the Gordon case]; and that it was proposed to make it the basis of the opinion, which, it appears by the report of the case, was to be subsequently prepared." [4] In a way this was a reaching out of the grave by Taney to direct the Court one last time.

During the 1864 Term the question of whether a state could tax bank property that consisted of securities of the United States was heard again. The Court had already ruled on this problem in the 1862 Term. The new case, known as the *Bank of the Commonwealth v. New York,* and twenty-four additional cases that were concerned with the same problem, grew out of the fact that following the adverse ruling the state of New York had modified its law in the hope that it might meet the objections of the Supreme Court.

The tax commissioners of New York, who sought to tax the securities, argued that "There is no jurisdiction in this court over any of the cases at bar. No question arises in either of them, under the Constitution of the United States. Their decision exclusively depended, in the Court of Appeals of New York, upon the Constitution and legislature of that State." [5]

But for the Bank of the Commonwealth it was argued that the Supreme Court had ruled that "In all cases involving the supremacy of the Consti-

---

[4] 117 U.S. 697.

[5] This discussion of the case of the Bank of the Commonwealth is based upon 17 L. Ed. 793-96.

tution of the United States, over state legislation, there can no longer remain a doubt that the power of the General Government, to borrow money . . . cannot in any way be impaired or affected by state legislation." It remained for the Supreme Court to determine whether the newly enacted New York statute altered the situation.

Justice Nelson delivered the unanimous decision of the Court just as he did when the problem was heard before. Although he admitted that the new law modified the situation somewhat, the Court sustained its earlier ruling and again supported federal supremacy.

One case dealt with during the term particularly embarrassed President Lincoln and his administration. This case, known as *The Providence Tool Company v. Samuel Norris*, brought memories of the confusion of the early days of the war. And it reflected badly upon a man to whom Lincoln had assigned a position of high public trust.

In July, 1861, with the war just beginning, the Providence Tool Company obtained a government contract to provide 25,000 muskets for the armed forces at a cost of twenty dollars apiece. An agent of the company, Samuel Norris, was influential in obtaining the contract.

Norris, who had led "a somewhat miscellaneous sort of life, in Europe and America," was in Washington when hostilities began. He was there "without any special purpose, but, as he stated, with a view of '*making* business—anything generally;' 'soliciting acquaintances;' 'getting letters;' 'getting any office,' etc."

He set out to meet persons who could provide him with personal contacts or letters to influence "Mr. Cameron, at that time Secretary of War, recommending him and his objects." He sought out Senators Henry B. Anthony and James F. Simmons of Rhode Island, demanding personal introduction to Cameron. Senator Anthony offered to write Cameron a note, but as to personal introduction, "Mr. Anthony declined . . . stating that since he had been Senator he had been applied to some hundred times, in like manner, and had *invariably* declined; thinking it discreditable to any Senator to intermeddle with the business of the department." [6]

But Norris got his introduction to Cameron. And Norris got the contract, too. Furthermore, Cameron expressed the wish "that he would make a great deal of money out of it." This fact, alone, discredited the Secretary of War, in whose hands war contracts rested.

In due course Samuel Norris and the Providence Tool Company disputed as to the amount of compensation. Norris claimed $75,000. The company maintained that all it promised was "liberal compensation." In

---

[6] This discussion of the case of *The Providence Tool Company v. Samuel Norris* is based upon 69 U.S. 45-56.

the federal circuit court in Rhode Island, Norris was awarded $13,500, and the case came before the Supreme Court on appeal.

The counsel for the company cited to the Supreme Court, in opposition to Norris's demand for more compensation, an earlier Supreme Court decision that stated that "it was an undoubted principle of the common law that it will not lend its aid to enforce a contract 'which tends to corrupt or contaminate, by improper influences, the integrity of our social or political institutions.' "

The counsel of Norris was intensely provoked by the defense developed for the company. "It is not easy to conceive [said James M. Blake, the counsel of Norris] of a more ungracious defence. Confessedly, the contract was procured through the exertions of Norris alone." Blake admitted that Norris sought the contract energetically, declaring, "Of course, he gave his time, spent his money, invoked the aid of acquaintances, solicited influence, waited about the ante-rooms, and went through such operations as persons seeking contracts at Washington generally go through; operations distasteful in the extreme to any man of independence; impossible, indeed, for such a man to undergo." Blake defended Norris as a man of high character and declared that there was no "allegation that Mr. Cameron acted corruptly." "Having got the contract through Norris's labor, [Blake asserted] having made an immense sum of it, the company now turn around, and plead the illegality of their agreements! Is this not base?"

The Supreme Court did not agree that this was base. It rightfully considered base the use of influence to obtain a government contract. With stinging rebuke Justice Field, speaking for the Court, declared: "Agreements for compensation contingent upon success suggests the use of sinister and corrupt means. . . . The law meets the suggestion of evil and strikes down the contract from its inception."

Samuel Norris, the Providence Tool Company, former Secretary of War Cameron—all smarted from the criticism of the Court's decision. Cameron's performance was a sorry spectacle and reflected badly upon the President. And the Court correctly upheld the public interest rather than sustain an agreement made with dishonest intent.

The December Term, 1864, dealt with two important cases involving enemies' property. One concerned *The Schooner Andromeda. The Andromeda* was captured with a cargo of cotton and hides off the Cuban coast on May 20, 1862. It was bound for Havana from Sabine, Texas, where it had received its cargo. Both vessel and cargo were condemned as enemies' property by the district court for the southern district of Florida, and appeal to the Supreme Court followed.

Chief Justice Chase delivered the opinion of the Court. He pointed out that *The Andromeda* engaged in the gulf trade during the entire war. Charles Caro and Company of Havana, to whom the cargo was consigned, sent no representative to the hearings in the district court. The Chief Justice declared that this confirmed the Court in the belief that "no part of the cargo belonged to Caro & Co., and that the original enemy character of the whole of it remained unchanged at the time of capture." [7]

The Court concluded, too, that Ashby, the master of the vessel, was its owner despite his claim that he sold it to one Alleyn, a neutral, resident in New Orleans. Ashby claimed that Alleyn sold the vessel to one Watson, a neutral, resident in Havana. In neither case, however, was there "change of possession, control, or employment." "There is not the slightest evidence [the Court stated] that either of the alleged sales was real, except the unsupported statement of Ashby." In upholding the district court's condemnation of *The Andromeda* and its cargo as enemies' property, the Supreme Court pointed out that the vessel and cargo could have been condemned as well for breach of blockade.

The other case involved Mrs. Alexander's cotton. In the spring of 1864 a joint expedition under Rear Admiral David D. Porter and Major General Nathaniel P. Banks proceeded up the Red River in Louisiana. A party from one of the gunboats, *The Quachita*, landed at the plantation of Mrs. Alexander where it seized seventy-two bales of cotton which had been saved from a conflagration set by retreating Confederates. The bales were hauled to the river, shipped to Cairo, Illinois, labeled as enemies' property, and sold on order of the federal district court for the southern district of Illinois, *pendente lite*.

Elizabeth Alexander claimed the proceeds of the sale, and the district court granted them to her. Upon appeal by the government the circuit court, as well, upheld her right to the proceeds. But the government and the captors of the cotton appealed the case to the United States Supreme Court.

At the heart of the case was the question of Mrs. Alexander's loyalty. It was established that "She was equally kind . . . to loyal persons and to rebels, whether sick or wounded." She had assisted in the building of a fort only a few miles from her plantation, but according to her testimony, she "did this only on compulsion." In her behalf, it was established that "She had particular friends among persons of known loyalty; but there were one or two Confederate officers who came to her house,— the testimony being, however, that they were attracted thither neither by Mrs. Alexander's politics nor by her cotton, but by the beauty of some 'young ladies' who resided with her and whom they went to

---

[7] This discussion of the case of *The Schooner Andromeda* is based upon 17 L. Ed. 849-51.

'visit.' " [8] Three weeks after the seizure of her property, Mrs. Alexander had taken the oath required by the President's proclamation of amnesty of December 8, 1863, a proclamation that provided for full pardon and restoration of all property with the exception of slaves.

For the United States it was argued that enemies' property seized by naval or military forces on land was prize "as much as in cases of naval capture on the high seas." But in behalf of Mrs. Alexander, it was contended that she was not disloyal. "It would be unreasonable [her counsel argued] to ask that a *widow*, sixty-five years old, of infirm health . . . who has lived in one spot . . . for thirty years, should leave the only home she has on earth, and follow the army . . . under penalty of being declared judicially a 'rebel,' and having her estate confiscated."

Chief Justice Chase delivered the decision. The Court decided that Mrs. Alexander's cotton was enemies' property. Chase asserted it was claimed that, although Mrs. Alexander remained in Confederate territory, she "has no personal sympathy with the rebel cause, and that her property therefore cannot be regarded as enemies' property." He declared that "this Court cannot inquire into the personal character and dispositions of individual inhabitants of enemy territory." He pointed out that if she had removed herself to a loyal state after taking the oath, her position as an enemy would have been altered.

The Court supported the capture as legal, but could not agree that Mrs. Alexander's cotton was "maritime prize." Citing the act of July 17, 1862, providing for the better government of the Navy, Chief Justice Chase said that property on land was excluded from the "category of prize for the benefit of captors." The proceeds from the sale of the cotton, therefore, could not be shared by the captors but had to be paid into the Treasury of the United States.

The Chief Justice explained that Mrs. Alexander, as a claimant, within two years after the end of the rebellion could sue in the court of claims to recover the proceeds from the sale of the cotton. "In this war," declared Chase, "by this liberal . . . legislation, a distinction is made between those whom the rule of international law classes as enemies. All, who have in fact maintained a loyal adhesion to the Union, are protected in their rights to captured as well as abandoned property."

END-OF-BLOCKADE CASES

Just as problems of blockade and prize caused the Supreme Court's greatest battle during the Civil War, questions of termination of blockade provided it with one of the last war-related problems that it faced during

---

[8] This discussion of the case of Mrs. Alexander's Cotton is based upon 69 U.S. 404-23. See also Jonathan T. Dorris, *Pardon and Amnesty under Lincoln and Johnson* (Chapel Hill, 1953), 395-96.

the war. No question as to disposition of prize hampered the Court after it handed down its ruling in the *Prize Cases*. But a new problem related to prize finally did develop, and the Court was called upon for a ruling. When does blockade terminate and by what means?

Differences of opinion on this question brought before the Court, a few days after Salmon P. Chase assumed his role as Chief Justice, the first of the *End-of-Blockade Cases*. During the December Term, 1864, three cases involving termination of blockade were heard. The question of blockade of New Orleans and other portions of Louisiana was at issue. The cases involved *The Steamship Circassian, The Schooner Venice,* and *The Schooner Baigorry*.

It was in the case of the British steamship *Circassian* that the Court first faced the problem and established a precedent that was applied in both the other cases. Argument of *The Circassian* came on December 19, and December 20, 1864; the decision was announced on January 30, 1865.

The merchant steamer *Circassian* was captured on May 4, 1862, by the United States vessel *Somerset* while attempting to violate the blockade at New Orleans and was condemned as prize in the district court for the southern district of Florida. Appeal to the Supreme Court largely involved the question of whether New Orleans, on the date that *The Circassian* was captured, was under blockade. The city was falling to Union naval and military forces late in April, 1862, and by May 1 Union forces had seized the city. With the city under the control of the Union did the blockade terminate?

The decision of the Supreme Court, after hearing the arguments of Jeremiah Larocque, A. F. Smith, and E. G. Benedict for *The Circassian*, and Edward Bates (he was no longer Attorney General) and Charles Eames for the United States, was that Union control of New Orleans did not terminate blockade. The new Chief Justice spoke for the majority. He stated that capture of the fortifications of New Orleans did not bring blockade to an end, "but, on the contrary, made it more complete and absolute." [9] Mere military occupation of an enemy city, the majority maintained, does not terminate blockade at once, but "It might ripen into a possession which would have that effect, as it did; but at the time of the capture it operated only in aid and completion of the naval investment." The blockade of enemy ports, the Court ruled, even after their seizure, terminated only when the United States proclaimed the end of blockade. Such a proclamation, coming soon after Union seizure of New Orleans, provided that the blockade would be lifted as of June 1, 1862.

In determining whether *The Circassian* was prize, Chief Justice Chase also applied the principles accepted by the Court in the *Prize Cases*. He

---

[9] This discussion of *The Circassian* is based upon 69 U.S. 135-60.

declared that *The Circassian,* chartered at Paris on February 11, 1862, planned to "proceed to Havre or Bordeaux . . . thence with her cargo to Havana, Nassau, or Bermuda, and thence to a port in America and 'run the blockade, if so ordered by the freighters.' " On the basis of the *Prize Cases* as well as the newly enunciated rule of end-of-blockade *The Circassian* was prize.

With the end of the war in sight the Supreme Court even yet was unable to rule unanimously on this vital problem. Justice Nelson, who had written the dissenting opinion in the *Prize Cases,* now dissented alone and filed a dissenting opinion. Justice Catron and Justice Davis, both of whom were absent, did not participate in the case.

Justice Nelson contended that blockade of New Orleans did not exist when *The Circassian* was seized. He declared that when New Orleans was captured the blockade ended because the port and city "no longer belonged to the enemy, nor were under its dominion, but were a port and town of the United States." Nelson explained that he felt it was his duty to dissent because he believed that the right of blockade was being pressed too far.

Within the next few weeks the Supreme Court handed down two additional decisions relative to end-of-blockade. The decision in the case of *The Schooner Venice* was announced on February 27, 1865. *The Venice,* with its cargo of over two hundred bales of cotton, was captured by the United States warship *Calhoun* on May 15, 1862, on Lake Pontchartrain. In United States district court the vessel and cargo were returned to the owner, David G. Cooke. The government of the United States and Joseph E. Lee Haven, commander of the *Calhoun,* appealed the decision to the Supreme Court.

Cooke was a British subject who had lived in New Orleans for about ten years. Early in April, 1862, he purchased *The Venice,* anchored it in Lake Pontchartrain, and proceeded to have necessary repairs made. When captured it was lying at anchor. Meantime the war in Louisiana was reaching a climax, and the vessel and cargo, when seized, were enemies' property.

When the Union established itself in New Orleans, General Benjamin F. Butler issued a proclamation, effective May 6, 1862, that provided: "All foreigners . . . claiming allegiance to their respective governments, and not having made oath of allegiance to . . . the Confederate States, will be protected in their persons and property. . . ." [10]

Chief Justice Chase and the Court ruled that Butler's proclamation applied to David G. Cooke. Chase pointed out that *The Venice* and its cargo could be deemed enemies' property only until May 6, the date Butler's proclamation was effective. *The Venice* did not try to run the

---

[10] This discussion of *The Venice* is based upon *ibid.,* 258-79.

blockade; its owner was not guilty of any act against the United States. Consequently, it was proper to return the vessel and cargo to the rightful owner, and the Court so ordered.

The third vessel involved in the *End-of-Blockade Cases* was *The Schooner Baigorry*. Chief Justice Chase handed down the decision in this case on March 8, 1865. *The Baigorry* was owned by foreigners who were residents of New Orleans. In May, 1862, it ran the blockade at Calcasieu Pass, Louisiana, an area possessed by the rebels.

Chief Justice Chase pointed out that "when the master of the Baigorry saw the Bainbridge, [the United States vessel that seized it] on the afternoon before the capture . . . he changed his course to avoid her." [11] Furthermore, Chase remarked, it appeared that the vessel delayed sailing from May 3 to May 26, attempting obviously "to get out without being seized. It goes to establish guilty intent." He explained that this case differed from *The Venice* "because of the employment of the vessel in enemies' trade, and because of the attempt to violate the blockade, and to elude visitation and search by the Bainbridge." Chase concluded that although the master and mate testified that they saw no blockaders, blockade "must be presumed to continue until notice of discontinuance, in the absence of positive proof of discontinuance by other evidence."

THE SLAVERS

Almost as if by a stroke of fate, on March 8, and March 10, 1865, the last two decision days of the term, the Supreme Court handed down decisions in four cases which concerned the nefarious slave trade. The war was ending; the Confederacy was fading; slavery was dying; and Lincoln was coming close to his fateful day. Even the Supreme Court, on the last day that it met during the war, contributed to the shattering of a way of life—a way of life that vanished as Confederate power vanished.

The Bark Reindeer, The Bark Sarah, The Bark Weathergage, The Brig Kate—slavers all—had their day before the Court just at the moment when all that they represented was rapidly being demolished. The Supreme Court spoke out earnestly and with deep conviction in three of these cases through a pre-Lincoln Justice, Nathan Clifford. And in the fourth, Chief Justice Chase vigorously condemned the illicit traffic in human beings that reflected grievously upon the standards and mores of the American people.

The Reindeer cleared from the port of New York and sailed for Havana on January 26, 1861.[12] Before the voyage began ownership of the vessel was transferred. The United States claimed that *The Reindeer*

---

[11] This discussion of *The Baigorry* is based upon *ibid.*, 474-81.

[12] This discussion of the case of *The Bark Reindeer* is based upon 17 L. Ed. 911-15.

was destined for the African slave trade but "Her shipping articles described the voyage as one from the Port of New York to one or more ports in Cuba, from thence to one or more ports in Europe, if required, and back to a port of discharge in the United States, or from Cuba back to the United States."

The vessel delayed in the port of Havana four months, during which her crew and master remained on board and drew full wages. The owner, Pierre L. Pierce of New York City, finally arrived in Havana and proceeded to make arrangements to sell *The Reindeer* to David Coggeshall. However, the vessel actually was chartered to Coggeshall for three years. The same officers and crew remained aboard, and the same plans for the vessel were continued.

The Reindeer cleared for Falmouth, England, on June 22, 1861, but encountered a storm, suffered severe damage, and made for Newport, Rhode Island. Upon arrival the vessel was seized when examination of her cargo revealed that she had on board, though unlisted on the manifest, "sixty-five water pipes . . . pickled fish, coarse salt, two barrels of lime . . . cases of medicines, medicinal herbs and lint, coarse sponges, and one demijohn of disinfecting liquid." Included in the manifested cargo were 117 pipes of rum, sixty-five half pipes of rum, sixteen pipes of biscuit, 8,740 pounds of tasajo, one bale and seventeen packages of hardware, wine, brandy, and gin. In addition, part of the cargo "innocently described in the manifest as hardware, consisted of saucepans, cooking pans, casks containing iron chains, padlocks and war knives." On board when the vessel was seized were two passengers, Pedro Garcia and Hato A. Pinto. Garcia finally admitted that he had once been to the African coast to obtain slaves, although he claimed to be merely a passenger on *The Reindeer*.

It was the conclusion of the Supreme Court that the "sale" and "charter" of the vessel were simulated to conceal the fact that she went to Havana to complete her fitment for the voyage to Africa for slaves. And the Court set up general principles to apply in cases of slavers. Justice Clifford pointed out that "Experience shows that positive proof in such cases is not generally to be expected, and for that reason among others the law allows a resort to circumstances as the means of ascertaining the truth. Circumstances altogether inconclusive, if separately considered, may, by their number and joint operations, especially when corroborated by moral coincidences, be sufficient to constitute proof."

The United States charged that *The Bark Sarah*, clearing the Port of New York for Cape Palmas in Africa in the spring of 1861, plotted to engage in the African slave trade.[18] Claimants of the vessel admitted the destination, and Justice Clifford declared that "it cannot be denied that

---

[18] This discussion of the case of *The Bark Sarah* is based upon *ibid.*, 906-09.

the destination would have carried her to market where it is known that the traffic in slaves is prosecuted." The Court ruled that examination of the cargo of the vessel branded it a slaver. Not only were there "Unusually large quantities of shooks for casks," on board, but also "Fifteen barrels of beef and pork were found on board not on the manifest, and sixteen barrels of bread, and six barrels of flour, and one tierce of rice, plainly marked for the homeward voyage."

A clerk at the customs house in New York City testified that it was his observance that vessels destined for the slave trade were transferred two or three times before a slaving expedition began. This was true of *The Sarah;* it was sold twice in March, 1861. In addition it was established that when the mate was employing a seaman for the voyage, he stated that "he was going black birding" and on another occasion declared that "the bark was going on a trading voyage to the African coast, and would probably bring back some negroes."

In upholding condemnation of the vessel Justice Clifford declared, "Plainly, the object of the law is to prevent the preparation of vessels in our ports for that trade; and consequently, the law looks at the intention, and confers the authority to take from the offender the means required to enable him to perpetrate the mischief."

The Bark Weathergage, too, was condemned as a slaver.[14] For its owner it was argued that the mere fact "that the bark was bound for the coast of Africa, with such a cargo on board as is usually taken there for the purposes of lawful trade, can raise no legal presumption against her."

The vessel, which came into the hands of a new owner prior to the beginning of this expedition, purported to be going, in the fall of 1860, to Hong Kong by way of Ambriz on the African coast. Fitment of the vessel incited suspicions. As Justice Clifford pointed out, on board were "seventeen coils of rope, three bolts of sail duck, eight anchors, coopers' tools, nails and almost every variety of article which is essential in the fitment of a slaver." The conclusion of the Justices was that "it seems to us, in view of the evidence in the case, that the manifest is a 'more complete one, in every respect, for engaging in the slave trade,' than any one heretofore presented to the Court." The Justices, furthermore, pointed out in condemning the vessel that trade from New York to Hong Kong, by way of Ambriz, was unknown.

The new Chief Justice, Salmon P. Chase spoke for the Court in another case involving a slaver. The facts in the case of *The Brig Kate* were not unlike those revealed by the other slavers.[15] *The Kate* arrived at New York from Havana in May, 1860. Following transfer of title to Charles

---

[14] This discussion of the case of *The Bark Weathergage* is based upon *ibid.,* 909-11.
[15] This discussion of the case of *The Brig Kate* is based upon *ibid.,* 878-80.

P. Lake, it set out for Cape Palmas in July, 1860, and was captured outside of New York Harbor.

When the vessel was seized, it was accompanied by a tug which conveyed the captain, Otto, and one Da Costa. Upon seizure of the tug, Da Costa pretended to be a stranger to Otto and feigned ignorance of the English language. But on board *The Kate* trunks were found bearing Da Costa's name, and soon it was apparent that ignorance of the language was mere pretense. Later it was established that Da Costa had been indicted four years earlier for participating in the slave trade. It was the conclusion of the Court that he was the real owner of *The Kate*.

Chief Justice Chase forcefully condemned the slave trade. It was appropriate that he, a violent antislavery leader, should as Chief Justice deal with cases concerning the slave trade at the time when the Confederacy was on the brink of destruction. "In considering this evidence, [said Chase] it is to be borne in mind, that for more than three hundred years the western coast of Africa has been scourged by the atrocities of the slave trade; and that this inhuman traffic, although at length proscribed and pursued with severe penalties by nearly all Christian nations, has continued, with almost unabated activity and ferocity, even to our times."

Chase pointed out that hopes for enormous gains were able to overcome fears that men had of forfeiture of property. He said that so long as any market for slaves existed, men would contrive more and more adroit means for carrying the trade through to completion. And he lamented that the crime could be disguised with effectiveness because "a very considerable traffic, regarded as legitimate, has sprung up and is carried on with the same African coast from which human cargoes are collected." "It does not seem unreasonable, [declared the Chief Justice] ... to require of the trader who engages in a commerce, which, altogether not unlawful, is necessarily suspicious from its theater and circumstances, that he keeps his operations so clear and so distinct in their character, as to repel the imputation of prohibited purpose."

So on this theme, the slavers, the Supreme Court of the United States ended its sessions of the Civil War. (It is to be noted that after the session adjourned, Chief Justice Chase went to Baltimore to hold circuit court in April, 1865. Here he heard only commonplace cases. Chase refused to enter other areas of his circuit until "the President or Congress, or both together, had proclaimed the restoration of peace and civil authority as paramount to the military authority." [16]) The strife was all but ended on the battlefield. The cause was won. The Union was saved. And in the Supreme Court, too, the struggle was ended, and a new era

---

[16] Schuckers, *Life of Chase*, p. 535.

had dawned. The Court, with considerably different personnel from that which existed when the war opened, faced the future, and a foreboding future it was. The end of the war solved part of the problems, while it served to intensify many others.

CHAPTER EIGHTEEN

Taney Absolved

HONOR DELAYED

With the death of Chief Justice Taney the most controversial figure in American constitutional history passed from the scene. In the eyes of those who disagreed with his attitude toward slavery and the war, his reputation was utterly destroyed. The result was that Republicans looked upon his death "as the removal of a barrier to human progress." [1] Nicolay and Hay, who themselves made a final evaluation of Taney that forecast the gradual improvement of his reputation, stated that upon his death "The general feeling found expression in the grim and profane witticism of Senator Wade, uttered some months before, when it seemed likely that the Chief-Justice would survive the Administration of Mr. Lincoln: 'No man ever prayed as I did that Taney might outlive James Buchanan's term, and now I am afraid I have overdone it.'" [2] They concluded, however, that "Toilsome and irreproachable as his life had been, so far as purity of intentions were concerned, it was marked by one of those mistakes [the Dred Scott decision] which are never forgiven. In a critical hour of history he had made a decision contrary to the spirit of the age, contrary to the best hopes and aspirations of the nation at large." [3]

An article that appeared in the *Atlantic Monthly* shortly after Taney's death best expressed the contempt for him which was widespread as the trial of the Union ended. "He did worse [declared this article] than torment and pervert language: he reversed its meaning. He denied the undoubted facts of history. . . . He slandered the memory of the founders of the government and the framers of the Declaration. He was ready to cover the most glorious page of the history of his country with infamy, and insulted the intelligence and virtue of the civilized world." [4]

There is irony in the fact that Taney's successor, within a year after he assumed office, revealed to Orville H. Browning that he had acquired a new feeling for Taney and a new appreciation of the problems he had faced. Browning recorded in his diary that on December 22, 1865, he

---

[1] Nicolay and Hay, *Abraham Lincoln*, IX, 386.

[2] *Ibid.*

[3] *Ibid.*, IX, 385.

[4] "Roger Brooke Taney," *The Atlantic Monthly*, February, 1865, XV, 160.

visited with Chase and in the course of conversation the Chief Justice uttered his new feelings. Chase remarked that he was "greatly shocked by the fierce, rude assault" upon Taney that recently had been made in the House of Representatives. He declared that Taney "was a man of great talents and attainments—a very able jurist—unusually kind and gentle in his nature, and of very pure and exalted character." [5]

Chase's attitude gained general acceptance with the passing years. Felix Frankfurter, who himself became a distinguished Justice of the Supreme Court, has summed up Taney's contribution to American constitutional development: "The devastation of the Civil War for a long time obliterated the truth about Taney. And the blaze of Marshall's glory will permanently overshadow him. But the intellectual power of his opinions and their enduring contribution to a workable adjustment of the theoretical distribution of authority between two governments for a single people, place Taney second only to Marshall in the constitutional history of our country." [6]

The resentments that lingered even after Taney was borne to the grave flashed fiercely shortly before the war ended. On February 8, 1865, Augustus Frank of New York reported to the House of Representatives that the committee on the library approved a proposal to place a marble bust of Chief Justice Taney in the courtroom where busts of the other Chief Justices stood. The House accepted the bill, which provided for an appropriation of one thousand dollars so that a joint committee of the House and Senate could contract to have a bust of Taney made, and requested that the Senate concur. [7]

Complications arose immediately in the United States Senate. Although Senator Trumbull reported the bill favorably from the committee on the judiciary on February 11, Senator Sumner prevented immediate consideration of the proposal. [8] He repeatedly blocked efforts to consider the bill and took advantage of the opportunity to attack Chief Justice Taney. He said, "I object to that; that now an emancipated country should make a bust to the author of the Dred Scott decision." [9] Trumbull, who was irritated by Sumner's stand, declared that the bill ought to be passed. He maintained that Taney, who presided over the Court for more than a quarter of a century, should not be deprived of this recognition. Trumbull said that Taney "added reputation to the character of the judiciary of the United States throughout the world," and that such a

<hr>

[5] Browning, *Diary*, II, 54 (December 22, 1865).

[6] Felix Frankfurter, "Taney and the Commerce Clause," *Harvard Law Review*, June, 1936, XLIX, 1302.

[7] *Cong. Globe*, 38th Cong., 2nd sess., p. 666.

[8] *Ibid.*, p. 742.

[9] The following debate concerning the bust of Taney is to be found in *Cong. Globe*, 38th Cong., 2nd sess., pp. 1012-17.

person "is not to be hooted down by an explanation that the country is to be emancipated. Suppose he did make a wrong decision. No man is infallible. He was a great and an able man."

By this time Charles Sumner was thoroughly aroused and ready for a fight. He declared that Taney had administered justice "wickedly" and had "degraded the judiciary." He forecast that "an emancipated country" would fasten upon Taney "the stigma which he deserves." And borrowing some of Trumbull's phraseology—he revamped and extended it—Sumner shouted, "The Senator from Illinois says that this idea of a bust is not to be hooted down. Let me tell that Senator that the name of Taney is to be hooted down the page of history."

At this point Reverdy Johnson of Maryland entered the fray to express astonishment at Sumner's intemperate statements. In urging that the Senate disregard Sumner, Johnson reminded the Senate that the Dred Scott decision was not made by Taney alone. "Every judge who has been at the head of that tribunal [Johnson continued] has his bust placed in that courtroom. Does the honorable member wish to have it unknown in future times that there was such a Chief Justice? I suppose he does; I presume he does; and why? Because he differed with him."

Sumner renewed his vigorous attack. He decried the effort that was being made to compliment "in marble" a man who, in his opinion, had done vast evil. Sumner said he did not seek the debate and regretted the need to speak bluntly, but he believed that the "wicked opinion of the Chief Justice" in the Dred Scott case was the "incident of our history," prior to the Civil War, "most deadly in its consequences." He suggested that the vacancy in the Supreme Court room be permitted to remain to "speak warning to all who would betray liberty." To show his contempt for the proceedings at hand, Sumner moved that the bill be amended to provide that a bust of Joshua R. Giddings, a violent antislavery leader of Ohio who had died recently, be placed in the Supreme Court room in place of a bust of Chief Justice Taney.

Trumbull arose, again, to denounce the efforts of Taney's opponents. He said to the Senate that he, for one, did not intend "to follow a departed brother into that other world for the purpose of denouncing him." With that, Sumner announced that he would withdraw his amendment so that the bill could be voted upon as reported.

But no such simple solution was to be permitted. Senator John P. Hale came to the support of Sumner. Hale argued that if a bust of Taney were placed in the Supreme Court room it would be inferred that Taney merited high honor. He demanded that such honor be denied Taney. "I apprehend Congress would not be willing to pass a general act [Hale argued] that whoever has heretofore, or shall hereafter be Chief Justice . . . should have a marble bust placed in the court-room.

If that was the character of the act, it would have no value at all." He summed up his views succinctly when he told the Senate that men of his inclinations urged that an "impartial posterity" be permitted to evaluate Taney and that in the meanwhile men should "let Judge Taney alone, let his memory alone, let his fame go for what it is worth."

Senator Henry Wilson of Massachusetts arose to lend support to Sumner and Hale, declaring that it was a crime to honor Taney, a man who, in his opinion, did more to plunge the nation into "this bloody revolution" than any other person. He asked the Senate how it could contemplate expenditure of one thousand dollars to honor Taney when the treasury was empty and when men "are fighting, bleeding, dying to defend their country, menaced by armed treason born of the Dred Scott decision." Wilson viciously attacked Taney and his role during the war: "In its hour of humiliation, trial, and agony, he never gave one cheering word nor performed one act to protect or save. He sank into his grave without giving a cheering word or a helping hand to the country he had vainly sought to place forever by judicial authority under the iron rule of the slavemasters."

Two others entered the heated exchange of views, Senator Benjamin F. Wade of Ohio and Senator John S. Carlile of Virginia. Wade said that the greater Taney's judicial skill was made to appear, the greater his sin against "light and knowledge" seemed. "It would be more for his fame if you could prove him a fool," maintained Senator Wade. But Senator Carlile denied that Taney had disgraced the bench and urged that the resolution pass so that Congress would avoid the stigma that would result if it denied Taney "the same mark of respect that has been shown to his predecessors."

Sumner gained the floor and retained it until the Vice President announced that the hour to adjourn until evening had arrived. During his remarks Sumner stated that "they who seek to canonize one of the tools of slavery" were responsible for the bitter debate and that "Taney shall not be recognized as a saint by any vote of Congress if I can help it." Agreement was reached to consider the bill further the next day, but it was not called up again. Antagonisms were too great in the days that the war was ending to honor the departed Chief Justice.

The bitterness of the debate was symptomatic of the rancor of the time, and Taney would have to wait almost a decade for the honor of having a bust placed in the Supreme Court room of the United States. During the war his role was a difficult one. He was right when it did not pay to be right; he was legalistic when it did not pay to be legalistic; he sought to maintain a "government of laws" when everything bowed before the imperative demands of military necessity. But Senator Charles Sumner was wrong when he declared that Taney would be "hooted down the page of history." Senator John P. Hale evinced far more perspicacity when he asked the Senate to let "impartial posterity" sit in judgment upon Taney. Posterity has done what Hale proposed it be permitted to do. But Hale would demur from its judgment. Despite all the impediment that Taney's policies would have been to the Union, he has been restored to his proper place in American constitutional development.

VINDICATION AT LAST

Many years after the war, at the time of his retirement in 1897, Justice Field declared to the members of the Supreme Court that when he was appointed in 1863 "Washington was one great camp, and now and then the boom of cannon could be heard from the other side of the Potomac." Despite the war, Field continued, the Court met as regularly scheduled and functioned as though no war raged so "we could not say *inter arma silent leges.*" [10]

And in his *Reminiscences* Justice Field had more to say about the Supreme Court during the war. Perhaps, as he reminisced his memory did not serve him too well; or, after a few decades had passed, he tended to idealize the role that the Court played during the conflict. At any rate the evidence only partly sustains what he stated in the following passage:

The Court and all its members appreciated the great difficulties and responsibilities of the government, both in the conduct of the war, and in effecting an early restoration of the States afterwards, and no disposition was manifested at any time to place unnecessary obstacles in its way. But when its measures and legislation were brought to the test of judicial judgment there was but one course to pursue, and that was to apply the law and the Constitution as strictly as though no war had ever existed. The Constitution was not one thing in war, and another in peace. It always spoke the same language, and was intended as a rule for all times and occasions. It recognized, indeed, the possibility of war, and, of course, that the rules of war had to be applied in its conduct in the field of military operations. The Court never presumed to interfere there, but outside of that field, and with respect to persons not in the military service within States which adhered to the Union, and after the war in all the States, the Court could not hesitate to say that the Constitution, with all its limitations upon the exercise of executive and legislative authority, was, what it declares on its face to be, the supreme law of the land, by which all legislation, State and federal, must be measured.[11]

Justice Field's reminiscences notwithstanding, it was not until quiet had been restored on the field of battle that the Supreme Court spoke out vigorously for the return of a rule of law. When the war was at an end and the Court did speak out, it spoke with a single voice—there was no division between the appointees of Lincoln and the pre-Lincoln

---

[10] 168 U.S. 715.

[11] Stephen J. Field, *Personal Reminiscences*, pp. 192-93.

appointees. Upon this fact rests the exoneration of Roger Brooke Taney. It demonstrates that Taney was not really wrong when he challenged Lincoln's arbitrary arrests. Rather, he was indiscreet and untimely.

Vindication of Chief Justice Taney's views came shortly after the war when the Supreme Court ruled against the government's exercise of military jurisdiction over Lamdin P. Milligan, a civilian seized and tried by army authorities during the conflict. In the Milligan case the Supreme Court reversed its decision in the case of Clement L. Vallandigham. Furthermore, the Milligan decision implied that Chief Justice Taney was correct in the stand he took in the controversy over John Merryman at the beginning of the war.

Once the war was over the Supreme Court's policy of refusing to take action that would endanger federal position was at an end. The Supreme Court did not restrain the administration while the war raged, but when the last shot was fired, the Supreme Court, even though it was dominated by Lincoln's appointees, called vigorously for a return to constitutional guarantees. Taney's "government of laws" was restored.

Lamdin P. Milligan was arrested on October 5, 1864, at his home and was taken to a military prison in Indianapolis. A military commission tried him on October 21 on the charge of joining the Order of American Knights for the purpose of overthrowing the government of the United States. The commission found him guilty, and the sentence—death by hanging—was to be carried out on Friday, May 19, 1865.

In Milligan's behalf a petition was filed on May 10, 1865, in the United States circuit court at Indianapolis requesting a writ of habeas corpus, it being claimed that a military commission had no jurisdiction over Milligan, a civilian.[12] The judges of the court disagreed on the decision; Judge David McDonald was unwilling to grant a writ of habeas corpus, but Circuit Justice David Davis concluded that the writ should be granted. The disagreement brought the case, on a certification of division, before the United States Supreme Court. The questions that were certified to the Court were: Should a writ of habeas corpus be issued? Should Milligan be discharged? Could a military commission exercise jurisdiction in this case? [13]

Not long after Milligan's arrest—William A. Bowles and Stephen Horsey were arrested with him—the war ended, and Andrew Johnson came to occupy the presidency upon the assassination of Lincoln. Justice Davis, who believed firmly that military commissions had no jurisdiction over civilians, talked to Governor Oliver P. Morton of Indiana and urged him to request President Johnson to commute Milligan's sentence. In the meanwhile Johnson postponed the execution.

On May 22, 1865, Governor Morton wrote a letter to be handed to

[12] 71 U.S. 7-8.
[13] New York *Tribune*, April 4, 1866, p. 4.

the President by Mrs. Milligan in which he urged commutation of the sentence to imprisonment.[14] And Morton sent John U. Pettit, speaker of the Indiana house of representatives, to Washington to confer with Johnson. Speaking in Richmond, Indiana, a few years later, Morton explained why he had intervened. He declared that although the conspirators had sought to take his life, to seize the state arsenal, and to release rebel prisoners in Indiana, their efforts had all come to nought. Since the rebellion was over and the peril was past, Morton explained, "I felt that, if they had been executed, it would be said that I might have saved them, and that, as I was the man whose life had been imperiled, it would be becoming in me to ask the President to spare their lives, and I did so." [15]

It was anticipated that the United States Supreme Court would decide the question of the authority of military commissions during the December Term, 1865. Edward Bates speculated in his diary how the Justices would view the case and quoted J. Hubley Ashton, the Assistant Attorney General, "I count on the following members being against the Commissions—*Nelson, Clifford, Grier,* and *Davis* (and *perhaps* Ch[ief] J[ustice] Chase[)]. I think *Swayne, Wayne,* and *Field* will be *certainly* in *favor* of the U.S.—Miller is doubtful!"

Bates was sorely perturbed by the prospect that partisan politics would dictate the views of the Justices. "Alas! Alas! that any judge of the S.[upreme] C.[ourt] of the U.S. [wrote Bates in his diary] should even be suspected of deciding such a case upon party or personal grounds—" It was Bates's conclusion that if the Justices upheld the legality of the military commissions, "the judges who give opinion that way will go down to posterity with characters as black as that of L[or]d. Ch[ief] J.[ustice] Saunders." [16]

The Milligan case was argued before the Court from March 5 to March 13, 1866. Milligan was represented by an array of distinguished talent: Jeremiah S. Black, David Dudley Field, James A. Garfield, J. E. McDonald, A. L. Roache, and John R. Coffuth. For the government there appeared Attorney General James Speed, Henry Stanbery, and Benjamin F. Butler.

Attorney General Speed and General Butler opened the case for the government by asserting that since a military commission "derives its powers" from martial law its decisions can be reviewed only by military authority.[17] Stanbery and Butler argued that neither residence nor pro-

---

[14] William D. Foulke, *Life of Oliver P. Morton, Including His Important Speeches* (Indianapolis, 1899), I, 428, n. 1.

[15] *Ibid.,* I, 430-31.

[16] Bates, *Diary,* 546-47 (February 16, 1866).

[17] The following treatment of the government's argument in the Milligan case is based upon 71 U.S. 9-21.

pinquity to the field of battle determines whether there is military authority over an individual. They maintained that the President could order the arrest of anyone who assisted the rebels. The government's counsel claimed for the President unlimited powers in time of war, declaring, "He is the sole judge of the exigencies, necessities, and duties of the occasion, their extent and duration." That was a bold and all-encompassing assertion of presidential authority.

Orville H. Browning, who had no sympathy with the government's counsel in the Milligan case, wrote in his diary that General Butler "spoke an hour and a half to day. His manner pompous, and his matter paltry. He is a weak man—a humbug." [18] Browning was as little impressed by Attorney General Speed. He termed Speed's efforts "a feeble, uninteresting, uninstructive harangue." [19]

The three leading attorneys serving in behalf of Milligan—David Dudley Field, James A. Garfield, and Jeremiah S. Black—argued persuasively against the contentions of the government's attorneys.[20] David Dudley Field demonstrated at length that both the circuit court and the Supreme Court had jurisdiction in this appeal, and he pointed out carefully that "military tribunals for civilians or non-military persons, whether in war or peace, are inconsistent with the liberty of the citizen, and can have no place in constitutional government." Chief Justice Taney, who surely was present in apparitional form to hear these arguments, must have smiled with favor as he heard his own position argued so brilliantly before the Court over which he had presided so long, but a Court which he could not carry with him in the years of civil strife.

And Taney, preternaturally, must have gained vast satisfaction as James A. Garfield declared to the Court that only if the Constitution were suspended could the military commission rightfully exercise jurisdiction over Milligan, a civilian active in an area that was not a battle area. Garfield maintained that opposite counsel was arguing that "martial law alone existed in Indiana; that it silenced not only the civil courts, but all the laws of the land, and even the Constitution itself; and that during this silence the executor of martial law could lay his hand upon every citizen; could not only suspend the writ of *habeas corpus*, but could create a court which should have the exclusive jurisdiction over the citizen to try him, sentence him, and put him to death."

Jeremiah S. Black denounced Speed's contention that Milligan could "be punished without being found guilty by a competent court or a jury." He denied that it was possible under the constitutional system of

---

[18] Browning, *Diary*, II, 65-66 (March 7, 1866).

[19] *Ibid.*, II, 66 (March 9, 1866).

[20] The following treatment of the argument in behalf of Milligan is based upon 71 U.S. 22-84.

the United States for a military tribunal to punish civilians who lived "in the midst of a community whose social and legal organization had never been disturbed by any war or insurrection, where the courts were wide open, where judicial process was executed every day without interruption, and where all the civil authorities, both state and national, were in the full exercise of their functions." The plea of necessity—that plea upon which so much of Lincoln's justification rested—Black rejected vehemently and affirmed that no plea "could give legal validity to that which the law forbids."

It fell to General Butler to reply to these imposing arguments.[21] He admitted that the courts were open in Indiana, but he maintained that they would not have remained able to function without the presence of federal troops. He implied, too, that if the military authorities had permitted freedom to the domestic foes of the United States, Indiana would have been hurled into insurrection. Butler cited the ruling in the Vallandigham case to support his contention that the decision of a military commission is reviewable only by military authority. Falling again upon the plea of necessity, Butler stated, "We do not ask anything outside of or beyond the Constitution. We insist only that the Constitution be interpreted so as to save the nation, and not to let it perish."

In concluding the government's case, Butler summed up the position of the government skillfully. His conclusion was a fine presentation of a view that was widely held:

We do not desire to exalt the martial above the civil law, or to substitute the necessarily despotic rule of the one, for the mild and healthy restraints of the other. Far otherwise. We demand only that when the law is silent; when justice is overthrown; when the life of the nation is threatened by foreign foes that league, and wait, and watch without to unite with the domestic foes within, who had seized almost half of the territory, and more than half the resources of the government, at the beginning; when the capital is imperilled; when the traitor within plots to bring to its peaceful communities the braver rebels who fights without; when the judge is deposed; when the juries are dispersed; when the sheriff, the executive officer of the law, is powerless; when the bayonet is called in as the final arbiter; when on its armed forces the government must rely for all it has of power, authority, and dignity; when the citizen has to look to the same source for everything he has of right in the present or hopes in the future,—then we ask that martial law may prevail, so that the civil law may again live, to the end that this may be a "government of laws and not of men."

On April 3, 1866, three weeks after the arguments were concluded, Chief Justice Chase announced the decision. The Court decided that military commissions such as the one that tried Milligan had no jurisdiction of the type assumed in the case, and it ordered the sentence of the

---

[21] Butler's reply is to be found *ibid.*, 84-106.

military commission set aside.[22] Chase's announcement created a sensation. The military commission that tried Milligan was without jurisdiction! The written opinions of the members of the Court were not immediately forthcoming, delay being provided so that the Justices could concentrate on their opinions after adjournment of the term. Chief Justice Chase said that he was "instructed to say that the opinion of the Court in this case will be read at the next term, when such of the dissenting judges as see fit to do so, will state their grounds of dissent." [23]

Orville H. Browning apparently knew beforehand what the Supreme Court would rule, the information being made available to him by Justice Grier. Browning noted carefully in his diary that on March 25, 1866, he attended Dr. Gurley's church with Grier and that Grier "told me" that the Court "had unanimously decided in favor of the Habeas Corpus, and against the Commissions." Grier revealed, too, that some of the Justices wished to apply the ruling only to the case at hand, although the majority "extended it to all military commissions for the trial of persons not in the Military or Naval Service." [24]

On December 17, 1866, shortly after the Supreme Court assembled for the December Term, the Justices delivered their opinions in the Milligan case. Justice David Davis spoke in behalf of the Court. It ruled unanimously that Milligan was held and tried illegally. This fact is all the more significant when it is remembered that of the nine Justices who comprised the Court at the time five were appointees of Lincoln. (Justice Catron died on May 30, 1865, and because of the struggle between Johnson and the Radicals no replacement had been made.)

Justice Davis remarked that to write the Milligan decision was an exceedingly difficult task, and it is not surprising that he had difficulty in phrasing it.[25] Nonetheless, it stands today, as it has stood from the day it was enunciated, as an irremovable bulwark of American civil liberties.

---

[22] Following the Court's ruling, Milligan was released on April 10 from confinement in a military prison at Columbus, Ohio. He was promptly seized by civil authorities in Indianapolis and was forced to give bail to gain his freedom. No case was pressed against him, however, and finally he was dismissed. Since he had been tried illegally by the military commission, in 1868 he filed a suit to collect damages. The case was tried in May, 1871, in the circuit court in Indianapolis, taking the form of *Milligan v. Hovey* (General Alvin P. Hovey was the military commander for the district of Indiana, 1864-65). Thomas A. Hendricks appeared for Milligan, and Benjamin Harrison appeared for the defendant. Judge Thomas Drummond, who presided, charged the jury that on account of the statute of limitations, Hovey was not to be held liable for acts prior to March 13, 1866. The jury had very little sympathy for Milligan, but realizing that the law provided damages in such a case, it brought in a verdict awarding Milligan five dollars. 17 Fed. Cas. 380-83. See also Foulke, *Oliver P. Morton*, I, 431-32.

[23] Indianapolis *Daily Herald*, April 14, 1866, p. 1.

[24] Browning, *Diary*, II, 67 (March 25, 1866).

[25] Pratt, "David Davis," p. 114.

Not only did Davis's opinion include a classic enunciation of American liberties, it provided also a key to an understanding of the role played by the Supreme Court during the four years of civil war.[26]

Justice Davis declared that although the Milligan case involved principles that were basic in the concept of American freedoms, the decision handed down would not and could not have been enunciated if the war were yet in progress. In a forcefully frank passage of the opinion, Justice Davis summarized the feelings of a majority of the Court during the years of battle and bloodshed:

During the late wicked Rebellion, the temper of the times did not allow that calmness in deliberation and discussion so necessary to a correct conclusion of a purely judicial question. *Then*, considerations of safety were mingled with the exercise of power; and feelings and interests prevailed which are happily terminated. *Now* that the public safety is assured, this question, as well as all others, can be discussed and decided without passion or the admixture of any element not required to form a legal judgment. We approach the investigation of this case, fully sensible of the magnitude of the inquiry and the necessity of full and cautious deliberation.

Here was vindication for Chief Justice Taney. Here was the answer to Taney's detractors and maligners, and it was an answer supplied by a Supreme Court in which there was a Republican majority.

Justice Davis announced that it was the decision of the Court that under the Habeas Corpus Act of 1863 the federal circuit court in Indianapolis had jurisdiction in the Milligan case, and further, that the court had the right and duty to certify the matters upon which its judges disagreed to the Supreme Court of the United States. As a Supreme Court Justice, Davis was sitting, along with the rest of the Court, in judgment of his own decision as Circuit Justice in Indianapolis.

He declared that it was the civil authorities and not the military authorities who had jurisdiction over Milligan. "This court has judicial knowledge [Davis affirmed] that in Indiana the Federal authority was always unopposed, and its courts always open . . . and no usage of war could sanction a military trial there for any offense whatever of a citizen in civil life, in nowise connected with the military service. . . ." Davis emphasized that soon after Milligan's military trial, "the Circuit Court met, peacefully transacted business, and adjourned. It needed no bayonets to protect it, and required no military aid to execute its judgements[sic]."

If the spirit of Chief Justice Taney were frequenting the Supreme Court while arguments were taking place concerning Milligan's arrest, surely it had been given leave to be present to hear Justice Davis discuss the significance of this case:

Milligan, not a resident of one of the rebellious states, or a prisoner of war,

---

[26] David Davis's opinion is to be found in 71 U.S. 107-31.

but a citizen of Indiana for twenty years past, and never in the military or
naval service, is, while at his home, arrested by the military power of the
United States, imprisoned, and, on certain criminal charges preferred against
him, tried, convicted, and sentenced to be hanged by a military commission,
organized under the direction of the military commander of the military
district of Indiana. Has this tribunal the *legal* power and authority to try and
punish this man? No graver question was ever considered by this court, nor
one which more clearly concerns the rights of the whole people; for it is the
birthright of every American citizen when charged with crime, to be tried
and punished according to law.

Four members of the Court—Chief Justice Chase, Justice Wayne,
Justice Swayne, and Justice Miller—agreed that Milligan was held illegally under the Habeas Corpus Act of 1863 and that the military commission had no authority over him, but they differed on "some important
particulars" and consequently formulated a statement of their own views.
The majority of the Court declared that Congress had no authority to
establish military commissions in loyal states even if it wished to do so.
Chase, Wayne, Swayne, and Miller were unwilling to deny, categorically,
to Congress the power to grant such jurisdiction to military commissions.
These Justices believed that at some future date an occasion might arise
necessitating the exercise of such power. "We think [wrote Chief Justice
Chase] that Congress had power, though not exercised, to authorize the
military commission which was held in Indiana." [27]

The Supreme Court, after peace was restored, had done what it consistently refused to do during the war. The majority was interested too
vitally in the Union to hamper the administration during the war, but
when peace was restored the Court was determined that a rule of law
should be restored, too. It asserted its just power in the Milligan case because comparative tranquillity had been restored. Chief Justice Taney's
plea for a "government of laws" had gone unheard in 1861 only because
it was untimely.

In the majority decision Justice Davis alluded to the fact that it could
not be expected that the United States would always be headed by a man
"sincerely attached to the principles of the Constitution." He pointed
out the dangers that lurked under our constitutional system if an un-
principled man gained the presidency. "Wicked men, ambitious of power,
[he wrote] with hatred of liberty and contempt of law, may fill the place
once occupied by Washington and Lincoln; and if this right is conceded,
and the calamities of war again befall us, the dangers to human liberty
are frightful to contemplate." [28]

Justice Davis revealed in a letter written to William H. Herndon on
September 10, 1866, that during the war he had apprised Lincoln that

[27] The views of Chase, Wayne, Swayne, and Miller are to be found *ibid.*, 132-42.
[28] *Ibid.*, 125.

military trials in areas where the federal courts were functioning freely
were "unconstitutional and wrong" and that the Supreme Court should
not uphold such trials. It was Davis's conclusion that Lincoln, himself,
opposed these trials, but that he put necessity first. In reference to the
Milligan case, Davis told Herndon: "When Joseph E. McDonald went to
Lincoln about these military trials and asked him not to execute the men
who had been convicted by the military commission in Indiana he
answered that he would not hang them, but added 'I'll keep them in
prison awhile to keep them from killing the Government.' " [29] This
demonstrated again Lincoln's basic policy. To Lincoln the argument of
emergency and necessity was sufficient.

By its decision in the Milligan case the Supreme Court hurled itself
into direct conflict with Radicals who were attempting to control the
policy of the government in the dark days of reconstruction. The
Milligan decision brought scorching criticism that in many ways was
similar to that which was showered upon the Court at the beginning of
the war.

The fears of the Radicals were perhaps best stated by the New York
Herald which suggested that if the Court saw fit to interfere in the
Milligan case, perhaps it would deliberately interfere with many of the
changes that resulted from the war. The *Herald* chose to assume that even
the abolition of slavery was endangered! Harking back to arguments
made in 1861 by Republicans who loathed the Democratic Court of
that day, the *Herald* warned the Republican-dominated Court that "by
increasing or diminishing the number of the Judges, the Court may be
reconstructed in conformity with the supreme decisions of the war."
How ironic it was that the *Herald* proceeded to say of this Court upon
which were five appointees of Lincoln: "A reconstruction of the Supreme
Court adapted to the paramount decision of the war looms into bold
relief as a question of vital importance." [30]

The *American Law Review* discussed the repercussions of the Milligan
decision at length. It pointed out that it was unfortunate—as indeed it
was—that some members of the Court saw fit to deliver *dicta* because in
so doing they obscured the fact that on the main issue there was complete harmony. "It is rare [the law review continued] that the whole
court agrees on any constitutional question: it is still more rare when
the court agrees to decide an important question in opposition to executive authority and the current popular feelings; and such unanimity is
too precious a thing to be hid under a bushel." [31]

---

[29] David Davis to William H. Herndon, September 10, 1866, quoted in Herndon
and Weik, *Herndon's Lincoln*, III, 556, note.

[30] Editorial, New York *Herald*, December 20, 1866, p. 4.

[31] "Milligan's Case," *American Law Review*, April, 1867, I, 575.

The Radicals continued to cry for reorganization of the Court. And the Court became further involved in the bitterness, the animosity of the Reconstruction period. Nonetheless, those who desired a peaceful and prompt restoration of the Union and those who were not blinded by Radical philosophy and desires, could agree with the Indianapolis *Herald* which said of the Milligan decision: "We express our thanks to the Supreme Court. It stands by Johnson in attempting to bring back Union and a government of laws. We congratulate the country that all but the fanatical Republicans and their disunion Congress are striving for peace and the Republic." [32]

A "government of laws"—that was the objective of Chief Justice Taney and the object of President Lincoln as well. And that was the object of the Supreme Court in the Milligan decision. In the broadest sense, the Milligan decision stands as a monument to the man who strove for a "government of laws" though the cause was not only unpopular but suspected, and the tide ran against him and everything for which he stood.

---

[32] Editorial, Indianapolis *Daily Herald*, April 5, 1866, p. 2.

Appendix

Justice Nathan Clifford, First Circuit (Maine, New Hampshire, Massachusetts, Rhode Island) Portland, Portsmouth, Boston, Newport, Providence.

Justice Samuel Nelson, Second Circuit (Vermont, Connecticut, New York) Windsor, Rutland, New Haven, Hartford, Canandaigua, Albany, New York City.

Justice Robert C. Grier, Third Circuit (New Jersey and Pennsylvania) Trenton, Philadelphia, Pittsburgh, Williamsburg.

Chief Justice Roger B. Taney, Fourth Circuit (Delaware, Maryland, Virginia, West Virginia, North Carolina) New Castle, Baltimore, Richmond, Lewisburgh, Raleigh.

Justice James M. Wayne, Fifth Circuit (South Carolina, Georgia, Alabama, Mississippi, and Florida) Charleston, Columbia, Savannah, Milledgeville, Mobile, Jackson, Appalachicola, Tallahassee, St. Augustine, Pensacola, Key West.

Justice John Catron, Sixth Circuit (Louisiana, Texas, Arkansas, Kentucky, Tennessee) New Orleans, Opelousas, Alexandria, Monroe, Shreveport, St. Josephs, Galveston, Brownsville, Austin, Tyler, Little Rock, Covington, Louisville, Frankfort, Paducah, Knoxville, Nashville, Huntingdon, (Carroll county).

Justice Noah H. Swayne, Seventh Circuit (Ohio and Michigan) Cleveland, Cincinnati, Detroit, Grand Rapids.

Justice David Davis, Eighth Circuit (Illinois and Indiana) Chicago, Springfield, and for Indiana, "at seat of government."

Justice Samuel F. Miller, Ninth Circuit (Wisconsin, Iowa, Missouri, Minnesota, Kansas) Milwaukee, Madison, Des Moines, St. Louis, St. Paul, and for Kansas, "at seat of government."

Justice Stephen J. Field, Tenth Circuit (California and Oregon) San Francisco, Los Angeles, Portland.

THE VALLANDIGHAM CASE

THE HOLT BRIEF IN THE VALLANDIGHAM CASE	THE WAYNE DECISION IN THE VALLANDIGHAM CASE
The appellate powers of the Supreme Court, as granted by the Constitution, are limited and regulated by the acts of Congress, and must be exercised subject to the exceptions and regulations made by Congress.	The appellate powers of the Supreme Court, as granted by the Constitution, are limited and regulated by the acts of Congress, and must be exercised subject to the exceptions and regulations made by Congress.
This case is believed not to be within either the letter or spirit of the	In other words, the petition before us we think not to be within the letter

grants of appellate jurisdiction of the Supreme Court. It is not believed to be a case "in law or equity," within the meaning of those terms as used in the third article of the Constitution; nor that the military commission is a court within the meaning of the term, as used in the 14th section of the judiciary act of 1789.

That there is no *express* act of Congress giving the Supreme Court . . . jurisdiction to revise, by writ of error, *habeas corpus,* or in any way, the proceedings of courts-martial or military commissions, will doubtless be conceded. If wrong has been done the applicant by the commanding officer who ordered his arrest, or by the military court who tried and sentenced him, his remedy is by action against them, not by review in this court of their proceedings.

or spirit of the grants of appellate jurisdiction of the Supreme Court. It is not in law or equity within the meaning of those terms as used in the 3d article of the Constitution. Nor is a military commission a court within the meaning of the 14th section of the Judiciary Act of 1789.

Whatever may be the force of Vallandigham's protest, that he was not triable by a court of military commission, it is certain that his petition cannot be brought within the 14th section of the act; and further, that the court cannot, without disregarding its frequent decisions and interpretations of the Constitution in respect to its judicial power, originate a writ of certiorari to review or pronounce any opinion upon the proceedings of a military commission.

LINCOLN ADDS "YOUTH" TO THE SUPREME COURT

MAY 30, 1860		MAY 1, 1861		DECEMBER 31, 1862	
Justice	*Age*	*Justice*	*Age*	*Justice*	*Age*
Taney	83	Taney	84	Taney	85
Daniel	76	—	—	—	—
McLean	75	—	—	—	—
Catron	74	Catron	75	Catron	76
Wayne	70	Wayne	71	Wayne	72
Nelson	68	Nelson	69	Nelson	70
Grier	66	Grier	67	Grier	68
Clifford	57	Clifford	58	Clifford	59
Campbell	49	—	—	—	—
				*Swayne	58
				*Miller	46
				*Davis	47
Average Age	69	Average Age	71	Average Age	65

---

* Appointees of Lincoln.

DECEMBER 31, 1863		DECEMBER 31, 1864	
Justice	*Age*	*Justice*	*Age*
Taney	86	—	—
Catron	77	Catron	78
Wayne	73	Wayne	74
Nelson	71	Nelson	72
Grier	69	Grier	70
Clifford	60	Clifford	61
*Swayne	59	*Swayne	60
*Miller	47	*Miller	48
*Davis	48	*Davis	49
*Field	47	*Field	48
		*Chase	56
Average Age	64		
		Average Age	62

* Appointees of Lincoln.

TOTAL NUMBER OF OPINIONS WRITTEN BY EACH JUSTICE DURING THE CIVIL WAR

	December Term, 1861		December Term, 1862		December Term, 1863		December Term, 1864	
	Majority	Minority	Majority	Minority	Majority	Minority	Majority	Minority
Taney	11	1	4	1	0	0	(**)	(**)
Catron	6	0	1	3	2	2	0	0
Wayne	7	4	3	2	4	0	2	1
Nelson	21	1	6	2	14	1	10	3
Grier	16	4	6	2	11	1	6	0
Clifford	9	1	6	3	12	1	8	3
Swayne	6	0	6	0	11	2	5	0
Miller	(*)	(*)	5	1	12	5	8	2
Davis	(*)	(*)	5	0	10	2	0	0
Field	(*)	(*)	(*)	(*)	12	0	5	2
Chase	(*)	(*)	(*)	(*)	(*)	(*)	12	0

* Not yet a member of the Supreme Court or not yet seated.
** Deceased.

Bibliography

MANUSCRIPT COLLECTIONS

Attorney General's Letter Books, 1861-65, National Archives.

George Bancroft MSS., Massachusetts Historical Society. Photoduplicates of significant items, Library of the University of Illinois.

James Gordon Bennett MSS., Library of Congress.

Blair Family MSS., Library of Congress. Papers of Francis P. Blair, Sr., Montgomery Blair, and Francis P. Blair, Jr.

James Buchanan MSS., Historical Society of Pennsylvania.

Simon Cameron MSS., Library of Congress.

Salmon P. Chase MSS., Library of Congress.

Salmon P. Chase MSS., Historical Society of Pennsylvania.

Nathan Clifford MSS., Maine Historical Society.

Caleb Cushing MSS., Library of Congress.

G. S. S. Davis MSS., New York Historical Society.

Edward S. Delaplaine Collection, Frederick, Maryland.

Thomas Ewing MSS., Library of Congress.

Edward C. Gardiner MSS., Henry C. Carey Section, Historical Society of Pennsylvania.

Joseph Holt MSS., Library of Congress.

Robert Todd Lincoln MSS., Library of Congress.

Hugh McCulloch MSS., Library of Congress.

Minutes of the United States Supreme Court, MSS., Clerk's File, Library of the United States Supreme Court.

Order Books of the United States Circuit Court at Cincinnati, MSS., vol. L, April 18, 1862-April 29, 1863; vol. M, October 6, 1863-October 23, 1863, United States District Court, Clerk's File, Cincinnati, Ohio.

Order Books of the United States Circuit Court at Indianapolis, MSS., vol. I, May 20, 1861-January 28, 1863; vol. J, February 2, 1863-April 1, 1865, United States District Court, Clerk's File, Indianapolis, Indiana.

William W. Orme MSS., Illinois Historical Survey, Urbana, Illinois.

Papers of the Attorneys General, 1861-65, National Archives.

Papers of the State Department, 1861-65, National Archives.

Franklin Pierce MSS., Library of Congress.

John Sherman MSS., Library of Congress.

Edwin M. Stanton MSS., Library of Congress.

Thaddeus Stevens MSS., Library of Congress.

Charles Sumner MSS., Widener Memorial Library, Harvard University. Photoduplicates of significant items, Library of the University of Illinois.

Roger B. Taney MSS., Library of Congress.

Roger B. Taney MSS., Maryland Historical Society.

Roger B. Taney MSS., New York Public Library.

R. W. Thompson MSS., Lincoln National Life Foundation, Ft. Wayne, Indiana.

Samuel J. Tilden MSS., New York Public Library.

Samuel Treat MSS., Missouri Historical Society.

Lyman Trumbull MSS., Library of Congress. Photoduplicates of significant items, Illinois Historical Survey.

United States House of Representatives Files, 37th and 38th Congresses (1861-65), Library of Congress.

United States Senate Files, 37th and 38th Congresses (1861-65), National Archives.

Benjamin F. Wade MSS., Library of Congress.

Elihu B. Washburne MSS., Library of Congress.

Gideon Welles MSS., Library of Congress.

PUBLIC DOCUMENTS

"Appointment of Officers to Fill Vacancies," *Senate Reports of Committees No. 80*, 37th Congress, 3rd session, Washington, 1863.

"Biographical Directory of the American Congress, 1774-1927: the Continental Congress, September 5, 1774, to October 21, 1778 and the Congress of the United States from the First to the Sixty-Ninth Congress, March 4, 1789, to March 3, 1927, Inclusive," *House Document No. 783*, 69th Congress, 2nd session, Washington, 1928.

Blatchford, Samuel, reporter, *Reports of Cases Argued and Determined in the Circuit Court of the United States for the Second Circuit*, 24 vols., New York, 1852-88.

Blatchford, Samuel, reporter, *Reports of Cases in Prize, Argued and Determined in the Circuit and District Courts of the United States for the Southern District of New York, 1861-1865*, New York, 1866.

California Reports (Supreme Court of the State of California).

Clifford, William H., reporter, *Reports of Cases Determined in the Circuit Court of the United States for the First Circuit, from October Term, 1861, to October Term, 1867*, 4 vols., New York and Boston, 1869-80.

Congressional Debates, 22nd Congress, 2nd session, December 3, 1832–March 3, 1833, Washington, 1833.

Congressional Directory, 38th Congress, 1st session, Washington, 1864.

Congressional Globe, 37th Congress, 1st session, July 4, 1861–August 6, 1861, Washington, 1861.

Congressional Globe, 37th Congress, 2nd session, December 2, 1861–July 17, 1862, Washington, 1862.

Congressional Globe, 37th Congress, 3rd session, December 1, 1862–March 3, 1863, and special session, March 4, 1863–March 14, 1863, Washington, 1863.

Congressional Globe, 38th Congress, 1st session, December 7, 1863–July 4, 1864, Washington, 1864.

Congressional Globe, 38th Congress, 2nd session, December 5, 1864–March 3, 1865, and special session, March 4, 1865–March 11, 1865, Washington, 1865.

Congressional Globe, 39th Congress, 1st session, December 4, 1865–July 16, 1866, Washington, 1866.

Congressional Globe, 40th Congress, 2nd session, December 2, 1867–November 10, 1868, Washington, 1868.

"Estimates of Appropriations," *House Executive Document No. 1*, 37th Congress, 2nd session, Washington, 1861.

"Estimates of Appropriations," *House Executive Document No. 2*, 38th Congress, 2nd session, Washington, 1864.

Federal Cases (Cases heard by the district and circuit courts of the United States, 1789-1880). Cited as 1 Fed. Cas. 1.

Iowa Reports (Supreme Court of the State of Iowa).

Lawyer's Edition of the United States Supreme Court Reports, vol. 17. (Includes materials that are not found in the official reports of the Supreme Court.) Cited as L. Ed.

"Proclamation Authorizing Suspension of the Writ of Habeas Corpus," *House Executive Document No. 6*, 37th Congress, 1st session, Washington, 1861.

Records and Briefs of the United States Supreme Court, Law Division, Library of Congress. (Records and briefs of all cases heard by the Supreme Court).

"Resolution of the Legislature of Iowa," *Senate Miscellaneous Document No. 73*, 37th Congress, 2nd session, Washington, 1862.

Schulz, George J., "Creation of the Federal Judiciary," *Senate Document No. 91*, 75th Congress, 1st session, Washington, 1938.

Scott, James B., ed., *Prize Cases Decided in the United States Supreme Court, 1789-1918, Including also Cases on the Instance Side in which Questions of Prize Law Were Involved*, 3 vols., Oxford, 1923.

"Suspension of the Writ of Habeas Corpus, Letter from the Attorney General," *House Executive Document No. 5*, 37th Congress, 1st session, Washington, 1861.

"United States Circuit Court for California," *House Executive Document No. 129*, 37th Congress, 2nd session, Washington, 1862.

United States Constitution.

United States Reports, vols. 65-71, 103, 117, 137, 168. (Official reports of the United States Supreme Court). Cited as 65 U.S. 1.

United States Statutes at Large.

War of the Rebellion: Official Records of the Union and Confederate Armies, 4 series, 128 vols., Washington, 1880-1901.

Woolworth, James M., reporter, *Cases Determined in the United States Circuit Courts for the Eighth Circuit by the Hon. Samuel F. Miller, L.L.D., One of the Associate Justices of the Supreme Court*, Chicago, 1870.

NEWSPAPERS

Atlanta *Daily Intelligencer*, July 1–July 15, 1867, Atlanta, Georgia.

Augusta *Daily Press*, July 1–July 15, 1867, Augusta, Georgia.

Baltimore *Sun*, January 19–February 28, 1862; July 10–July 25, 1862; December 1–December 20, 1862; Baltimore, Maryland.

Chicago *Daily Tribune*, January 1, 1861–December 30, 1862; July 6, 1867; June 27, 1886; Chicago, Illinois.

Indianapolis *Daily Herald*, April 4–April 5, 1866; December 18–December 19, 1866; Indianapolis, Indiana.

Louisville *Daily Journal*, September 16, 1861–October 15, 1861, Louisville, Kentucky.

Memphis *Daily Appeal*, January 1–December 31, 1862, Memphis, Tennessee.

Memphis *Daily Bulletin,* January 1–December 31, 1862, Memphis, Tennessee.
New York *Daily Tribune,* May 28, 1861–December 31, 1864; April 3–April 6, 1866; December 18–December 31, 1866; June 10, 1884; New York City.
New York *Herald,* July 17, 1862; October 14, 1864; December 6–December 8, 1864; December 10, 1864; December 14, 1864; April 3–April 6, 1866; December 17–December 20, 1866; July 6, 1867; New York City.
New York *Times,* January 1, 1861–December 31, 1864; April 3–April 9, 1866; July 1–July 15, 1867; May 12, 1918; New York City.
New York *World,* March 1, 1861–April 15, 1865; July 1–July 15, 1867; New York City.
Philadelphia *Inquirer,* July 1–July 15, 1867, Philadelphia, Pennsylvania.
Richmond *Enquirer,* July 1–July 15, 1867, Richmond, Virginia.
Savannah *Daily Republican,* July 1–July 15, 1867, Savannah, Georgia.
Washington *Daily Globe,* July 17, 1862, Washington, D. C.
Washington *Daily Morning Chronicle,* November 3, 1862–April 17, 1865; July 1–July 15, 1867; Washington, D. C.
Washington *Daily National Intelligencer,* April 4, 1861–April 15, 1865; July 1–July 15, 1867; Washington, D. C.
Washington *Evening Express,* July 1–July 15, 1867, Washington, D. C.
Washington *Evening Star,* April 1, 1861–February 3, 1863; July 1–July 15, 1867; Washington, D. C.
Washington *National Republican,* January, 1862; July 1–July 15, 1867; Washington, D. C.

Books, Works, Articles

Adams, Charles Francis, *Richard Henry Dana: A Biography,* 2 vols., 3rd ed., rev., Cambridge, 1891.
"Address of Mr. Justice Miller Delivered before the Iowa State Bar Association at Des Moines, May 13, 1879," *Albany Law Journal: A Weekly Record of the Law,* XX, 25-29, Albany, July 12, 1879.
Angle, Paul M., "Lincoln and the United States Supreme Court," *Bulletin of the Abraham Lincoln Association,* no. 47, pp. 3-10, Springfield, May, 1937.
Angle, Paul M., "Lincoln and the United States Supreme Court: A Postscript," *Bulletin of the Abraham Lincoln Association,* no. 47, supplement, pp. 1-3, Springfield, June, 1937.
Appleton's American Annual Cyclopedia, vol. III, New York, 1871.
Ascher, Leonard, "Lincoln's Administration and the New Almaden Scandal," *Pacific Historical Review,* V, 38-51, Glendale, California, March, 1936.
Basler, Roy P., ed., *The Collected Works of Abraham Lincoln,* 9 vols., New Brunswick, New Jersey, 1953-55.
Bates, Ernest S., *The Story of the Supreme Court,* Indianapolis, 1936.
Beale, Howard K., ed., *The Diary of Edward Bates, 1859-1866,* American Historical Association, *Annual Report for 1930,* vol. IV, Washington, 1933.
Binney, Horace, "The Privilege of the Writ of Habeas Corpus under the Constitution," *Fahnestock Pamphlets,* XXXIX, no. 2, 1-50, Philadelphia, 1862.
Black, Chauncey F., and Smith, Samuel B., eds., *Some Account of the Work of Stephen J. Field as a Legislator, State Judge, and Judge of the Supreme Court of the United States,* New York, 1881.

Blair, Francis P., Sr., to John A. Andrew, November 19, 1864, Massachusetts Historical Society, *Proceedings*, LXIII, 88-89, Boston, 1931.

Boudin, Louis B., *Government by Judiciary*, 2 vols., New York, 1932.

Bourne, Edward G., et al., eds., *Diary and Correspondence of Salmon P. Chase*, American Historical Association, *Annual Report for 1902*, vol. II, Washington, 1903.

Boutwell, George S., *Reminiscences of Sixty Years in Public Affairs*, 2 vols., New York, 1902.

Boyd, Andrew, compiler, *Boyd's Washington and Georgetown Directory Containing also a Business Directory of Washington, Georgetown, and Alexandria, 1864*, Washington, 1864.

Boyd, William H., compiler, *Boyd's Washington and Georgetown Directory containing a Business Directory of Washington, Georgetown, and Alexandria, Congressional and Department Directory, and an Appendix of Much Useful Information, 1860*, Washington, 1860.

Callender, Clarence N., *American Courts: Their Organization and Procedure*, 1st ed., New York, 1927.

Carson, Hampton L., *The History of the Supreme Court of the United States, with Biographies of all the Chief and Associate Justices*, 2 vols., Philadelphia, 1902.

Carson, Hampton L., *The Supreme Court of the United States: Its History*, Philadelphia, 1902.

Clifford, Philip Greeley, *Nathan Clifford: Democrat (1803-1881)*, New York, 1922.

Conkling, Alfred, *A Treatise on the Organization, Jurisdiction, and Practice of the Courts of the United States, with an Appendix of Practical Forms*, 4th ed., revised and enlarged, Albany, 1864.

Connor, Henry G., *John Archibald Campbell, Associate Judge of the United States Supreme Court, 1853-1861*, Cambridge, 1920.

Corwin, Edward S., "The Dred Scott Decision in the Light of Contemporary Legal Doctrines," *American Historical Review*, XVII, 52-69, New York, October, 1911.

Corwin, Edward S., *The Twilight of the Supreme Court: A History of our Constitutional Theory*, New Haven, 1934.

Countryman, Edwin, "Samuel Nelson," *The Green Bag*, XIX, 329-34, Boston, June, 1907.

Countryman, Edwin, *The Supreme Court of the United States, with A Review of Certain Decisions Relating to Its Appellate Power under the Constitution*, Albany, 1913.

Cummings, Homer, and McFarland, Carl, *Federal Justice: Chapters in the History of Justice and the Federal Executive*, New York, 1937.

Dent, Thomas, "David Davis of Illinois—A Sketch," *American Law Review*, LIII, 535-60, St. Louis, July, 1919.

Donald, David, ed., *Inside Lincoln's Cabinet: The Civil War Diaries of Salmon P. Chase*, New York, 1954.

Dorris, Jonathan T., *Pardon and Amnesty under Lincoln and Johnson*, Chapel Hill, 1953.

Dunning, William A., *Essays on the Civil War and Reconstruction and Related Topics*, New York, 1931.

Ellis, John B., *The Sights and Secrets of the National Capital: A Work Descriptive of Washington City in All Its Various Phases*, New York, 1869.

Ellison, Joseph, "The Currency Question on the Pacific Coast during the Civil War," *Mississippi Valley Historical Review*, XVI, 50-66, Cedar Rapids, June, 1929.

Ewing, Cortez A. M., *"The Judges of the Supreme Court, 1789-1937, A Study of Their Qualifications*, Minneapolis, 1938.

Fairman, Charles, ed., "Justice Samuel F. Miller and the Barbourville Debating Society," *Mississippi Valley Historical Review*, XVII, 595-601, Cedar Rapids, March, 1931.

Fairman, Charles, *Mr. Justice Miller and the Supreme Court: 1862-1890*, Cambridge, 1939.

Field, Henry M., *The Life of David Dudley Field*, New York, 1898.

Field, Stephen J., *Personal Reminiscences of Early Days in California, with Other Sketches*, published privately, 1893.

Foote, Henry S., *Casket of Reminiscences*, Washington, 1874.

Foulke, William D., *Life of Oliver P. Morton, Including His Important Speeches*, 2 vols., Indianapolis, 1899.

Frankfurter, Felix, "Taney and the Commerce Clause," *Harvard Law Review*, XLIX, 1286-1302, Cambridge, June, 1936.

Frankfurter, Felix, and Landis, James M., *The Business of the Supreme Court: A Study in the Federal Judicial System*, New York, 1927.

Gregory, Charles N., *Samuel Freeman Miller*, Iowa City, 1907.

Gregory, Charles N., "Samuel Freeman Miller, Associate Justice of the Supreme Court of the United States," *Yale Law Journal*, XVII, 422-42, New Haven, April, 1908.

Grice, Warren, *The Georgia Bench and Bar: The Development of Georgia's Judicial System*, Macon, 1931.

Haines, Charles G., *The Conflict over Judicial Powers in the United States to 1870*, New York, 1909.

Harper, Robert S., *Lincoln and the Press*, New York, 1951.

Hart, Albert Bushnell, *Salmon Portland Chase* (John T. Morse, Jr., ed., *American Statesmen Series*, vol. 28), Cambridge, 1899.

Herndon, William H., and Weik, Jesse W., *Herndon's Lincoln, The True Story of a Great Life: The History and Personal Recollections of Abraham Lincoln*, 3 vols., Chicago, 1889.

Hockett, Homer C., *The Constitutional History of the United States, 1776-1876*, 2 vols., New York, 1939.

Hodder, Frank H., "Some Phases of the Dred Scott Case," *Mississippi Valley Historical Review*, XVI, 3-22, Cedar Rapids, June, 1929.

"Hon. Noah H. Swayne, Memorial Proceedings of the Ohio State Bar Association," *Reports of the Ohio State Bar Association*, V, 41-48, Columbus, 1885.

"Hon. Robert C. Grier," *The Western Jurist*, V, 37-38, Des Moines, January, 1871.

Hutchinson, Thomas, compiler, *Boyd's Washington and Georgetown Directory containing also a Business Directory, Congressional and Department Directory, and an Appendix of Much Useful Information, 1862*, Washington, 1862.

Hutchinson, Thomas, compiler, *Boyd's Washington and Georgetown Directory containing also a Business Directory, Congressional and Department Directory, and an Appendix of Much Useful Information, 1863*, Washington, 1863.

Ingersoll, Henry H., "John Catron," *Great American Lawyers*, IV, 241-76, Philadelphia, 1908.

Johnson, Allen, et al., eds., *Dictionary of American Biography*, 21 vols., New York, 1928-44.

Jones, Francis R., "Robert Cooper Grier," *The Green Bag*, XVI, 221-24, Boston, April, 1904.

Kasson, John A., to Charles Aldrich, November 10, 1893, *Annals of Iowa*, series III, I, 252, Iowa City, January, 1894.

Klaus, Samuel, ed., *Ex Parte: In the Matter of Lambdin P. Milligan, Petitioner*, New York, 1929.

Lathrop, H. W., "Judge Miller's Appointment to the Supreme Court," *Iowa Historical Record*, VII, no. 1, 16-17, Iowa City, January, 1891.

Lawrence, Alexander A., *James Moore Wayne: Southern Unionist*, Chapel Hill, 1943.

McCulloch, Hugh, *Men and Measures of Half a Century: Sketches and Comments*, New York, 1900.

McIntyre, J. W., ed., *The Writings and Speeches of Daniel Webster*, 18 vols., Boston, 1903.

McLaughlin, Andrew C., *A Constitutional History of the United States*, New York, 1935.

Marshall, Jessie A., ed., *Private and Official Correspondence of Gen. Benjamin F. Butler during the Period of the Civil War*, 5 vols., Norwood, Massachusetts, 1917.

Mikell, William E., "Roger Brooke Taney," *Great American Lawyers*, IV, 77-194, Philadelphia, 1908.

Miller, Samuel F., to Mrs. James W. Grimes, August 28, 1888, *Iowa Historical Record*, VII, 88-89, Iowa City, April, 1891.

"Milligan's Case," *American Law Review*, I, 572-75, Boston, April, 1867.

Morse, John T., Jr., *Diary of Gideon Welles, Secretary of the Navy under Lincoln and Johnson*, 3 vols., Cambridge, 1911.

Myers, Gustavus, *History of the Supreme Court of the United States*, Chicago, 1918.

Nicolay, John G., and Hay, John, *Abraham Lincoln: A History*, 10 vols., New York, 1886.

Nicolay, John G., and Hay, John, eds., *Abraham Lincoln: Complete Works, Comprising His Speeches, Letters, State Papers, and Miscellaneous Writings*, 2 vols., New York, 1894.

"Noah H. Swayne," *American Law Review*, XVIII, 693-95, Boston, July-August, 1884.

Parker, Joel, "Habeas Corpus and Martial Law: A Review of the Opinion of Chief Justice Taney, in the Case of John Merryman," *Fahnestock Pamphlets*, XXXIX, no. 15, 1-49, Philadelphia, 1862.

Pease, Theodore C., and Randall, James G., eds., *The Diary of Orville Hickman Browning (Collections of the Illinois State Historical Library*, vol. XX) vol. I, Springfield, 1925.

Pierce, Edward L., *Memoir and Letters of Charles Sumner*, 4 vols., London, 1893.

Pomeroy, John N., Jr., "Stephen Johnson Field," *Great American Lawyers*, VII, 3-51, Philadelphia, 1909.

Pratt, Harry E., "David Davis, 1815-1886," doctoral dissertation, University of Illinois, 1930.

Proceedings of the Bench and Bar of the Supreme Court of the United States in Memoriam Samuel F. Miller, Washington, 1891.

Randall, James G., *Constitutional Problems under Lincoln,* rev. ed., Urbana, Illinois, 1951.

Randall, James G., "Has the Lincoln Theme Been Exhausted?" *American Historical Review,* XLI, 270-94, New York, January, 1936.

Randall, James G., *Lincoln the President,* 3 vols., New York, 1945-53.

Randall, James G., *The Civil War and Reconstruction,* Boston, 1937 and 1953.

Randall, James G., "The 'Rule of Law' under the Lincoln Administration," *The Historical Outlook,* XVII, 272-78, Philadelphia, October, 1926.

Randall, James G., and Current, Richard N., *Last Full Measure,* New York, 1955.

"Robert Cooper Grier," *American Law Review,* V, 365, Boston, January, 1871.

Rodell, Fred, *Nine Men: A Political History of the Supreme Court from 1790 to 1955,* New York, 1955.

"Roger Brooke Taney," *The Atlantic Monthly,* XV, 151-61, Boston, February, 1865.

Rose, John C., *Jurisdiction and Procedure of the Federal Courts,* 4th ed., revised and enlarged by Byron F. Babbitt, Albany, 1931.

Rose, Walter M., "Notes on the U.S. Reports," Lawyers Edition, 2nd edition, extra annotated, vol. 17, Rochester, New York, 1931.

Salter, William, *The Life of James W. Grimes, Governor of Iowa, 1854-1858; A Senator of the United States, 1859-1869,* New York, 1876.

Sandburg, Carl, *Abraham Lincoln: The War Years,* 4 vols., New York, 1939.

Schuck, Oscar T., *History of the Bench and Bar of California Being Biographies of Many Remarkable Men, a Store of Humorous and Pathetic Recollections, Accounts of Important Legislation, and Extraordinary Cases, Comprehending the Judicial History of the State,* Los Angeles, 1901.

Schuckers, Jacob W., *The Life and Public Services of Salmon Portland Chase, United States Senator and Governor of Ohio; Secretary of the Treasury, and Chief-Justice of the United States,* New York, 1874.

Sellery, George C., "Lincoln's Suspension of the Habeas Corpus as Viewed by Congress," *Bulletin of the University of Wisconsin, History Series,* I, 213-86, Madison, April, 1907.

Smith, Charles W., *Roger B. Taney: Jacksonian Jurist,* Chapel Hill, 1936.

Spear, Samuel T., *The Law of the Federal Judiciary: A Treatise on the Provisions of the Constitution, the Laws of Congress, and the Judicial Decisions Relating to the Jurisdiction of, and Practice and Pleading in the Federal Courts,* New York, 1883.

Speech of Alexander A. Lawrence, February 1, 1940. Copy made available to the author on February 13, 1940, by Miss Ola M. Wyeth, librarian of the Georgia Historical Society.

Steiner, Bernard C., *Life of Roger Brooke Taney: Chief Justice of the United States Supreme Court,* Baltimore, 1922.

Stern, Horace, "An Examination of Justice Field's Work in Constitutional Law," *Great American Lawyers,* VII, 52-85, Philadelphia, 1909.

Stern, Horace, "Samuel Freeman Miller," *Great American Lawyers,* VI, 541-85, Philadelphia, 1909.

Sterne, Simon, "The Salaries of the U.S. Supreme Court Justices," *The Counsellor*, I, 93-98, New York, January, 1892.

Strong, Henry, "Justice Samuel Freeman Miller," *Annals of Iowa*, series III, I, 241-57, Iowa City, January, 1894.

Swisher, Carl B., *Roger B. Taney*, New York, 1935.

Swisher, Carl B., *Stephen J. Field, Craftsman of the Law*, Washington, 1930.

Tyler, Samuel, *Memoir of Roger Brooke Taney, L.L.D.*, Baltimore, 1872.

Van Fossan, W. H., "Clement L. Vallandigham," *Ohio Archaeological and Historical Publications*, XXIII, 256-57, Columbus, 1914.

Veeder, Van Vechten, "A Century of Federal Judicature," Parts III-IX, *The Green Bag*, XV, 127-38; 181-91; 223-32; 281-89; 323-32; 419-29; Boston, March-September, 1903.

Warden, Robert B., *An Account of the Private Life and Public Services of Salmon Portland Chase*, Cincinnati, 1874.

Warren, Charles, *A History of the American Bar*, Boston, 1911.

Warren, Charles, *Congress, the Constitution, and the Supreme Court*, Boston, 1925.

Warren, Charles, *The Supreme Court in United States History*, new and rev. ed., 2 vols., Boston, 1928.

Weisenburger, Francis P., *The Life of John McLean: A Politician on the United States Supreme Court (Ohio State University Studies, No. 15)*, Columbus, 1937.

White, Horace, *The Life of Lyman Trumbull*, Cambridge, 1913.

Willoughby, Westel W., *The Constitutional Law of the United States*, 2nd ed., 3 vols., New York, 1929.

Willoughby, Westel W., *The Supreme Court of the United States: Its History and Influence in Our Constitutional System (Johns Hopkins University Studies in Historical and Political Science*, vol. VII), Baltimore, 1890.

Index

Crenshaw, The Schooner: mentioned, 109; captured, 112; condemned, 116

Crier of the Supreme Court: duties of, 103

Crittenden, John J.: suggested for Supreme Court, 25; appointment feared by Swayne, 60; member of Supreme Court bar, 103; is lawyer for Andres Castillero, 160

Cumberland County, Pennsylvania: birthplace of Grier, 22

Currie, William; part owner of *The Brig Amy Warwick*, 110

Curtis, Benjamin R.: member of the Supreme Court bar, 103; represents the United States in the New Almaden Mine case, 160

Cushing, Caleb: is recommended for the Supreme Court, 4; is told that Taney resigned, 4 n.

Czar Nicholas: referred to by Swett, 80

Da Costa: passenger on board *The Brig Kate*, 221

Dana, Richard H., Jr.: member of Supreme Court bar, 103; represents government in the *Prize Cases*, 109; saves government from defeat, 109; argument in the *Prize Cases*, 110-11; awaits decision, 113; supports Evarts for Chief Justice, 192

Daniel, Peter V.: tribute by Black, 3; delay in filling seat of, 3; native of Virginia, 25

Danville, Pennsylvania: Grier practiced law in, 22

Dartmouth College: Clifford hoped to attend, 22

Davis, David: comments on election of 1860, 2; aspires to Supreme Court, 51, 70, 72; served in Illinois legislature and courts, 57; fears Browning, 71, 72; aids Lincoln in 1858 and 1860, 74; appointed to Supreme Court, 74, 77-78; friends urge appointment, 75, 76, 78; thanks Lincoln for appointment, 78; press praises appointment, 79; retains political interests, 81, 82; laments over burdensome duties, 81; finally resigns from Supreme Court, 82; annoyed by Lincoln, 82; friendship with other Justices, 98; favors W. W. Orme for clerk, 103; attitude on legal tender in postwar period, 147 n.; serves on circuit, 176-77; opposes suppression of Chicago *Times*, 175-76; asks Swayne to hold circuit court, 175; rumors of Chief Justiceship

for, 189; supports Swayne for Chief Justice, 191; speculation on vote in Milligan case, 229; writes Milligan decision, 232-34; opposes military trials, 234-35

Davis, Garrett: explains court packing, 87; makes attack upon Lincoln, 123

Davis, H. Winter: corresponds with David Davis, 2; predicts changes in Supreme Court, 2; urges appointment of David Davis, 75

Davis, J. C. Bancroft: statement on case of *Gordon v. The United States*, 211

Davis, Jefferson: grants letter of marque, 178

December Term, 1860: vacancy exists on Supreme Court, 3; nation faces dissolution, 3; ends as Lincoln assumes power, 3

December Term, 1861: Supreme Court ready to meet, 37-38; Bates anticipates little activity during, 38; California land cases prominent in, 157; no war case heard during, 157-58

December Term, 1862: Supreme Court assembles for, 79; forty cases heard during, 158; wartime cases appear, 158; *Prize Cases* decided, 158; California land cases prominent in, 158; hears cases concerning United States securities, 211

December Term, 1863: decides Vallandigham case, 147; hears Legal Tender case, 147; decision in Milligan case and Roosevelt case handed down, 163; quarrel of Swayne and Miller takes place in, 166

December Term, 1864: memorial to Taney given, 187; delays pending appointment of a Chief Justice, 203; Chase appointed, 210; new Attorney General appointed, 210; deals with enemies' property, 213; hears cases involving the slave trade, 218

December Term, 1866: Supreme Court assembles for, 232

Dennison, William: urges Swayne appointment, 59-60; attends Taney funeral, 186; uninformed about Chase appointment, 204; appointed Postmaster General, 204

Dickinson, Daniel S.: is urged for Chief Justice, 188-89

Dickinson College: attended by Taney, 14; Grier graduate of, 22

Dimick, Justin: commandant at Fort Warren, 182

BOOKS ABOUT ABRAHAM LINCOLN

The Historian's Lincoln: Pseudo-History, Psychohistory, and History
Edited by Gabor S. Boritt

Lincoln and the Economics of the American Dream
Gabor S. Borritt

Lincoln and the Tools of War
Robert V. Bruce

The Inner World of Abraham Lincoln
Michael Burlingame

Lincoln, Land, and Labor, 1809-60
Olivier Fraysse; translated by Sylvia Neely

The Lincoln Murder Conspiracies
William Hanchett

Out of the Wilderness: The Life of Abraham Lincoln
William Hanchett

"We Cannot Escape History": Lincoln and the Last Best Hope of Earth
Edited by James M. McPherson

Constitutional Problems under Lincoln
James G. Randall

Lincoln the President: Last Full Measure
J. G. Randall and Richard N. Current

"Right or Wrong, God Judge Me": The Writings of John Wilkes Booth
Edited by John Rhodehamel and Louise Taper

Lincoln's Supreme Court
David M. Silver

Lincoln's Preparation for Greatness: The Illinois Legislative Years
Paul Simon

The Shadows Rise: Abraham Lincoln and the Ann Rutledge Legend
John Evangelist Walsh

Herndon's Informants: Letters, Interviews, and Statements
about Abraham Lincoln
Edited by Douglas L. Wilson and Rodney O. Davis, with the assistance of Terry Wilson

Lincoln before Washington: New Perspectives on the Illinois Years
Douglas L. Wilson

The University of Illinois Press also publishes semiannually
The Journal of the Abraham Lincoln Association.